ITALIAN FILM IN THE SH~~~~~~ ~~ ~~~~~~~~~~

In recent years there has been a surge of Italian films that deal with Fascism, anti-Semitism, and the Holocaust. This trend marks a distinct departure from the postwar reluctance to represent these deeply sensitive subjects in film. In addition to Roberto Benigni's internationally acclaimed *Life Is Beautiful* (1997), there have appeared a number of other Italian films that deal with the Holocaust, many of which have not been available to foreign audiences. Millicent Marcus's *Italian Film in the Shadow of Auschwitz* looks at this development, attributing the new acceptance not only to international influences, but also to a domestic audience that is increasingly willing to face its collective demons and a cultural industry ready to produce its own forms of historic testimony. Throughout the book, Marcus brings a variety of critical perspectives to bear on the question of how Italian filmmakers are now confronting the Holocaust, especially in light of the sparse output of Holocaust films produced in Italy from 1945 to the early 1990s. What emerges is a penetrating look at how film is being used to address a profoundly disturbing chapter in the history of humankind.

The study features in-depth analyses of five recent Italian films: Ricky Tognazzi's *Canone inverso*, Ettore Scola's *Concorrenza sleale*, Andrea and Antonio Frazzi's *Il cielo cade*, Alberto Negrin's *Perlasca*, and Ferzan Ozpetek's *La finestra di fronte*. In addition, the book includes a DVD of Scola's short film *'43–'97*, which has previously been unavailable outside of Italy.

(Goggio Publication Series, Toronto Italian Studies)

MILLICENT MARCUS is a professor in the Department of Italian at Yale University.

TORONTO ITALIAN STUDIES

Goggio Publication Series
General Editor: Olga Zorzi Pugliese

MILLICENT MARCUS

Italian Film in the Shadow of Auschwitz

UNIVERSITY OF TORONTO PRESS
Toronto Buffalo London

© University of Toronto Press Incorporated 2007
Toronto Buffalo London
Printed in Canada

ISBN 978-0-8020-9188-8 (cloth)
ISBN 978-0-8020-9189-5 (paper)

Printed on acid-free paper

Goggio Publication Series, Toronto Italian Studies

Library and Archives Canada Cataloguing in Publication

Marcus, Millicent
  Italian film in the shadow of Auschwitz / Millicent Marcus.

  (Toronto Italian Studies)
  (Goggio publications series)
  Includes bibliographical references and index.
  ISBN 978-0-8020-9188-8 (bound)
  ISBN 978-0-8020-9189-5 (pbk.)

  1. Motion pictures – Italy – History.   2. Holocaust, Jewish (1939–1945),
  in motion pictures.   3. Jews in motion pictures.   4. National socialism
  and motion pictures.   I. Title.   II. Series.   III. Series.

  PN1995.9.J46M37 2007   791.43′658094509045   C2007-901365-1

This book has been published with the aid of a grant from the Emilio Goggio
Chair of Italian Studies, University of Toronto.

University of Toronto Press acknowledges the financial assistance to its
publishing program of the Canada Council for the Arts and the Ontario
Arts Council.

University of Toronto Press acknowledges the financial support for its
publishing activities of the Government of Canada through the Book
Publishing Industry Development Program (BPIDP).

For Allan

Contents

Acknowledgments   ix

Historical Background Sketch   3

PART I   Weak Memory: From the End of the Second World War to
the End of the Cold War, with a Foray into the 1990s

1. Ghost Stories: An Introduction   13

   Grief Work   13

   The Case of Rosetta Loy's *La parola ebreo*   20

2. A Diaphanous Body of Films   28

   Soon After (1947–9): *L'ebreo errante, Il grido della terra, Il monastero
   di Santa Chiara*   30

   The Second Wave (1960–6): *Tutti a casa, Kapò, L'oro di Roma,
   Sandra, Andremo in città*   35

   Breaking New Ground (the 1970s): *Garden of the Finzi-Continis,
   Diario di un italiano, The Night Porter, Seven Beauties, La linea del
   fiume*   46

   A Dearth of Films, Offset by the Arrival of the TV Mini-series
   (the 1980s): *L'ebreo fascista, Storia d'amore e d'amicizia, La Storia,
   Gli occhiali d'oro*   62

   After the Thaw (the 1990s): *Jona che visse nella balena, 18.000 giorni
   fa, Life Is Beautiful, The Truce*   70

PART II   Recovered Memory: Contemporary Italian Holocaust Films in Depth

3. The Haunting Strains of Holocaust Memory: Ricky Tognazzi's *Canone inverso* (Making Love)   85

4. A Childhood Paradise Lost: Andrea and Antonio Frazzi's *Il cielo cade* (The Sky Is Falling)   99

5. The Alter-Biography of the Other-in-Our-Midst: Ettore Scola's *Concorrenza sleale* (Unfair Competition)   111

6. The Holocaust Rescue Narrative and the End of Ideology: Alberto Negrin's *Perlasca: Un eroe italiano* (Perlasca: The Courage of a Just Man)   125

7. The Present through the Eyes of the Past: Ferzan Ozpetek's *La finestra di fronte* (Facing Windows)   140

Postscript – A Glimpse at 2004: *Il servo ungherese* (The Hungarian Servant) and *La fuga degli innocenti* (The Flight of the Innocents)   153

Epilogue: The Holocaust, the Cinema, and 'the Italian Case' in Ettore Scola's '43–'97   161

Bibliography   169

Film Index   175

General Index   179

Acknowledgments

This book would have remained forever in the shadows of uncertainty had it not been for the support of the many friends, associates, and sympathizers who helped me bring it to the light of the printed page. My own personal willingness to begin to confront the horror of the Holocaust, and the challenge of its representation on screen, dates back to 1986 when my colleague at the University of Texas, Seth Wolitz, invited me to participate in a panel discussion of Claude Lanzmann's newly released *Shoah*. Since then, my scholarly interest in the issue developed into a pedagogical one at the University of Pennsylvania, where I team-taught an undergraduate course entitled 'Representations of the Holocaust in Literature and Film' with Al Filreis of the English department, and this collaboration helped me to confront head on the intricate critical problems, along with the emotional turmoil, of such an enterprise. At Penn I also taught graduate courses specifically on the literature and film of the Shoah in Italy, and it is to the students of those classes that I owe an inestimable debt of gratitude for the rich and probing conversations that emerged from our seminar sessions. But it was not until 2003 that this interest coalesced into a book project, thanks to the invitation by Olga Pugliese to become Visiting Goggio Professor at the University of Toronto. There I taught a graduate course on Italian Holocaust representation, and gave a series of public lectures that would form the nucleus of *Italian Film in the Shadow of Auschwitz*. The passionate commitment of my students in that course, along with the unstinting support of the departmental chair, Domenico Pietropaolo, were of the greatest help to the elaboration of my scholarship on the subject. What enabled me to expand the lectures into a full-fledged book-length study was the warm encouragement of Ron Schoeffel, my editor at the University of Toronto Press. Without his good counsel, I never would have had the motivation to extend my inquiry beyond the close reading of a limited sample of films. He convinced me of the wisdom of broadening the scope of my investigation, and it is thanks to his promptings that I discovered the hitherto 'shadowy' body of films that preceded the cinematic upsurge of Holocaust representations in the 1990s. In addition, I would like to thank Ani Deyirmenjian, who has worked with me regarding film stills; managing editor Anne Laughlin, who has been generous and accommodating beyond measure; and my patient, learned, and meticulous copy-editor, John St James. I am extremely grateful to Peter Bondanella and Gaetana Marrone for their supportive and constructive commentary on a provisional draft of the manuscript. I also owe heartfelt thanks to the Italian department of the University of Toronto for granting Goggio funds towards the publication of my text.

Since the incubation period for this book coincided with my seven years on the faculty at the University of Pennsylvania, it is to the students, faculty, and administration of Penn that I owe my most sustained debt of gratitude. Regular exchanges of news about scholarly developments of mutual interest with my colleague Victoria Kirkham were of the greatest help to me during this time, as was the generous and continuous logistical support of Nicola Gentili and Robert Cargni. My warm thanks go to the deans at Penn for granting me a semester's leave of absence to work full-time on my study. At Yale, my project very much benefited from the support of my department chair, Giuseppe Mazzotta; of my colleague Risa Sodi, who profoundly shares my research interests; of Daniel Leisawitz, who expertly prepared the index; and of the department's senior administrative assistant, Ann DeLauro. The experience of team-teaching with my colleague in the Department of History at Yale, Frank Snowden, has been extremely important to me in finalizing my thinking about postwar Italian historiography on the subject of Fascist anti-Semitism and the Shoah. With regard to the technological aspects of my project, special thanks go to Phil Kearney and Jude Breidenbach of the Yale Center for Media Initiatives and to Marcus Aden, a member of the faculty support staff at Yale's Information Technology Services.

Other important venues and sources of encouragement for my project have come from my involvement in two sessions organized by the chair of the Department of Religion at the College of William and Mary, Marc Lee Raphael, whose publications of the proceedings (2003 and 2006) in

The Representation of the Holocaust in Literature and Film, volumes 1 and 2, included two essays that appear in revised form in this book. They are 'Ghost Stories: The Haunted History of the Italian Holocaust and the Case of Rosetta Loy,' and 'Weak Memory: From the End of WWII to the End of the Cold War.' Another conference crucial to my project was organized by Joshua Zimmerman at Yeshiva University in 2002. My paper, entitled 'Return of the Repressed: Italian Film and Holocaust Memory,' which synthesized some of the introductory material of this book, was published in *Jews in Italy under Fascist and Nazi Rule, 1922–5.* An earlier version of my current chapter on *Unfair Competition*, entitled 'Ettore Scola's *Concorrenza sleale*: The Alter-Biography of the Other-in-our-Midst' appeared in *Incontri con il cinema italiano.*

I never could have uncovered the archival treasures that emerged from my research without the generous, and often heroic, help of my Italian collaborators. At my 'home base' of the Mediateca Regionale Toscana in Florence, the librarian Umberta Brazzini has been the steadfast facilitator of all my efforts over the years. Emiliano Madiai, Cristina Dell'Orso, and Piero Matteini have also offered me precious technical and film historical advice whenever I called upon them to do so, and the director of the Mediateca, Roberto Salvadori, has been extremely supportive of my research needs. The Centro di Documentazione Ebraica Contemporanea in Milan has provided rich resources for my project, and the film librarian, Irene De Francesco, gave me unlimited access to the centre's video collection. Conversations with Liliana Picciotto were also of the utmost help to my thinking with regard to my discoveries at the CDEC. Thanks to a lead by an American colleague, Virginia Picchietti, I came upon the holdings of Il Pitigliano at the Centro di Cultura Ebraica in Rome, where Michaela Vitale and Vally Debach made available to me important video and print materials. One of my most important 'informants' on the contemporary Italian scene has been my dear friend Carla Montemagno – it was she who brought to my attention the 'case' of Giorgio Perlasca, and the important filmic representation of this unlikely 'eroe italiano.'

But the undisputed hero of this research saga is Roberto Perpignani, editor, faculty member of the Centro Sperimentale, and, most of all, friend, who intervened twice to further my project. In one instance, he provided me with access to a rare film – *La linea del fiume* – whose only extant copy lies in the vaults of the Cineteca Nazionale in Rome. Perpignani literally sat with me as I viewed the footage, frame-by-frame, on the editing equipment of the facility. As a result, not only did I gain knowledge of this elusive text, but I had the most intimate possible experience of the medium of film in all its concrete materiality. But Perpignani came to my aid in a matter of far greater consequence to my project as a whole. It was he who approached Ettore Scola on my behalf to ask for the rights to '43–'97. Perpignani went to incredible lengths to explain my study to Scola, and then to physically squire the 35-mm original of the film through the digitizing process. In a very real sense, then, Perpignani is the 'producer' of my book's DVD.

By far the most extraordinary benefactor of my project has been Ettore Scola himself, who gave me permission to duplicate his miniature masterpiece for the DVD that accompanies this text. In his 10-minute film, Scola manages to say everything I aspire to prove in my book-length study about the relationship between the best Italian cinema and the life of the country to which it bears witness. My only hope is that *Italian Film in the Shadow of Auschwitz* can begin to justify the great gift that Scola has conferred upon me.

ITALIAN FILM IN THE SHADOW OF AUSCHWITZ

Historical Background Sketch

'Because of the large dimensions of the camp, the complexity of its organization, and the number of those who found death there,' writes Roberto G. Salvadori, 'the name of Auschwitz has justly become emblematic, summarizing all of the forms that Nazi persecution took toward the Jews and other ethnic groups, in its crudest phase.'[1] Yet in the Italian case, the synecdochal force of Auschwitz, its power to conjure up the entire *univers concentrationnaire* of which it was but one example, should not supersede its literal meaning. For Jewish Italy, Auschwitz was the material destination of eleven of the fifteen transports that led 6806 victims to their death between October 1943 and December 1944.[2] For Italian Jews, Auschwitz was not the synecdoche, but the synonym, for annihilation.

By a kind of atrocious historical coincidence,[3] the first Nazi round-up in Italy struck at the oldest Jewish settlement in all of Europe – that of Rome, whose records date back at least as far as 4 BC, preceeding the well-known influx of Hebrew captives from the Roman conquest of Jerusalem in AD 70, so notoriously depicted in the bas-reliefs on the

---

1 Roberto G. Salvadori, *Auschwitz perché: La realtà del male* (Arezzo: Limina, 2004), 13. Unless otherwise noted, all translations from the Italian are mine.
2 A detailed list of these transports, including dates, places of departure and arrival, and numbers of victims and survivors, may be found in *Discriminazione e persecuzione degli ebrei nell'Italia fascista*, ed. Ugo Caffaz (Florence: La Giuntina, 1988), 81–4.
3 According to Liliana Picciotto, Naples had been the original target of the Nazis' first round-up of Italian Jews. See her fundamental article 'The Shoah in Italy: Its History and Characteristics,' in *Jews in Italy under Fascist and Nazi Rule, 1922–1945*, ed. Joshua D. Zimmerman (New York: Cambridge University Press, 2005), 212.

arch of Titus.[4] At the height of the imperial period, this community reached a peak of 50,000 inhabitants, and it would provide the seedbed for the Jewish settlements that would spring up throughout Italy in the centuries to come. Those populations would be further enlarged by the arrival of immigrants from Germany and France after the Black Plague of 1348 (for which Jews were often made the scapegoats), from Spain and its territories after the 1492 expulsions, and from the Middle East, creating communities of great internal variety and complexity – veritable microcosms of diasporic Judaism. The Jews of Venice, for example, had five separate synagogues catering to the ritual needs of their diverse *scole*, or cults: the *Scola tedesca* and the *Scola Canton* (both Ashkenazic); the *Scola spagnola* and the *Scola levantina* (both Sephardic); and the *Scola italiana*. The Roman Jewish community was similarly arrayed among a plurality of *scole* – the *Tempio*, the *siciliana*, the *catalana*, the *nova*, and the *castigliana*.[5]

Throughout its two-thousand-year history, Italian Judaism was beset by restrictions, taxations, and repressions, relieved by sporadic bouts of tolerance (thanks to the eclecticism of Renaissance humanist thought, from the fifteenth to mid-sixteenth century, and thanks to the human-rights advances of the Enlightenment [12–13]). But no term better sums up the Italian Jewish predicament than that of the ghetto – a word of Venetian origin referring to the area previously occupied by the city's iron foundaries (*gettare* means to cast, but the German immigrants transformed the soft Italian *g* sound to the more guttural *gh*) where this minority was forced to reside in isolation from the Christian world. The material wretchedness of ghetto life is well known – residents were not only confined to a limited living space that became ever more crowded and unsanitary as the population expanded, but they were generally restricted to the least lucrative of livelihoods – street peddling, rag-picking, selling used clothing and goods – and were subject to onerous taxation, all of which kept the community in a state of chronic indigence (13). Added to these physical hardships were a host

---

4 For this, and much of the following material on the history of Italian Jewry, I am deeply indebted to Susan Zuccotti's pioneering English-language study *The Italians and the Holocaust: Persecution, Rescue and Survival* (Lincoln: University of Nebraska Press, 1996), 12. Henceforth, page references to this work will be included in the body of my text.

5 See Anna Foa, *Ebrei in Europa: Dalla Peste Nera all'emancipazione* (Milan: Mondadori, 2001), 162.

of spiritual and psychological ones – the age-old suspicion that Jews practised ritual murder, the Church-sponsored accusations of deicide, and the intense pressure to convert meant that Jewish identity itself was under constant assault during the ghetto years (14). But despite these highly documented adversities, ghettoization is now being 're-evaluated,' according to historian Anna Foa, who argues that forced segregation favoured powerful currents of internal cultural renewal and the elaboration of a vital and coherent collective sense of self.[6] No longer considered simply a restrictive and deleterious barrier to a better condition, the self-enclosure of the ghetto is now being viewed in a very different light, as protective and reassuring, representing 'the concrete realization of those invisible walls that the Law had constructed around the identity of the Jewish people, to protect it and conserve it.'[7]

All this was radically to change during the Risorgimento period, when the ghettos were abolished and Jews were granted full citizenship under the constitutional monarchy that united Italy in 1870. Proud of their emancipated status, Jews embraced their *italianità*, enlisting enthusiastically in the military, rising to leadership positions in the government, and participating whole-heartedly in all aspects of civic life (15–18). Mussolini's regime, from its onset in 1922, inspired the same devout loyalty from Jewish quarters as had previous national governments, and Jews enrolled in the Fascist party in proportions equal to those of their Christian compatriots (23–4). Unlike Hitler's rise to power in 1933, Mussolini's founding of his dictatorship in the 1920s had no corollary in racism – Il Duce's rhetoric did not assume anti-Semitic overtones until the second decade of his regime, when it could serve the dual purpose of humouring his ally to the north and creating an innovation in a Fascist domestic ideology gone stale. 'There were ... many restless youths, unhappy with the few novelties introduced by Fascist culture,' writes Ugo Caffaz. 'There was a need to create an element of rupture with the bourgeois past, it was necessary to "understand" that the racial question stood at the base of the foundation of the new Fascist society, of the new Italy.'[8] Far from being an imposition by Hitler on an unwilling partner in the Axis of Steel, as has been com-

---

6 On this 'rivalutazione del ghetto,' see Foa's incisive historiographic commentary, especially ibid., 287–8.

7 Ibid., 160.

8 See the Introduction to *Discriminazione e persecuzione degli ebrei nell'Italia fascista*, 12.

monly held,[9] the move toward 'Aryanization' was a spontaneous gesture on the part of Mussolini, eager to ingratiate himself with his German partner and searching for a racial 'other' against which Italian national identity could be consolidated from within. For this purpose, Mussolini mounted a vicious anti-Semitic campaign in the press, culminating in the Racial Laws of 1938–9, and heralded by a proclamation, designed to give the program a veneer of scientific authority, issued on 26 July and published in the August edition of the newly founded journal *Difesa della razza* (Defence of the Race). Entitled 'Il manifesto della razza,' and signed by 'a group of Fascist scholars, professors of Italian universities,'[10] the document made the following claims:

1. Human races exist.
2. There exist great races and small races.
3. The concept of race is purely biological.
4. The population of today's Italy is of Aryan origin and its civilization is Aryan.
5. The contribution of huge masses of men [of alien races] in historical times is a legend.
6. There now exists a pure 'Italian race.'
7. It is time for Italians to proclaim themselves frankly racists.
8. It is necessary to make a clear distinction between Mediterraneans of Europe (Western), on the one hand, and Orientals and Africans, on the other.
9. Jews do not belong to the Italian race.
10. The purely European physical and psychological characteristics of the Italians must not be altered in any way.[11]

Between September 1938 and June 1939, the Fascist government spewed out a series of laws that effectively condemned this tiny and

---

9 For a challenge to this conventional wisdom, see Jonathan Steinberg, *All or Nothing: The Axis and the Holocaust, 1941–43* (London and New York: Routledge, 2002), 225. Accordingly, Philip V. Cannistraro argues that the 1938 Racial Laws represented no sudden change in Fascist thinking, but were deeply rooted in policies and public pronouncements made by Il Duce throughout the second decade of his rule. See 'Mussolini and Fascist Anti-Semitism: Turning Point of a Regime,' in *The Italian Jewish Experience*, ed. Thomas P. DiNapoli (Stony Brook, NY: Forum Italicum Publishing, 2000), 133–9.

10 See Caffaz, ed., *Discriminazione e persecuzione degli ebrei nell'Italia fascista*, 19.

11 Ibid., 19–21. For reasons of space, I have translated only the titles of the ten *proposizioni*, omitting the explanatory paragraphs that follow each one.

highly assimilated minority (amounting to slightly more than 0.1 per cent of the total population),[12] to what Fabio Galluccio has called a 'civic death.'[13] On 5 September Jews were banned from attending public schools and expelled from all faculty ranks. On 17 November Mussolini issued the most comprehensive set of anti-Semitic rules, setting limitations on property and business ownership by Jews, barring them from mixed marriages, military service, and the employment of Christian domestic help and denying them positions in banks, insurance companies, or government offices (36). The 17 November document also confronted the thorny question of who was a Jew, taking into account cases of mixed parentage and expedient baptism (1 October 1938 serving as a pivotal date) and providing for a Byzantine series of exceptions, exemptions, and so on (36–8). Further anti-Semitic regulations were issued throughout 1939, including the 29 June edict that categorically banned Jews from serving as notaries and allowed only those eligible for exemptions to practise medicine (human or veterinary), law, accounting, engineering, architecture, chemistry, agronomy, journalism, pharmacy, or mathematics (39). To complete the social ostracism of its Jewish subjects, Fascist policy prevented them from owning radios (*the* mass medium par excellence in 1930s Europe and lifeline to the outside world), listing their names and numbers in telephone directories, placing obituaries in local newspapers, giving public lectures, or attending vacation resorts (40).

This heinous and incremental assault on the rights of an indigenous minority met with no resistance on the part of the Italian public. The laws were implemented, with varying degrees of rigour, throughout the land and the positions vacated by Jews in the numerous faculties, professions, and offices from which they were expelled were easily filled by willing replacements among the gentile population. Perhaps most shocking was the silence of the cultural elite, which failed to make any show of political opposition or moral outrage in the face of such injustice. 'There were no intellectuals, writers, journalists, leaders of public opinion, *maitres-à-penser* disposed to raise their voices against the racial laws,' writes Furio Colombo. 'Few approved the laws openly; many others only pretended to do so. But neither was there any real opposition on the part of those who would subsequently become

---

12   In 1938 there were 47,000 Jews, in a country of 45 million.
13   See Fabio Galluccio, *I Lager in Italia* (Civezzano: Nonluoghi, 2003), 29.

heroes and chiefs of the Resistance. The Pope remained silent (even if the Catholic Church provided significant help), and lost a great opportunity to reaffirm his moral leadership.'[14]

Much has been made of the distinction between the Jews' predicament under the Fascist Racial Laws from 1938 to 1943, and their far more dire plight under the Nazi occupation from 1943 to 1945. September 8, 1943, was the watershed date, when the government of King Victor Emmanuel III and Marshal Pietro Badoglio – the latter appointed to replace Mussolini after *Il Duce*'s ouster on 25 July – signed an armistice with the American, French, and British Allied forces, precipitating the German occupation of the country and the agonizing twenty-month campaign of liberation. For Italian Jews, September 8 signalled the divide between discrimination and persecution, between legally sanctioned segregation, on the one hand, and atrocity and death, on the other. Further proof of the vital distinction between Italian and German anti-Semitism is the exemplary behaviour of the civilian populace during the Nazi occupation period, when much was done, on the private and minor institutional level, to thwart the workings of genocide.[15] It is thanks to the massive efforts of individual Italians – who hid Jews in their homes, participated in rescue networks, procured false identity papers and food ration cards, while local churches and lay Catholic organizations offered sanctuary in monasteries, convents, and orphanages (despite the official neutrality of the Vatican) – that a significant majority of the Jewish population survived. In addition, Italian military forces in Croatia, Greece, and southern France went to extravagant lengths to protect the Jews in their charge.[16] This profoundly generous and humanitarian attitude towards a persecuted minority helped bolster the Italians' own emerging self-image as either victims of the Nazi-Fascist war machine (e.g., the 115,000 soldiers who died, ill-equipped and abandoned by their German allies on the Russian Front) or as heroic Resistance fighters, all of which contributed persuasively to the stereotype of *italiani brava gente* (Italians, good folks).

Though the undeniable differences between Fascist and Nazi racist programs cannot help but mitigate our judgment of the Italian case,

14 See Colombo's introduction to Zuccotti, *The Italians and the Holocaust*, xvi.
15 See, for example, Steinberg, *All or Nothing*, 228–9, 240–1.
16 For a detailed account of this fortunate tendency, see Zuccotti's chapter 5, 'Italians and Jews in the Occupied Territories,' in *The Italians and the Holocaust*, 74–100, and Steinberg, *All or Nothing*, especially Part I, Phases Two and Three.

there is no question that Mussolini's policies laid the foundations for the genocidal program to come. Once the deposed Mussolini was reinstated on 23 September 1943, by German fiat, as the leader of Fascist Italy (renamed the Republic of Salò, with its capital on the shores of Lake Garda), his Black Shirts gladly collaborated with their Nazi counterparts to carry out the Final Solution. With a bureaucratic infrastructure firmly in place, thanks to the institutionalized anti-Semitism of the Racial Laws, the work of identifying, capturing, detaining, and deporting this populace could be carried out with relative ease. 'Prior to the German occupation' writes Liana Picciotto,

> the Italian Fascist regime had worked to instill anti-Judaism in public opinion, had already passed anti-Jewish laws, had kept its records on Jews constantly up to date, and had already set up a special department in the interior ministry named the Department for Demography and Race, in charge of managing and implementing anti-Jewish policies ... [I]n Italy, the first building blocks of the edifice of anti-Semitism were put in place by Fascism at the time of the monarchy and not by Nazism, thus paving the way for the extermination planned by the latter.[17]

In the context of the Shoah, what the Italians have to atone for, then, is not their own behaviour under the Nazi occupation of 1943–5, during which time their actions were admirable when they were not indeed heroic, but the passive acceptance of a long-lived regime whose racist policies were the first cause in the chain of events leading to the deaths of 8529 of their Jewish compatriots. This number, which amounts to 26.24 per cent of the Italian Jewish population of 1943, includes the 6806 deportees mentioned above, plus 322 who died by suicide or escape attempts while detained in Italy, and another 950 who went missing.[18] The collective task of coming to terms with this agonizing historical chapter – one that has been a residual 'blind spot,'[19] an object of repression and avoidance of mass accountability – is finally coming to the cultural forefront. In the case of Italian film, the shadow cast by Auschwitz is no longer an obstruction to the screening of this narrative, but a darkness that has found its place in the cinematic chiaroscuro of the present age.

17 Picciotto, 'The Shoah in Italy,' 210.
18 For these statistics, see ibid., 219–21.
19 This is Furio Colombo's apt term. See his introduction to Zuccotti's *The Italians and the Holocaust*, xvii.

PART ONE

Weak Memory:
From the End of the Second World
War to the End of the Cold War, with
a Foray into the 1990s

1 Ghost Stories: An Introduction

Grief Work

The fifteen survivors of the Roman Jewish community who returned from Auschwitz in 1945 were like ghosts, wrote Elsa Morante. 'Erano figure spettrali come numeri negativi, al di sotto di ogni veduta naturale, e impossibili perfino alla comune simpatia. La gente voleva rimuoverli dalle proprie giornate come dalle famiglie normali si rimuove la presenza dei pazzi, o dei morti' (They were spectral figures, like negative numbers, beneath all natural sight, inconceivable even for common friendliness. People wanted to censor them from their days as normal families remove the mad or the dead).[1] But it was not just their wasted appearances that rendered these survivors ghostly in the eyes of their compatriots. If by ghosts we mean the souls that return from the hereafter to remind us of unfinished business, like the spirits of the unburied in Greek antiquity who wandered the earth as a grim memento of their family's failure to meet their interment obligations, or like the spectre of Hamlet's father who incited the Danish prince to avenge his murder at the hands of Claudius, then the Auschwitz survivors performed a similar, admonitory function. These returnees from the world of death brought tidings that disturbed the fragile postwar peace of the living, that troubled the consciences of their compatriots who had acquiesced to a regime that institutionalized anti-Semitism and helped implement the 'Final Solution' for 8529 of Italy's Jews. Unwilling or unprepared to con-

---

1 Elsa Morante, *La Storia, Romanzo* (Turin: Einaudi, 1974), 377. The English is from Elsa Morante, *History, A Novel*, trans. William Weaver (New York: Random House, 1984), 321.

front the consequences of their passive and inadvertent complicity in genocide, most Italians closed their ears to the reports brought back by these ghostly messengers. 'Presto essi impararono che nessuno voleva ascoltare i loro racconti' (Soon they [the returnees] learned that nobody wanted to listen to their stories),[2] Morante concluded, and indeed not even she, the author of the impassioned survey of history written 'from below,' would give Rome's Auschwitz survivors a sustained voice. This unlistened-to story, this news that made people turn away, shrinking into the attitudes of indifference or outright denial that Primo Levi so fearfully anticipated during the long nights in Auschwitz,[3] has been the story of Italy's relationship to Holocaust history from the end of the Second World War through the 1980s. Among contemporary filmmakers, it is Ettore Scola who pointedly remarks on Italy's silence with respect to this chapter 'poco frequentato e poco edificante della nostra Storia' (little revisited and hardly edifying, of our History).[4]

Of all possible cultural venues for working through this troubled history, it is the cinema that surprises us most with its reticence. Filmmakers working in a realist tradition known for its courage in facing sociopolitical injustices past and present, show a surprising reluctance to confront Mussolini's racial laws and the ensuing genocidal campaign. Historian Niccolò Zapponi, for example, finds it significant that the inaugural film of neo-realism, *Rome, Open City*, 'avoided venturing into the most wretched, and least "open" area of the city: the Ghetto.'[5] 'In fifty years of Italian cinema,' Paolo Finn notes, there has been 'a decidedly limited production of works regarding this topic' – a topic that constitutes 'one of the most despicable and dramatic pages in our history, *never adequately reconsidered*' (emphasis mine).[6] Fascist anti-Semitism and the fate of the Jews under the Nazi occupation of Italy is 'a theme absolutely unpleasant to mass audiences,' according to Finn,

---

2 Ibid. in both the Italian and English editions.
3 For this oft-repeated nightmare, see Primo Levi, *Se questo è un uomo, La tregua* (Turin: Einaudi, 1989), 53–4 and 191. For the English translations, see Levi, *Survival at Auschwitz*, trans. Stuart Woolf (New York: Touchstone, 1996), 59–60, and *The Reawakening*, trans. Stuart Woolf (New York: Touchstone, 1995), 55.
4 See the preface to the screenplay of *Concorrenza sleale* (Turin: Lindau, 2001), 5.
5 Niccolò Zapponi, 'Fascism in Italian Historiography, 1986–93: A Fading National Identity,' *Journal of Contemporary History* 29 (October 1994), 565. I am grateful to Julie Doochin, a Master's student in History at the University of Pennsylvania, for calling my attention to this important article.
6 See Finn's review of Ettore Scola's *Concorrenza sleale* in *Cinemasessanta* 42 (March–April 2001), 21–2.

because' it would have raised *unresolved questions* about our embarrassing recent past' (emphasis mine).[7] And yet, is not this precisely what the Italian *cinema d'impegno* (*engagé* cinema) was designed to do? Neorealist filmmakers Rossellini, De Sica, and Visconti in the 1940's and their successors in the realist tradition, the Tavianis, the early Bertolucci, and Pasolini, revelled in *temi sgradevoli* (unpleasant themes): Fascist psychopathology, postwar unemployment, the social neglect of the elderly, worker exploitation, the plight of the subproletariat. When treating historical subjects they did so in order to make the *passato* indeed *prossimo* – linked to the present in causally significant ways, reading history, in Gramscian terms, as 'current politics in a nutshell.'[8] Far from avoiding unresolved social issues, Italian cinema offered itself as the medium for raising them – the movie screen as collective sounding board for the acknowledgment, through representation, of the tensions and contradictions at the basis of the Italian national self.

Given the relative dearth of films on Fascist anti-Semitism and the Holocaust to emerge from Italy during the postwar era, the interest on the part of directors in recent years is all the more dramatic and noteworthy. Films to treat the Shoah since 1990 include Roberto Faenza's *Jona che visse nella balena* (Jonah Who Lived in the Whale, 1993), Gabriella Gabrielli's *18.000 mila giorni fa* (18,000 Days Ago, 1994), Benigni's *La vita è bella* (Life Is Beautiful, 1997), Francesco Rosi's *La tregua* (The Truce, 1997), Andrea and Antonio Frazzi's *Il cielo cade* (The Sky Is Falling, 2000), Ricky Tognazzi's *Canone inverso* (distributed under the English title *Making Love*, 2000), Ettore Scola's *Concorrenza sleale* (Unfair Competition, 2001), Ferzan Ozpetek's *La finestra di fronte* (Facing Windows, 2003), Massimo Piesco and Giorgio Molteni's *Il servo ungherese* (The Hungarian Servant, 2004), and the made-for-TV films *Senza confini* (Without Borders) by Fabrizio Costa (2001), *Perlasca* by Alberto Negrin (2002), and *La fuga degli innocenti* (The Flight of the Innocent) by Leone Pompucci (2004).

This outpouring of films on Fascist anti-Semitism and the Final Solution did not occur in a vacuum, however; it is a sign of what Fabio Girelli-Carasi has greeted as the belated emergence of a Jewish discourse in the Italy of today.[9] At the institutional level, this recent public impulse to memorialize the plight of Italian Jewry has taken several

---

7 Ibid., 22.
8 Antonio Gramsci, *Il Risorgimento*, ed. Maria Corti (Turin: Einaudi, 1952), 114.
9 Fabio Girelli-Carasi, 'Italian-Jewish Memoirs and the Discourse of Identity,' in *The Most Ancient of Minorities*, ed. Stanislao G. Pugliese (Westport, CT: Greenwood Press, 2002), 191–9.

conspicuous forms, including legislation approved in 2000 to establish 'Il Giorno della Memoria' every year on January 27, the day of the liberation of Auschwitz, and a law passed in 2003 mandating the foundation of a Museo Nazionale della Shoah in Ferrara.

How do we account for this surge of interest in the Holocaust after so many years of relative silence? Or, to return to my initial conceit, why are Italians from the 1990s on finally willing to be haunted by this history, finally ready to accept the morally disquieting messages brought by the ghostly emissaries from Auschwitz? In addressing this question, I will adopt a two-fold strategy – both psychoanalytic and political-historical – approaching Italy's recent openness to the Nazi genocide in terms of Freudian *Trauerarbeit* (grief-work) and attributing the timing of this development to a set of concrete circumstances that arose in the 1990s.

In psychoanalytic terms, the ghosts that make such guilt-inducing claims on us, that compel us to take up the issues left unresolved at their death, might be seen as psychic projections of those in whom the mourning process has remained incomplete. For Eric Santner, who theorizes Nazism and the Final Solution 'under the sign of massive trauma,' mourning is the appropriate therapeutic means for 'elaborating and integrating the reality of loss or traumatic shock.'[10] The ability to construct a healthy group identity, according to Santner, is predicated on a cultural willingness to grapple with historical trauma; in other words, to undertake the collective work of mourning. The aim of such *Trauerarbeit*, however, must be two-fold. In a Freudian context, mourning requires a particular form of remembering that allows the libido gradually to disengage from the object of loss. This is accomplished through a carefully calibrated process of libidinal reinvestment or hypercathexis of the object of memory before the bereaved psyche can finally let go, and move on to invest in more appropriate objects, according to the dictates of the pleasure principle.[11] When the loss that

---

10 See Eric Santner, 'History beyond the Pleasure Principle: Some Thoughts on the Representation of Trauma,' in *Probing the Limits of Representation: Nazism and the 'Final Solution,'* ed. Saul Friedlander (Cambridge, MA: Harvard University Press, 1992), 144.

11 The task is 'carried out bit by bit, at great expense of time and cathectic energy, and in the meantime the existence of the lost object is psychically prolonged. Each single one of the memories and expectations in which the libido is bound to the object is brought up and hyper-cathected, and detachment of the libido is accomplished in respect of it.' Sigmund Freud, 'Mourning and Melancholia,' in *The Standard Edition of the Complete Psychological Works of Sigmund Freud*, vol. 14, trans. and ed. James Strachey (London: Hogarth Press, 1953–74), 245.

is mourned involves traumatic shock, then *Trauerarbeit* must accomplish a further task – that of allowing the psyche to experience the anxiety that was absent at the time of the original occurrence, for it is the very absence of such anxiety that lies at the heart of trauma.[12] In Santner's study, the kind of cultural manifestations that will achieve the goals of Freudian mourning are defined in polar opposition to what the critic calls 'narrative fetishism' or representations that stave off anxiety by expunging 'the traces of the trauma or loss that brought the narrative into being in the first place.'[13] By contrast, we can infer that successful narratives of mourning will rehearse the history of devastation and horror without resorting to anxiety-calming expedients.

It is in this sense that we may see Italy's recent impulse to revisit the Holocaust in the arts as a way of undertaking the mourning work necessary to overcome traumatic shock. The outpouring of texts and films on the subject may be understood as a form of Freudian repetition compulsion, of *fort-da* activity,[14] in order to belatedly experience and symbolically contain the anxiety that had been repressed at the time of the event. To achieve the work of Freudian *Trauerarbeit*, therefore, Italian Holocaust representation must bring its Jewish victims vividly and convincingly back to life in order to tell the story of their destruction and, with them, the destruction of the integrity and wholeness of the Italian *communitas* to which this minority belonged. Or, to invoke Michele Sarfatti's metaphor of the Italian body politic, 'Those who decided to persecute them performed an actual mutilation, tearing a piece of living flesh from the nation ... The Jews represented a bone, a muscle, a lung, in sum, an essential living part.'[15] In mourning the fate of its Holocaust victims, then, Italy is also mourning the demise of a certain all-inclusive myth of community, with the accompanying sorrow and anxiety that such a loss entails.

---

12 For Freud's discussion of traumatic neurosis as a shock whose necessary anxiety is not experienced by the victim, see 'Beyond the Pleasure Principle,' in *The Standard Edition*, vol. 18, 32.

13 Santner, 'History beyond the Pleasure Principle,' 144.

14 This refers to the important conclusions reached by Freud upon observing his grandson as the child invented a game to cope with the anxiety over his mother's absence. Repeatedly causing his favourite toy to disappear (accompanied by his exclamation *fort*, meaning 'go away') and to reappear (greeted by the exclamation *da*, meaning 'there'), the child symbolically enacted his sense of loss of, but also his power to regain, the object of love. See Freud, 'Beyond the Pleasure Principle,' 18, 15–16.

15 Michele Sarfatti's indictment is quoted in Galluccio, *I Lager in Italia* (Civezzano: Nonluoghi, 2003), 32.

It remains to be seen, however, why the 1990s, in particular, should be the time for this cultural overture towards the plight of the Jews in Italy under Fascist and Nazi rule. In Fabio Girelli-Carasi's terms, why would a Jewish discourse arise at this particular historical juncture? Most intriguing for me is the hypothesis that links such a development to the end of the Cold War, whose ideological polarization had prevented any serious engagement with Holocaust history, and to the consequent loosening of the stranglehold that Left-Right oppositional thought had on historiography.[16] It should come as no surprise that the postwar Right would be loath to revisit one of Fascism's most despicable chapters, but the Left's stake in avoiding the issues of the Racial Laws and the subsequent genocidal campaign is less obvious. Such avoidance may stem from the need to protect a certain understanding of Second World War history that privileges anti-Fascism as the foundation on which the progressive movement in postwar Italian politics based its claim for legitimacy. Any emplotment of the wartime past that threatened the 'Resistance master narrative' – and the plight of Italian Jewry certainly qualifies as such a threat – would have to be overlooked in order to maintain the prestige and authority of this foundational account.[17] With the fall of the Berlin wall in 1989, the collapse of the Soviet Union in 1991, and the following dissolution of the Italian Communist Party, the selective reading of Second World War history could give way to the other stories, or indeed, the stories of 'the other,' that emerged from this highly charged past. In terms of the Shoah, it was as if the floodgates had finally been opened, and the belated work of confronting this anguished episode in Italian national history could finally begin. Historian Niccolò Zapponi connects this development to what he calls a 'global change in culture' motivated by the 'the ever more widespread drive toward rethinking the 'fascist'

---

16 On the European level, Annette Wieviorka gives the following explanation for the Cold War suppression of Holocaust history. The Left's insistence that fascism had not ended with the Second World War, but endured in all contemporary non-Communist regimes, and the Right's assertion that concentration camps were not the exclusive province of the Nazis, but that they were alive and well in the Soviet gulags, meant that the role of the *Lager* in the extermination of European Jewry was entirely overlooked. See *Déportation et génocide: Entre la mémoire et l'oubli* (Paris: Plon, 1992), 20. I would like to thank Liliana Picciotto for calling my attention to Wieviorka's work.

17 See Zapponi, 'Fascism in Italian Historiography,' 555. For an anecdotal report of the way in which the Resistance dominated the Italian historical imagination (and pedagogy), see Galluccio, *I Lager in Italia*, 9.

event from the *Jewish* point of view ... A through examination of this question would entail establishing in what way, during the past two decades (approximately), the whole of the Western world has rethought its identity with respect to the Nazi massacres.'[18] In this important formulation, Zapponi acknowledges the need for a comparative and indeed international approach to the question – an approach that exceeds the scope of my current, narrowly focused study, but whose challenge, it is to be hoped, will be met by scholars more competent than I to take up its global dimensions.

Another important factor in explaining the current impulse to revisit the plight of the Jews under Fascist and Nazi rule has been the influx of Third World immigrants, which prompts Italians to reconsider their relationships to the 'other in our midst' and acknowledge the extremes to which intolerance may lead. In order to dramatize the continuity between the past and the present of racial intolerance, Ettore Scola made the stunning short film entitled *'43–'97*, which is be the subject of detailed analysis in my epilogue and may be viewed on the DVD accompanying this book. In another example of the need to remember the lessons of the Shoah as contemporary Italy struggles to accommodate waves of immigrants from the Third World, the television station RAIUNO chose to frame the broadcast of Roberto Faenza's Holocaust film *Jona che visse nella balena* with a series of questions aimed at the viewing audience. The film was thus presented as a highly interactive event involving written queries that streamed across the bottom of the frame during relevant episodes within the narrative, accompanied by a phone number to which viewers could call in their answers. The questions read as follows: 'Is racial hatred dead, or could it arise again?' 'Is it possible to pardon without forgetting?' And, finally, transforming an aphorism uttered by one of the characters into a query: 'Is it right to always look upwards and never hate anyone?' The relevance of Faenza's film to Italy's struggle to accept its new multi-ethnic identity was reinforced by an interview with Jonah Oberski – author of the memoirs on which the film was based – who concluded with a blanket condemnation of racism in all of its possible forms.

A factor not to be discounted in the Italian cultural openness to a Jewish discourse is the evolving position of the Roman Catholic Church in this regard. A series of events under the papacy of John Paul

---

18 Zapponi, 'Fascism in Italian Historiography,' 550.

II marked major steps forward in Vatican–Jewish relations, beginning with the pontiff's visit to Auschwitz in 1979. But perhaps the most important milestone in this recent history of interfaith healing was John Paul II's acceptance of Chief Rabbi Elio Toaff's 1986 invitation to the synagogue in Rome. The first pope to ever enter a Hebrew place of worship, John Paul II named the Jews 'nostri fratelli prediletti e, in un certo modo, si potrebbe dire i nostri fratelli maggiori' (our favorite brothers and, in a certain way, you could say, our older brothers).[19] During this eventful visit, the pontiff invoked the ecumenical work of John XXIII, whose Vatican II council reached out to embrace diversity, and he reaffirmed the 1965 declaration by Paul VI, entitled 'Nostra Aetate,' that dismissed the long-standing and virulent charge of deicide against the Jewish people. In March of the Jubilee Year 2000, John Paul's path of interfaith reconciliation led him to Yad Vachem in Jerusalem, where he declared the Church to be 'profondamente rattristata per l'odio, gli atti di persecuzione e le manifestationi di antisemitismo dirette contro gli ebrei da crisitiani in ogni tempo e in ogni luogo.' (profoundly saddened by the hatred, the acts of persecution and the manifestations of anti-Semitism directed against Jews by Christians in every time and in every place).[20]

The Case of Rosetta Loy's *La parola ebreo*

Arguably the most obvious explanation for the impulse to historical retrospection in the 1990s has been the rise of right-wing extremism and the rehabilitation of Italian Fascism under the guise of Gianfranco Fini's Allianza Nazionale, one of the three parties involved in Silvio Berlusconi's coalition government from 1994 to 1995, and then again from 2001 to 2006. It was precisely this development that led Rosetta Loy to write her searing memoir *La parola ebreo* (1997, published in English under the title *First Words: A Childhood in Fascist Italy,* 2000), which interweaves her experiences as the child of a well-to-do Catholic family with the persecution history of the Roman Jews under Fascist and Nazi rule. 'I asked myself, how come I wrote this book now, when

---

19 See 'Ringraziamo il Signore per la ritrovata fratellanza e per la più profonda intesa tra la Chiesa e l'Ebraismo,' *L'osservatore romano,* 14–15 April 1986, 1.

20 Quoted in Marco Politi, 'La Chiesa non dimentica gli orrori dell'Olocausto, '*La repubblica,* 24 March 2000, 2.

I could have written it a long time ago?' Loy stated in an interview that I will quote at length (in translation) for its crucial importance to the argument at hand.

> In my case it was, in particular, the victory of Berlusconi that gave me a terrible shock: it was a way for me to understand what my parents had experienced at the victory of Fascism. During the elections I thought, 'No, Berlusconi can't win, who could vote for Berlusconi and Fini?' I was truly convinced. The evening in which victory was proclaimed I was alone. It was a terrible moment: I felt as if something which I had deeply believed in had been broken ... I had always thought that amidst the highs and the lows, terrorism, etc., that a process was extending itself. Instead, it's as if I had seen the tide beginning to rise on the other side. This awareness was very important for me, the triggering motive. And I understood that in some way, if there is not an awareness of what we have behind us, it's useless to try to move ahead. Because, first of all, we must come to terms with ourselves, all of us must all come to terms with ourselves, with the most hidden things, concealed in the folds. And only afterwards, I think, can we say that we are free to move ahead.[21]

In this dramatic account of the genesis of *La parola ebreo*, Loy offers a strong argument for the relevance of the approach that I am proposing – that of Santner's psychoanalytic model, grounded in the concrete political-historical circumstances of Italy in the 1990s. The very term 'shock' that Loy uses to signal her response to Berlusconi's victory alerts us to the traumatic power of the past, which can so easily be conjured up by contemporary political occurrences. In connecting her reactions in the 1990s to those of the Fascist generation, Loy seeks to address the historical trauma by re-experiencing it through writing and acknowledging the anxiety that the original event had kept under repression. Such a psychologically fraught return to the past can, according to Loy, help her compatriots to therapeutically 'fare i conti' (come to terms) with themselves and reap the cognitive and moral benefits necessary for the construction of a contemporary Italian national self.

The absence of anxiety that Freud ascribes to the original traumatic incident takes the form, in Loy's case, of the child's carefree perspec-

---

21 'Per Rosetta Loy la memoria è anche assunzione di responsabilità,' http://www .wuz.it/archivio/cafeletterario.it/intervista/loy.html.

tive on events. Oblivious to the meaning of the history to which she bears witness, Loy's childhood focalizer registers these happenings within the protective confines of her innocence. By alternating between the benign routine of life in a privileged Roman household and the dire predicament of the city's Jews, Loy puts into play two forms of cognition – one lodged in the consciousness of the child, experiencing fragmentary perceptions of persecution history without an awareness of their significance, and one lodged in the consciousness of the adult, whose knowledge of the genocidal future of the Roman Jews compels her to insert passages of straightforward historical reportage amidst the annals of childhood. As a result, in every instance of such narrative shifting from first-person reminiscence to third-person persecution chronicle (and there are twelve of them that punctuate the text), Loy enacts the cognitive journey from obliviousness to the full-fledged awareness afforded by historical hindsight. The narrator makes explicit this back and forth movement when she reports from the perspective of 1939–1940, before the onset of catastrophe: 'dovranno accadere cose terribili perchè io torni a visitare quel tempo e guardi nel pozzo dove la signora Della Seta, i Levi, e quel bambino che vedo trotterellare tra una finestra e l'altra stanno scivolando giù senza che ne arrivi il minimo fruscio' (Some terrible things will happen to make me go back and visit that time, to look down into the well that Signora Della Seta, the Levis, and the little boy across the road are sliding into with not the slightest sound).[22] It is, of course, macro-history that will retroactively govern her selection of childhood scenes out of the infinity of other possible autobiographical emplotments that could have structured her text.

In the transitions between third-person historical reportage and first-person reminiscence, Loy insists on contrasting the turbulence of the one set of events with the relative stasis of the second. After the Japanese attack on Pearl Harbor and the U.S. entry into war, for example, Loy marvels: 'Ancora niente turba l'ordine di via Flaminia' (98) (Still nothing disturbs the order in Via Flaminia, 117), and after the promulgation of the 1938 Racial Laws, she admits 'Nelle mie giornate nulla è cambiata ... E se al professore Luzzatti è stato proibito di poggiare il

---

22 Rosetta Loy, *La parola ebreo* (Turin: Einaudi, 1997), 57. For the English translation, see *First Words: A Childhood in Fascist Italy*, trans. Gregory Conti (New York: Henry Holt, 2000), 69. Henceforth, page references to Loy's novel, in both languages, will be included parenthetically in the body of the text.

suo orecchio irsuto sulla mia schiena calda di febbre, è l'orecchio appena unto, morbido e tiepido del professore Vanuttelli ad ascoltare i miei bronchi' (56) (My days haven't changed at all ... And although Dr Luzzatti has been prohibited from laying his hairy ear on my feverish back, I have the soft, warm, slightly oily ear of Dr Vannuttelli to listen to my lungs, 67). There could be no better way to characterize the obliviousness of the childhood perspective than this description of the coddled little girl, whose already limited sphere of awareness is further diminished by the fever that turns perception in on itself. The sickness of the Italian body politic, plagued by anti-Semitism, is registered only peripherally by the child's own sick body, which translates the substitution of the Jewish family doctor for a gentile one into the difference in tactile sensation produced by the pressure of two different ears on the feverish skin of her back. For us, as readers, the difference is catastrophic, leading us to understand that while Dr Luzzatti and his co-religionists were struggling against the external assaults of the racist state on their social well-being, the child Rosetta need only worry about the internal bodily threat of the microbes that attend the usual round of childhood illnesses. Given the girl's elevated and protected social status, the loss of the long-time family doctor will not amount to any lapse in medical care, but only a slight, nearly imperceptible change in bedside manner. Significantly, that change will be registered not by the eyes, with their privileged access to intellection (we are never told how the two men look), but by the skin on the patient's back, through the lower, more primitive and animal sense of touch.

Had Loy not chosen the powerful and provocative title *La parola ebreo* (literally, The Word Jew) for her text, she might have considered the poetically suggestive *Al di là di quelle finestre* (On the Other Side of Those Windows). Such a title would have aligned her childhood voyeurism with the time-honoured poetic trope for representing consciousness and the way in which the outside world impinges upon it. Using the room, the window, and the view into the apartment across the street as metaphors for the child's insulated perspective as it indulges its curiosity about 'the other,' Loy stages the young Rosetta's evolution of consciousness at this lookout point on Via Flaminia. 'Posso guardare nell'appartamento al di là della strada dove dai vetri aperti le tende dondolano all'aria' (3) (I can look into the apartment on the other side of the street and see the curtains there swinging in the breeze, 3), she states in the opening paragraph of the text. It is through this window that Rosetta catches fleeting glimpses of family life in the facing apartment, and there that she observes a party to celebrate the *bris*, or circumcision, of a new baby boy. When she asks her German governess if the festivities are for a baptism, the *Fräulein* snarls, 'No, certo che non ... sono ebrei' (3) (Certainly not ... they are Jews, 3). Thus, Rosetta's first exposure to *la parola ebreo* is through the spiteful and dismissive retort of her governess, while the ceremony of the *bris*, marking the initiation of a Jewish male child into his ethnic community, coincides with Rosetta's initiation into a European community that will ultimately deny that child's right to live his life at all. From Rosetta's *tabula rasa* perspective, however, the governess's contempt for the family across the street is absurd. 'Al di là di quelle finestre, vedo passare bambine con i fiocchi in testa simili al mio, signore con le perle e i corpi fasciati da morbidi vestiti di maglia come quelli della mamma' (4) (Inside the apartment across the street I can see little girls with bows in their hair just like mine, and ladies wearing pearl necklaces, draped in soft knit dresses like the ones my mother wears, 4). To the child Rosetta, the family in the facing apartment is the specular image of her own, with the elegant clothing and accessories that betray a common adherence to bourgeois canons of good taste. The insistence on such terms as *simili* and *come*, and the fact that the individuals sighted are gendered female, only heightens the sense of identification that binds the child voyeur to the objects of her curiosity.

Rosetta neither meets any members of the family in the facing apartment nor does she ever learn their names. They remain fleeting images, as if in a movie imperfectly projected, whose screen will eventually go blank. Rosetta's sporadic glimpses of life in the facing apartment continue beyond the time of the 1938 Racial Laws ('ogni tanto intravedo quel neonato diventato una palla cicciottella che ficca la testa tra una colonnina e l'altra della balaustra del balcone,' 57) [every once in a while I get a glance of the newborn baby, who is now a chubby little ball sticking his head out between the columns of the railing on the balcony, 68]), but by the summer of 1942, the curtains are drawn shut and this life is forever concealed from her view. Also nameless, for the most part, is the succession of pupils who suddenly and inexplicably come to occupy the benches of Rosetta's schoolroom, only to mysteriously disappear a short time later.

Unlike these nameless characters who flit in and out of her life, the Jewish neighbours within Rosetta's building are vividly personalized and portrayed. Giorgio Levi, her brother's playmate, and Signora Della Seta, the kindly matron who brings gifts to cheer up Rosetta during her various childhood illnesses, become the foremost referents of *la parola ebreo*. In a passage of surpassing poignancy, Loy describes her final vision of the Signora, caught as if in a cinematic freeze frame, in the act of giving Rosetta and her siblings a precious gift of boiled bass on the day of their departure from Via Flaminia. This portrait of Signora Della Seta is overlaid with the knowledge of 'le cose terribili che dovranno accadere' (the terrible things that will happen), making the following description stand as a funerary monument, an effigy on the tomb that history will so woefully deny her.

Nessuno ancora sa che un interrogativo smisurato nascerà dalla sua immagine muta mentre ci consegna quel pesce adagiato fra ciuffetti di prezzemolo verde. In quella giornata di luglio la sua immagine si è dissolta lasciando nella memoria un'impronta quasi fosse stampata in trasparenza su una garza, senza che sia possibile, mai più ritrovarne il corpo che intercettava la luce o il movimento di quando si sedeva in salotto, il fruscio della gonna. (108)

Nobody knows yet how great a question will envelop that mute image of Signora Della Seta as she hands us the fish, lying there among sprigs of green parsley. Her image dissolves on that July morning, leaving its mark on my memory as if silk-screened onto fabric. But it will never again be possible to find the living body that intercepted the sunlight or to capture the movement she made when she sat down in our living room, the rustling of her skirt. (128–9)

In this beautiful tribute to Signora Della Seta's last and defining gesture, Loy assumes a fluid narrative position that oscillates between pre- and post- Holocaust time. Written in the present tense from the perspective of the morning in 1940 when the episode occurred, Loy flashes forward to a future of historical knowledge that will cast an *interrogativo smisurato* (immeasurable question) over the remembered event. The nature of this question becomes clear in the very next sentence, which concerns the mystery of *il corpo mai ritrovato* (the body that was never found). Loy's chose of verb, *nascerà* (will be born), is therefore excruciatingly ironic, given the mega-death from which it arises. But irony does not exhaust the poetic richness of this passage, which traces the transformation of Signora Della Seta from fully embodied character, to image, to a mere imprint on the transparency of gauze. The progressive dematerialization of this figure to the gossamer lightness of a veil has special power in the Holocaust context, for it refers not only to the gradual weakening of remembrance but also to the atrocious fate of genocide victims, for whom there is no identifiable corpse, no bodily trace, that could 'give birth' to an image in memory.

But it is the family in the apartment across the street to which I wish to return, for their namelessness, and their existence on the other side of the window that stands for consciousness, makes them the Italian Jewish Every Family, whose predicament was observed, in *campo lungo* (long shot), by the majority of their gentile compatriots. Loy's act of retrospectively assembling the miscellaneous bits and pieces of her childhood memories into a coherent narrative of genocide stands for Italy's collective attempt to come to terms with this agonizing chapter in national history. Loy recounts that when asked to give a lecture in Paris on the Racial Laws, she began with a personal reminiscence about how Giorgio Levi was forced to carry his bicycle up many flights of stairs because the concierge had barred him from using the elevator on the grounds of his ethnicity. This memory triggered an avalanche of related ones, and hence the writing of *La parola ebreo* began.

Of the readings that most influenced her own approach to the Holocaust in Italy, Loy finds in Morante's *La Storia* the key to her own ethical engagement with the plight of Italian Jewry. What struck Loy most, from her own position of social privilege, was Morante's insistence that no one is immune to the onslaughts of history. 'It is useless to say "it doesn't touch me," "it's not important to me," it touches everyone, because it is the belonging to the collectivity that makes us understand history. The collectivity determines me, marks my life and to understand this has a very strong consciousness-raising effect.'[23] It was Loy's impulse to imaginatively overcome class barriers and to be able to identify with the humblest victims of history – with the Idas and the Useppes and the Davides of *La Storia* – that enabled her to write her own impassioned text of witness. Indeed, such was the impact of *La Storia* on Loy that it inspired her to take up and elaborate on Morante's somewhat oblique approach to Holocaust chronicle. 'Presto essi impararono che nessuno voleva ascoltare i loro racconti' (Soon they learned that no one wanted to hear their stories). Morante had written of the fifteen ghostly survivors of Auschwitz who returned to Rome in

---

23 'Per Rosetta Loy la memoria è anche assunzione di responsabilità.'

1945. It would take over four decades for their stories to reach willing ears, and for Italy to be able to begin the work of mourning required by the mass trauma of genocide. For this to happen, a form of historical memory had to arise that would incorporate the occurrence of loss and traumatic shock into the Italian collective consciousness. If the conjuring act of Rosetta Loy is any indication, then Italy's recent willingness to accept its haunted history marks an important step in the process of learning to live with these unquiet ghosts.

2 A Diaphanous Body of Films

'I didn't know that behind certain famous ruins, there was a neighbour-hood that used to be called the ghetto. One day, many years ago, a friend of mine took me there.'[1] This voice-over narration, which leads us into the 1982 television mini-series *Storia d'amore e di amicizia* (Story of Love and Friendship) encapsulates an entire postwar history of igno-rance, inadvertent neglect, or downright repression of the Jewish pre-dicament under the Fascist and Nazi regimes. Especially significant is the fact that the ghetto provided the setting for the most horrific 'signa-ture' event of the Italian Holocaust – the 16 October 1943 round-up of Rome's Jewish community, bound for extermination at Auschwitz. In spatial terms, the voice-over narrator reveals the 'behindness' of this history – its obstruction by the other foregrounded histories that have upstaged or cancelled the dark and uncomfortable 'back' story of Italy's Jews. It is a history that has indeed been ghettoized, and to enter it, like the voice-over narrator, we need a guide who will open its gates and lead us within it exclusive confines.

The 'behindness' of this history extends, as previously argued, to its cinematic representation. Film critics Paolo Finn and Raffaella Anto-nutti put it succinctly: 'In fifty years of Italian cinema we find a decid-edly limited production of works regarding this topic'[2] Both my own film-viewing experience and my reading in the field supported this conventional wisdom on the paucity of Italian films dedicated to the

---

1 Unless otherwise noted, all quotes from the films will come from my translations of the Italian transcribed directly from the soundtracks.
2 See Paolo Finn and Raffaella Antonutti, 'Quando il cielo cade,' *Cinemasessanta* 41 (Sept.–Oct. 2000), 24. For a related comment, see Galluccio, *I Lager in Italia*, 10.

Shoah throughout most of the postwar period. While that indeed proved to be the case, in pursuing my research I was surprised to discover a body of films on the subject that seemed to have escaped critical notice. The relative obscurity of this corpus supported my impression of weak Holocaust memory, for such works, with a few high-profile exceptions (*Kapò*, *Garden of the Finzi-Continis*, *Seven Beauties*, and *The Night Porter*) had no impact on the course of Italian film history, and as a result, they created no continuous tradition, no genealogy, no cumulative discourse, no representational traces. In other words, these films did not talk to each other.[3] It was as if each filmmaker who embarked on a Holocaust narrative had to do so from scratch, without a prior tradition to draw upon, to elaborate and complicate, to polemically react against, or to transgressively rewrite. This meant that the body of Italian Holocaust films was an amorphous and incoherent one, where individual works did not hark back to a linear genealogy, but to a variety of isolated cinematic ancestries. Due to such discontinuity, the minor films that emerged within this oeuvre did not gain the kind of visibility that a more conspicuous cinematic body would have conferred even upon its less acclaimed examples. (I am thinking here of the vast and uneven welter of films dedicated to the representation of Fascism, or of the social critiques levelled, with varying degrees of success, by the practitioners of the *commedia all'italiana* and the *cinema politico* genres. Films within these categories *do* talk to each other, and as a result, individual works, even those of little merit, gain notice as part of a collective and on-going cinematic conversation.)

Without such a representational memory, the Holocaust films to emerge in this postwar period have more in common with concurrent cinematic production than with previous Italian works on the subject. Thus, what I am calling the 'second wave films' (1960–6) share with other works of the time a tendency towards melodramatically tinged sentimental romance, while the mid-1970s auteurist production flirts with the sexual brinksmanship of that tumultuous period. In the survey that follows, patterns will indeed surface, but they will do so more as a result of the surrounding cinematic context than of any conscious attempt on the part of filmmakers to locate their work within a specific discourse on the Italian Jewish plight.

---

3 For this argument, I am deeply indebted to Liana Picciotto, who shared her insights with me in a conversation at the Centro di Documentazione Ebraica Contemporanea in Milan on 15 July 2004.

Soon After (1947–9)

Within the scarce, diffuse, and heterogeneous production of Italian films concerning the Shoah, there is a subgroup that shares a decided tendency to internationalize this history, to project its horrors outside the realm of domestic Jewry. Significantly, the first Italian film to broach Holocaust subject matter, *L'ebreo errante* (The Wandering Jew, 1947) represents Judaic identity as inherently rootless and nomadic, and in so doing, absolves the host country from responsibility for the fate of its itinerant guests. Most disturbing is the linkage that this film establishes between the Shoah and the charges of deicide that gave pseudo-theological justification to anti-Semitism throughout the Common Era. According to the legend that the film's title evokes, the diaspora itself was seen to be divine punishment for complicity in the condemnation and crucifixion of Christ – a crime that the Holocaust served to expiate, if not for the Jewish people as a whole, then at least for the film's protagonist, whose story was clearly identified with the entire course of the Israelites' dispersion from the Holy Land. Directed by the renowned Goffredo Alessandrini, and benefiting from the high-profile acting talents of Vittorio Gassman and Valentina Cortese, *L'ebreo errante* offered a prestigious venue for the staging of this troubling historical parable.

Set in Frankfurt in 1935, the film opens with the visit of Matteo, a mysterious wanderer, to the home of the well-known scientist Dr Lukas Epstein in the hopes of a cure for a malady that is metaphysical in origin. In an extensive flashback that returns us to the man's origins as a wealthy financier in ancient Jerusalem we learn that Matteo had mocked Jesus on the road to crucifixion, prompting the curse that would resound throughout the rest of the film: 'Il mio cammino è breve ormai, ma tu camminerai nei secoli dei secoli finchè la verità non è discesa in te' (By now my path is brief, but you will walk for century after century until the truth has come to you). Another temporal leap, this time to 1940, finds Matteo living in Paris as a prosperous banker who forfeits his social privilege to join his co-religionists in an unnamed concentration camp, where he organizes a rebellion and escapes with his beloved, the beautiful and virtuous Esther. In the end, Matteo chooses to sacrifice his life for the safety of one hundred fellow prisoners being held hostage against his surrender. The protagonist's final utterance, 'Il mio cammino è finito' (My journey is over) recalls Jesus' prophetic pronouncement on the Via Crucis, signalling the Wandering Jew's atonement for the guilt incurred by his original failure to accept salvation in Christ.

Though Matteo never formally converts, the film gives strong indications of his final arrival at the *verità* that Jesus had intimated during their encounter on the road to Calvary. Throughout *L'ebreo errante*, the power to work miracles has been associated with the Christian redemptive process. The ancient Matteo's wife Sarah had predicted that a miracle was needed to save their fatally ill son and that 'the Nazarene' would be its purveyor. Dr Epstein had divined that a miracle could indeed cure Matteo of his malaise – the miracle of 'human brotherhood' – and within the narrative present of the film, it is Esther who is the medium of that transformation, the catalyst who can change Matteo's narcissism and cynical pursuit of self-interest into *caritas*. Thanks to this conversionary process, Matteo can now expiate his two-thousand-year-old rejection of Christ's message by enacting his own *imitatio Christi*, his own martyrdom in the name of human solidarity.

Even more disturbing than the Christianization of this Holocaust narrative is the written inscription of the film's final frames. 'Thus the sacrifice was performed in the love of all mankind,' the text reads, 'as it was in the word of the Lord. And a hope illuminated the heart of a people that an implacable fanaticism wanted to erase from the earth.' This conclusion confers the authority and prestige of a presumptive biblical source on the preceding narrative, and in so doing clinches the troubling argument about the exemplarity of Matteo's story: his personal sacrifice stands for the Holocaust's collective expiation of the Jews' crime against Christendom, and his two thousand years of exile from human concourse is emblematic of the plight of all Jewry since the time of their 'original sin.' 'I was rejected, chased away by everyone like a dog, like my people that I repudiated,' Matteo explains to Dr Epstein during the fateful visit to the scientist's home early in the film. Accompanying the stricken man's voice-over narration is a montage of official-looking documents blaming Jews for the Black Plague of 1348 in Frankfurt, for example, or expelling them from the kingdom of Spain in 1492, in what amounts to a whirlwind tour of exilic history.[4] Matteo,

---

4 The edicts read as follows: (1) 'L'imperatore Carlo IV ordina: la popolazione ebraica di Francoforte sarà garante del pagamento delle spese straordinarie causate dalla peste nera.' (2) 'Ferdinando e Isabella di Castiglia. Ordiniamo che tutti gli ebrei e figli di ebrei abbandonino il territorio del Regno entro novanta giorni pena la confisca dei beni e la morte.'

then, is Jewish 'Everyman,' the quintessential rejecter of Christ whose geographic wandering allegorizes the moral straying of the unredeemed. In offering Matteo the historical venue for absolving his guilt, the Holocaust provides, by atrocious implication, both the just punishment and the redemptive sacrifice of a people in need of salvation.

Where the theme of wandering in *L'ebreo errante* is seen as a moral condition whose only remedy is the *imitatio Christi* of the story's protagonist, in *Il grido della terra* (The Cry of the Land, Duilio Coletti, 1948) the diaspora is portrayed as a historical injustice that can be remedied through a collective journey to the Jewish place of origin. This film is the most overtly Zionistic of our entire corpus, and though its main characters are displaced German Jews as well as Israeli freedom fighters, the story makes Italy its starting point and assigns a pivotal role to the Italian who pilots their ship to the Promised Land.

The film begins in 1947 in a displaced-persons camp located somewhere in southern Italy.[5] Among the *dramatis personae* introduced in the camp are Dr Tannen, a German Jewish survivor of Auschwitz, Dina, the fiancée of his son Davide (who had emigrated to Palestine before the war), and Ari, an Israeli assigned to bring refugees to the Holy Land. After a harrowing voyage to Palestine, Dr Tannen, Dina, and Ari are reunited with Davide, but conflicts immediately arise because the latter, believing in armed rebellion, has joined the Haganah. Davide comes to a violent end after his capture during an attack on British army headquarters, and George Birkmore, an English friend and former co-combatant, along with Ari and David, in the Allied campaign for the liberation of Italy, is executed by the Haganah in retaliation. The film's redemptive promise is only realized in its final scene as the Kibbutz leader announces 'Now, to work' and the young people gather their farming tools to answer *il grido della terra.*

Coletti's film both idealizes and critiques the Zionist dream. Hebrew singing, folkloristic dancing, and a sense of festive abundance surround the arrival of the émigrés to their destination. When the ship's captain admires the fruit offered to him by a lovely local maiden, he is greeted with an account of the Israeli success story. 'A thousand tons of fruit a year,' boasts one young man. 'Five years ago, when my father and I first came, [the harvest was] not even five tons.' As the guest of

---

5 In actual fact, Italian *campi di smistamento* were way stations for many European Jews in transit to Palestine.

honour at this celebration, the ship's captain becomes the focalizer of the Zionist scene. His wonder takes the form of a wish-fulfilment fantasy. 'It's the dream of every sailor – a piece of land, peace, calm.' Of utmost importance is his role as the film's representative Italian – the kind-hearted, nautically skilled, and courageous Genoese captain who facilitates the dream of *aliyah* (return to the Holy Land). 'This journey has great meaning for me ... bringing these desperate people here. I feel like a Good Samaritan rather than a sailor. I hope to come back someday, not in this old wreck of a ship but in one like those I used to sail, with my flag.'

But the Zionist dream is not without its nightmarish underside. When Dr Tannen gushes, 'How beautiful and good everything is here. Now I understand the dream of my son,' he reveals precisely what thwarts its realization: the violent militancy of Davide and his ilk. George Birkmore's leadership role in the British occupying army personalizes the conflict and reveals the extremist effects of fanaticism. Of the three friends who celebrated that Utopian moment of Liberation, it is only Ari who survives, and with him the film celebrates the activist stance of one who rejects the recourse to violence, and who heeds the 'cry of the land' to beat the proverbial swords into plowshares.

Il monastero di Santa Chiara (The Monastery of Saint Clare, Mario Segui, 1949) is the first of our films to have an exclusively Italian focus – a cultural rootedness that brings with it a profound debt to the indigenous postwar cinematic tradition of neorealism. Echoes of *Rome, Open City* (Rossellini, 1945) pervade *Il monastero di Santa Chiara*, from details of casting to the use of music-hall characters, to the pairing of a Gestapo chief with a glamorous and corrupt henchwoman. More importantly, each film is so firmly ensconced in its urban setting that, in one case, *romanità* and, in the other, *partenopeità* (Neapolitan-ness) become full-fledged thematic concerns. Finally, both *Open City* and *Il monastero di Santa Chiara* contaminate their neorealist historicity with the conventions of melodrama – conventions that, in the case of the Neapolitan film, revert to the etymological root of the genre as literally a drama set to music, and that recall the local traditions of the *sceneggiata*, the popular theatrical form involving sentimental stories and musical interludes.

The generic identity of *Il monastero di Santa Chiara* is foregrounded by the film's narrator, a vaudeville impresario who concludes his story with the comment 'It is said that we sing too much. But how can we help it?' 'You are right,' his addressee responds. 'Songs don't kill anyone.' Especially noteworthy is the fact that the narrator's interlocutor is none other than Alberto Moravia, who begins the film by walking into the impresario's office and announcing his name, to which the Neapolitan gentleman replies, 'Does this story really interest you?' Moravia's laconic affirmation, 'Sure, that's why I came here,' serves as the invitation to begin, and the narrator proceeds to tell the tale of Esther De Veroli, vaudeville singer of Jewish descent, who has a romantic liaison with SS officer Rudolph Stassen and is hidden in the convent of Santa Chiara, only to be arrested by the Gestapo soon after Stassen's suicide for love. Esther is freed when the Americans liberate Naples, but is caught in a trap laid by ex-Nazis wanting to extort money from Enrico (played by a young and earnest Nino Manfredi!), an admirer of the singer who has made a fortune in the black market. Shot down by Greta Muller, her rival for Stassen's affections, Esther dies in the arms of Enrico.

As the above storyline suggests, Esther's Jewish origin is a mere plot device for making her the object of special Nazi persecution and hence heightening the stakes of her romance with Rudolph. The only time that her religious identity comes into play is in the conversion narrative that underlies Esther's story. Music becomes the venue for the conversionary message in the guise of three full-length singing performances that punctuate *Il monastero di Santa Chiara*. Esther's first appearance on screen is as a garishly made-up, extravagantly costumed Marlene Dietrich surrogate, singing 'Lily Marlene' to an audience of ogling Neapolitan men and appreciative Nazi guards. This music-hall routine finds its antidote in a symmetrically placed performance towards the film's end in which the protagonist, now cleansed of make-up and demurely dressed, sings before a public of reverential men and women the song 'Monastero di Santa Chiara,' whose most conspicuous line celebrates 'Napoli come'era' (Naples like it was) as a paean to an authentic, pre-war local identity.

If these two vaudeville routines, positioned towards the beginning and the end of the film, mark the secular rebirth of a city ready to embark on a new life, the song sung at the mid-point of *Il monastero di Sant Chiara* testifies to a conversion of a different sort. During her stay in the convent, presented as a privileged space of beauty and *caritas*, a bombing raid occurs in which Esther refuses to take shelter with the nuns. Terrified by the fury of the explosives raining down on the building, Esther runs through the convent to be greeted with the heavenly strains of the sisters who are singing Schubert's arrangement of 'Ave Maria.' Eavesdropping on their gathering, Esther is shown in extreme close-up as the camera intercuts between her wondrous eyes and the image of Christ on the cross. The scene has all the trappings of an epiphany. At the film's end, the dying Esther hears these heavenly strains once more. Rising up, in ecstasy, to the music of the 'Ave Maria,' she marvels, 'How much light ... they are singing' in an unmistakable evocation of a deathbed conversion.

The Second Wave (1960–6)

Though Luigi Comencini's *Tutti a casa* (Everybody Home, 1960) is not a Holocaust narrative in any sustained sense, the film does dedicate important footage to the plight of Italian Jewry and gives this history a prominent place in the protagonist's journey to enlightenment. Comencini's film is a tragicomic treatment of the period between the armistice of 8 September 1943 and the popular uprising in Naples that overthrew the Nazi-Fascist regime in the prelude to the Allied liberation of the city on 1 October. This loosely structured series of vignettes follows a group of Italian soldiers after the disbanding of the army on 8 September as they make their way, in varying numbers, from northern Italy to Campania. The film's focalizer, Second Lieutenant Innocenzi (Alberto Sordi), begins as an uncritically loyal supporter of the Fascist military mission, but undergoes a gradual and revolutionary moral awakening as his journey progresses, so that, by the end of *Tutti a casa*, he is inspired to take up arms and join the partisan struggle. Among the experiences that lead to Innocenzi's conversion are two encounters with the Holocaust – the second of which offers a fully fleshed out character whose story serves to epitomize the Italian Jewish plight.

At a certain point in their odyssey, the disbanded soldiers meet up with Silvia Modena, a gentle and lovely young woman who endears herself to the entire group. Especially smitten with her is Codegato, a peasant whose naivety borders on simple-mindedness and who takes it upon himself to carry her belongings. When her suitcase falls open and objects of considerable value topple out, Silvia feels obliged to reveal her Jewish identity. She explains to Codegato that her parents were deported while she was away at school, and that upon returning to the empty house, she fled with what possessions she could gather. Codegato, unfazed by the revelation of Silvia's ethnicity, responds with characteristic ingenuousness, 'Ordunque, siamo tutti cristiani, no?' (Well then, we're all Christians, no?), reflecting the peasant use of the religious designation to mean 'generic human being.' In the tragic ending to this episode, Codegato dies saving Silvia from capture by Nazi assailants.

Though the above vignette is a fully realized and exemplary story of the Jewish plight, there is an earlier encounter that is far more indicative of the Italian impulse towards Holocaust representation. In this scene, Innocenzi and his sidekick Ceccarelli (Serge Reggiani) witness the slow progress of a cargo train whose human passengers are crying out for relief from thirst. All that is visible from the grating on the small upper windows of the rail cars are hands reaching out to drop notes by the side of the tracks. Once the train has passed, Innocenzi and Ceccarelli notice the lone figure of a young girl, dressed in white, purposefully and carefully collecting the bits of paper left by the deportees. The figure of this child is fraught with significance for our study. While she is filmed realistically and takes her place among the many other flesh-and-blood characters who arbitrarily stray into the path of Innocenzi's journey, her angelic whiteness and her gesture of supreme, almost superhuman compassion suggest her profoundly emblematic status with respect to the film's literal level. In gathering these scraps of paper that would otherwise be carried off by the winds of oblivion, she is the receiver of witness, the custodian of memory, the answer to the victims' plea that their testimony be heard. But her youth is a highly ambiguous signifier. On the one hand, it is the guarantor of that innocence (and here the pun on the surname of the film's protagonist is laden with irony) which makes her the perfect vehicle of Holocaust truth. On the other hand, because she is a child, and by definition helpless within the greater scheme of things, this collector of messages is unable to act upon them in any effectual way. Together with her youth, the little girl's solitude serves as a powerful indictment of the adult world's collective acquiescence and indifference to atrocity.

The figure of the compassionate young gatherer of messages also has strategic importance for what we might call the 'representational history' of the Holocaust. Though *Tutti a casa* dedicates only a small segment to the Italian Jewish plight, that segment is rich with potential, suggesting an infinity of possible narratives that could spin off from this particular moment in the plot. Each of the many notes that drop along the tracks of the deportation train could be a Holocaust text in its own right, containing the nucleus of a story that could be fully developed to tell its own unique and vivid account of a life heading towards extinction. In the young girl who collects and receives these messages, Comencini is acknowledging the enormity of this history's representational challenge – to properly memorialize its victims, to fashion public narratives capable of transmitting the richness of these private lives and the tragic injustice of their loss.

Gillo Pontecorvo's *Kapò* (1960) marks the first of the Italian Holocaust films to win widespread acclaim, thanks to the lustre of its international cast – led by Susan Strasberg (daughter of Lee Strasberg, director of the Actor's Studio) and Laurent Terzieff – and to the moral cogency of its storyline. As his casting suggests, Pontecorvo's film too participates in the internationalizing strain of Italian Holocaust representations, and it does so by setting the initial scenes in Paris, before proceeding to concentration camps in Germany and Poland. Significantly, the promised land for which the protagonist yearns after liberation is not her Parisian one, by now destroyed and unretrievable, nor the Palestinian destination of the Zionist dream, but an imagined village in the Soviet Union, a place of communitarian, if not outright communist-utopian, belonging. Within this context, *Kapò* traces the unmaking and the redemption of Edith, a fourteen-year-old bourgeoise who leaves her music teacher's house one day to find her parents and Jewish neighbours being herded off for deportation. She joins them on their journey to Auschwitz, but is saved from immediate extermination by a mercenary *kapò*, Sophia, and a kindly doctor, who confers upon Edith the identity of a newly deceased inmate, a Frenchwoman named Nicole Niepo, interned as a common thief. Wearing the black triangle used to designate criminals, rather than the red badge of the political prisoner or the yellow star of Jewish ethnicity, Edith/Nicole will have the best possible chance of survival. Arguably the most powerful scene in the film, this episode marks Edith's abrupt and violent coming of age, with the spectacle of her naked parents being ushered towards the gas chambers as she gives voice to the last vestiges of a dying childhood identity: 'Mamma, no, stop, Mamma ... Mamma ... Mamma ...' 'If you want to live, you must put on this outfit' the doctor tells Edith, handing her the filthy garments he has just removed from her predecessor's corpse. An urgent, intensely distilled lesson on survival follows. 'Your number is 10,099,' the doctor instructs Edith, while tatooing the digits on her forearm. As he sheers off her thick and luxurious head of hair, the physician continues his prescription for 'health.' 'You must live and not think of anything else. Live and that's all. You are no longer a Jew. Try to live.' Of utmost significance to this pedagogy is the doctor's reference to the category of *kapò* – a species to be heeded and feared, and an anticipation of Edith/Nicole's future self. For now, she is an identity-less creature who will morph into something intermediate and fluid before assuming this nefarious guise. Pontecorvo will meticulously chart Edith/Nicole's downward course in her determination to 'live and that's all.' This means stealing the precious potato that the benevolent Teresa had been hoarding; it means escaping selection by baring her breasts to distract the Nazi officer from seeing her ulcerated hands; it means callously flaunting her survival tactics before those who are not so fortunate; it means prostituting herself to the German commander for extra food; and finally, it means acceding to the rank of *kapò*.

This process does not take place in a moral void – Pontecorvo presents several powerful alternatives to Edith/Nicole's path of self-degradation. There is Prisoner 9711, a political activist who is unstinting in her efforts to sabotage the workings of the camp, and who is punished by public execution. There is Teresa, who offers to use her knowledge of German for the benefit of the Resistance and who serves as Pontecorvo's mouthpiece for the maintenance of moral virtue and human dignity in the face of insuperable odds.[6] In lines that may well have been inspired by Primo Levi's Steinlauf, Teresa insists that Nicole perform her morning ablutions as a gesture of defiance against Nazi efforts to reduce the prisoners to the level of subhuman filth.[7] Even Georgette, a common criminal who is not averse to killing Nicole's cat out of vindictiveness, is redeemed by her connection with the other members of the barracks.

Nicole's moral deterioration comes to a halt towards the end of the film, when a batch of Soviet prisoners, let by the handsome and charismatic Sasha, arrives at the camp, and Nicole forms a bond of solidarity with them. Anticipating the approach of Soviet troops and the expected Nazi massacre of all prisoners, Sasha's group devises an escape plan that will require the intervention of the reformed *kapò*, who readily agrees to collaborate, unaware that her mission will be a fatal one. Just moments before she is to throw the switch that will defuse the electrified fence and allow the inmates to flee, Sasha informs Nicole that in so doing she will surely die. Deluded and demoralized, Nicole nonetheless completes her mission, and with her dying words she recites the 'Shema Yisrael,' the defining prayer of Judaism, in a return to her pre-

---

6 For an insightful interpretation of this pivotal character, see Annette Insdorf, *Indelible Shadows: Film and the Holocaust* (Cambridge: Cambridge University Press, 2002), 149.

7 For his vivid portrait of Steinlauf, see Primo Levi, *Survival at Auschwitz*, trans. Stuart Woolf (New York: Touchstone, 1996), 40–1.

fallen self. With this act of martyrdom, Nicole becomes Edith and Sasha is left to live with the guilt of his decision to sacrifice his beloved for the common good.

Much to the surprise of Pontecorvo and his collaborator Franco Solinas, *Kapò* met with great commercial success, garnering the director international acclaim and an Oscar nomination for best foreign film. In technical terms, *Kapò*'s black-and-white photography and rough imagistic texture gave powerful expression to the brutality of its content. Pontecorvo went to considerable lengths to achieve such visual violence, even quarrelling with his cinematographer Aleksander Sekulovic and resorting to post-production expedients to simulate the desired crudeness of image. In the end, however, the filmmaker himself began to have doubts about the excessive severity of *Kapò* and yielded to co-scriptwriter Franco Solinas's insistence on the mitigating device of the romance between Sasha and Edith/Nicole. 'In the phase of scriptwriting,' Pontecorvo confessed,

> we reached a crisis when we confronted the idea that the film was too harsh, that it was necessary to put in a love story. Initially, I was convinced that this would have ruptured the unity of the film. But when arguing about it, even Solinas was convinced. Then I changed my mind; it seemed to me that the story functioned, and the sentimental interlude no longer bothered me. Once the film was fully assembled, I again found the little love story to be indigestible, but by then it was too late. Despite this, the film has kept its edge; it is quite modern, I think.[8]

A year later, Pontecorvo's generic mix of historical realism and sentimental romance would reappear in Carlo Lizzani's *L'oro di Roma* (The Gold of Rome) the chronicle of Gestapo commander Kappler's scheme to extort 50 kilograms (110 lbs) of gold from the members of the Jewish community on the eve of the 16 October deportations. *L'oro di Roma* is introduced by an on-screen text that asserts Lizzani's truth claims in bearing witness to the Shoah, despite the film's fictional overlay. 'The facts narrated in this film are true,' the inscription begins. 'Nonetheless there is no reference to persons who really existed.' Over the final frames of *L'oro di Roma* we read the following affirmation of the film's referential impulse: 'The facts recounted in this film are true and the

8 Quoted in Massimo Ghirelli, *Gillo Pontecorvo* (Florence: La Nuova Italia, 1978), 14.

producers and authors thank the Comunità Israelitica of Rome for permitting us to use the locations where the tragic events took place.' What emerges from these opening and closing inscriptions is the film's conflicted generic identity – fictional and romantic, on the one hand, documentary and tragic, on the other. The film's aspirations to historical authenticity, underwritten by on-location shooting, are reinforced by the austere use of black-and-white photography and the forthright, almost ethnographic attention to the details of Roman Jewish life – the recording of the synagogue service, the solemn and dignified wrapping of Simone in traditional prayer garb before his suicide, the funeral rites performed over his body.[9] Within this strongly referential context, the film chronicles forty-eight hours of frantic efforts to comply with the Nazi demand for gold on the part of a minority already severely straitened by the Racial Laws and the privations of war. The community's reactions to the Nazi order span a vast gamut of behaviours that come to transcend the specificity of the situation at hand and lead the film in the direction of historical typology. Individual characters become typical, in a Lukácian sense,[10] reacting in paradigmatic ways that could lend themselves as much to the challenges of the early 1960s as to those of a previous, though certainly far more dire, historical scenario. There is the Conciliator (the leader of the Jewish community, who organizes the collection of gold and mediates between Gestapo and ghetto), the Activist (Davide Sermoneta, who refuses to comply and chooses the path of armed resistance), the Holy Man (the rabbi, who renounces worldly action and entrusts himself into the hands of a merciful God), the Perennial Victim (the community elder, who claims that diasporic Judaism has always been obliged to pay tribute to inhospitable hosts), the Coercer (Signora Rosa, who bullies and shames everyone into obedience), the Well-Intentioned Outsiders (non-Jews, who offer gold out of solidarity or pity). The one character who escapes such historical typology is Giulia, engaged to the gentile Massimo De Sanctis – and it is she who introduces hybridity into the genre of Lizzani's film. Played by the pop-

---

9 In 'Representations of Judaism and the Jewish Experience in Italian Cinema,' a paper presented at the 2005 meeting of the American Association of Italian Studies, Virginia Picchietti offers a superb study of what she labels a 'semiotics' of Jewishness. On Lizzani's carefully researched portrayal of Roman Jewish religiosity, see Gualtiero De Santi, *Carlo Lizzani* (Rome: Gremese, 2001), 41.
10 See Georg Lukács, *Realism in Our Time: Literature and the Class Struggle*, trans. John and Necke Mander (New York and Evanston: Harper & Row, 1964), 122–3.

ular starlet Anna Maria Ferrero, sporting stylish bouffant hair and iri-
descent lipstick, Giulia is encoded as the protagonist of sentimental
romance whose beauty and charm invite all the operations of that
generic formula. Her fiancé, deeply in love with Giulia and desperate to
save her, becomes a surrogate for the audience – our entrée into the
ghetto, our vehicle for identifying with the plight about to overtake the
'other.' Giulia, who transitions between the Jewish and Christian
worlds within the film and who must definitively decide between the
two, actually undergoes baptism in order to marry Massimo and escape
the fate of her co-religionists. But she abandons the consolations of her
sentimental romance plot at the film's end when, returning to the ghetto
one last time, she sees its occupants rounded up for deportation and
makes the anguished decision to join them. Like Nicole/Edith at the
end of *Kapò*, Giulia re-embraces the Jewish identity that she had previously disavowed in order to survive. But the redemptive function of the
love plot in Pontecorvo's film – Sasha's love for Edith brings her back to
Judaism – undergoes a complete reversal in *L'oro di Roma*, whose hero-
ine must reject romance in order to reclaim her Jewish identity.

It is impossible to overestimate the importance of location (*i luoghi*) in
this film, where the life of the Jewish community is deeply enmeshed in
the spaces of Roman topography. 'Is it true that the Jews are among the
most ancient of Roman citizens, and that they don't pass under the arch
of Titus because their ancestors were led there in defeat?' Kappler asks
as he is about to deliver his terrible ultimatum: the delivery of the req-
uisite gold or the surrender of two hundred Jewish hostages. The many
shots of the film in locations within the ghetto wed the community to
its setting, marked by a series of picturesque corners, fragments of
fluted columns, arches embedded in walls, cobblestone streets, all pre-
sided over by the dome of the synagogue at one point and the Teatro di
Marcello at another. The antiquity, and indeed the profound Roman-
ness of these *luoghi*, offers visual answers to Kappler's rhetorical question, making the Jewish community an integral part of the city's
historical past while it maintains a distinct identity (ghettoized, arch-of-
Titus-averse, etc).

It is in the final sequence that *L'oro di Roma* achieves its full expressive
grandeur with a montage of still shots of the ghetto, now emptied of
life. The scene begins as Massimo arrives by bicycle along a winding
street against the background of the Teatro di Marcello. The camera
pans past Massimo along the uneven surface of a wall to stop at a dead
end before cutting to a close-up of the young man as he calls out the

name of his beloved. Running through a courtyard to the street that leads to the synagogue, Massimo beholds its empty interior in a scene that takes us back to the film's opening moments, likewise set in the sanctuary during what was then a crowded and solemn holiday service. There follows a rapid-fire montage of seventeen still shots that survey the world of the ghetto now devoid of life: a number of picturesque street corners, the underside of a baroque fountain, a wall of windows with laundry hanging outside, a street with a fallen bicycle, another with an overturned chair, yet another with a man's lost hat, and finally an abandoned kitten on a ledge. For most of the sequence, the soundtrack consists of footsteps echoing in the emptiness, and it concludes with the desperate sobs of Massimo, whose figure we see in an extreme high-angle shot prostrate atop an outdoor staircase that seems to lead nowhere. This montage of emptiness represents a kind of visual mourning – it is the *mise-en-scène* of loss, as if the space itself were grieving for those who had been exiled from it.[11]

Of the great postwar Italian auteurs, Visconti will be the first to broach the Holocaust, but he will do so through a perverse strategy of non-representation. In other words, the Shoah will be relegated to the narrative pre-history of his film *Vaghe stelle dell'Orsa* (1965, distributed in the English-speaking world under the title *Sandra*) and will be recalled through the ghostly, literally veiled image of the protagonist's father, Emanuele Luzzatti, a renowned Jewish scientist who died in Auschwitz. In the film's narrative present, Sandra (played by Claudia Cardinale) and her new husband, Andrew Dawson, travel from Paris to her ancestral home in Volterra, where the family is gathering to celebrate the donation of the villa grounds to the city in honour of Luzzatti's memory. As an outsider to the family circle, Andrew seeks to unravel the web of suspicions, guilty passions, and squalid intrigues that bind together its members: Sandra believes that her mother and her second husband, the lawyer Gilardini, had conspired to deliver Luzzatti into the hands of the SS, and is bent on revenge; Gianni, her brother, is eager to undermine Sandra's marriage to Andrew and lure her back to their sibling *folie à deux*; and Gilardini is out to prove that Sandra's accusations of betrayal are a mere cover-up for her incestuous affair with her brother.

---

11 Annette Insdorf sees in this final scene the spectre of extinction for Roman Jewry as a whole. See *Indelible Shadows*, 141.

Within this tangled network of familial passions and resentments, the Shoah becomes simply one more pretext for melodramatic plot developments.[12] It is significant that Visconti made *Vaghe stelle dell'Orsa* at a turning point in his career, when his commitment to critical realism and historical accountability had given way to 'more internalized, existential' concerns.[13] Several passages in the film foreground Visconti's tendency to subordinate history, in this case Holocaust chronicle, to the generic requirements of melodrama. 'We want to show love and respect for our father by testifying to his tragic fate,' Sandra explains in a formulation that puts Holocaust testimony to the service of this dysfunctional family romance. Similarly, she will later justify her pathological bond with her brother in terms of their paternal source and their common ethnicity. 'We had nothing to be ashamed of,' she claims. 'We had a passionate loyalty to the memory of our father and of our race.' It is Gianni who exposes the psychological mechanisms behind Sandra's approach to the Holocaust past. 'You went to the concentration camp to re-live the Calvary of our father, to hide your love for me,' he charges, refusing to ascribe his sister's motives to any genuine quest for historical meaning. The inappropriateness of Gianni's New Testament allusion in this context parallels, on the rhetorical level, what he claims to be the inappropriateness of Sandra's reasons for investigating her father's experience of the Shoah. Again, melodrama gains the upper hand. In another sign of the subordination of history to familial psychodynamics, the mother turns Jewishness into a weapon against her alienated and avenging daughter. 'You're afraid, aren't you?' she snaps. 'Your father? Do you want to hear the truth about your idol? You have Jewish blood like him. You are corrupt, like him! Small, dirty vices. Secret vices.'

As a result, the Shoah comes to occupy but one of the many layers of buried pasts within the world of the film. There is the infinite regress of literary sources for this story, going back to the Electra of Sophocles and Euripides, *Remembrance of Things Past* (specifically, Proust's references to César Franck, whose *Prelude, Chorale and Fugue* punctuates the soundtrack at strategic points throughout the film), to Eugene O'Neill's

---

12 Accordingly, Insdorf argues that Visconti privileges the brother-sister incest bond over the daughter's quest to learn the truth about her father's Holocaust ordeal. See *Indelible Shadows*, 127.

13 For this observation, see Henry Bacon, *Visconti: Explorations of Beauty and Decay* (Cambridge: Cambridge University Press, 1998), 125.

Mourning Becomes Electra, to Jean Cocteau's *Les enfants terribles* (the motif of incest), to D'Annunzio's *Forse che sì, forse che no* (the Volterrean setting and the sexually prodigious protagonists), and, of course, to Bassani's *Garden of the Finzi-Continis* (the intense brother-sister bond, the isolated hot-house existence, the topos of the garden).[14] The environment of Volterra itself is rich with hints of 'underneathness,' of a layering of civilizations past: the city's Etruscan ancestry is recalled in allusions to the ancient walls as well as in a conversation held in a museum full of funerary urns; its classical period is evoked in a brother-sister exchange that takes place in a Roman cistern; and its Baroque moment is celebrated in a visit to the Church of San Giusto. If Volterra is portrayed as a palimpsest, it is one whose buriedness threatens to block all access to what lies below, thanks to the city's geologically precarious position, perched on the constantly eroding *balze* (cliffs).

The subterranean past of Volterra's history finds its domestic equivalent in the locked rooms of the family villa – the mother's vacated suite can only be entered with a special key, and Sandra's bedroom is strategically closed off to intruders. The Holocaust fate of Sandra's father remains similarly sealed, creating a void within the film. No image is more indicative of this absence than that of the enshrouded bust of the man that awaits unveiling at the dedication ceremony to take place at the film's end. It is only during this ceremony that any real traces of Judaism emerge – a rabbi presides over the rites, and a brief Hebrew prayer is recited, followed by a passage from Isaiah. Significantly, we do not learn the father's name until this final moment in the film, and when the bust is finally unveiled, we see it only fleetingly. The camera denies us the opportunity to lavish any visual attention on this object of Sandra's obsessive and unhealthy love. As a result, Luzzatti remains a cipher, just as the Shoah itself remains outside representation in Visconti's film.[15]

Andremo in città (We'll Go to the City, 1966) marks an important collaboration between the cinema and literature of Holocaust representation. Based on the eponymous novel by Edith Bruck, a Hungarian

---

14 For most of the titles in this list, I am indebted to Lino Miccichè, *Luchino Visconti: Un profilo critico* (Venice: Marsilio, 1996), 51.

15 Another Visconti film, *The Damned* (1969), will make oblique reference to the Holocaust in the secondary character of Lisa, a Jewish child who is molested by Martin and consequently takes her own life.

survivor of the camps who settled in Italy and wrote extensively, both in fictional and autobiographical formats, of her experiences, the film was made by her husband, Nelo Risi, brother of the better known and more commercially oriented Dino. Featuring the young and willowy Geraldine Chaplin in the role of the film's protagonist, Lenka, *Andremo in città* functions as a star vehicle for a fledgling actress whose image becomes a visual obsession for Risi's infatuated camerawork. To offset the unseemly focus on Lenka as icon, the film offers the unglamorous austerity of its black-and-white photography and the intrinsic interest of its quaint, Middle European village environment.

Located in rural Yugoslavia, the film tells the story of Lenka's relationship with Miscia, her blind younger brother for whom her eyesight serves as a window onto the world. Orphaned of their Greek Orthodox mother and their Jewish father Rasco Vitas, who has been reportedly killed in the war, Lenka and Miscia must fend for themselves in a society increasingly hostile to its Semitic minority. Lenka is not without a support system, however. The partisan Ivan is in love with her, and her father Rasco indeed returns from the battle front, giving the lie to reports of his death. Rasco eventually sacrifices himself to save Ivan, who has been hurt and is hidden in the family's attic. When the SS eventually come to take Lenka and Miscia away, they do not reveal the whereabouts of Ivan, who thus survives to carry on the partisan struggle.

Andremo in città takes its title from Lenka's voice-over narration at the film's very start, when she and Miscia wait by the railroad tracks of their rural village. 'Every day before the train slows down, it whistles. It doesn't actually stop, but it slows down. I always tell Miscia that we must be ready to jump on, up-and-over, and off we go. Once we've boarded, it's done.' In the film's opening scene a train passes by transporting a human cargo that Lenka refuses to describe to her sightless brother. 'Is it going to the city? Miscia asks. 'All trains go to the city,' Lenka affirms. 'And what is the train like? Tell me, what it is like,' the boy persists. 'It's a train that I've never seen before,' Lenka concludes, leading him away from the tracks. It is this unknown train that will indeed lead them *in città* in the film's final scene, as Lenka cradles her brother in her arms and paints an illusory landscape of the wonders that adorn the way. By superimposing an imaginary superstructure on the horrific reality of the Shoah to maintain the morale of a mercifully benighted young boy, the film offers clear intimations of Benigni's game plan in *Life Is Beautiful*.

Breaking New Ground (the 1970s)

De Sica's 1970 filmic adaptation of Giorgio Bassani's magisterial *Garden of the Finzi-Continis* forms a strategic bridge between the cluster of films of the early 1960s (soon after the time of the novel's release) and the cinematic works that represent the Shoah in the mid-1970s.[16] Bassani's text shares with *Kapò*, *L'oro di Roma*, and *Andremo in città* a narrative of sentimental romance that ends with the sacrifice of the female protagonist to the forces of Holocaust history. De Sica's film version of *Il giardino dei Finzi-Contini* looks ahead to the more sexually explicit treatments of the 1970s and brings to the foreground a cinematic self-consciousness that complicates the less sophisticated realism of its predecessors.

Set in Ferrara in the period between 1938 and 1943, the film tells the story of Giorgio, a university student from a bourgeois Jewish background, who becomes infatuated with his lovely, aristocratic, and inaccessible co-religionist, Micol Finzi-Contini. Despite the increasingly tightened restrictions on Jewish life imposed by the Racial Laws, the Finzi-Continis' estate remains a haven of privilege, and Giorgio avails himself of the invitations to use the family's tennis court once expelled from the recreation club of the city. Proximity to Micol only increases the young man's ardour, but to no avail, as she continues to rebuff his awkward advances. A journey to visit his brother Ernesto in Grenoble exposes Giorgio to news of Nazi persecution, yet this does not deter the young man from returning to Fascist Italy, and to the amorous entrapment of Ferrara. The film ends with the round-up of the city's Jewish population, including the Finzi-Continis and Giorgio's father, who informs Micol of his son's escape from capture.

Central to both novel and film is the image of the garden – a topos that functions on a number of levels, linking the story's setting to its biblical exemplar in Eden, with all the aesthetic and moral significance of such a comparison. Like its Edenic model, the garden of the Finzi-Contini estate is a place of surpassing beauty, luxury, and exclusivity where Micol, together with her brother Alberto, has led a hothouse existence in total isolation from the outside world. With the onset of the Racial Laws, the Finzi-Continis' reclusiveness finally breaks down, and

---

16 For a fuller treatment of *Il giardino dei Finzi-Contini*, with particular emphasis on the relationship between De Sica's film and Bassani's text, see my *Filmmaking by the Book: Italian Cinema and Literary Adaptation* (Baltimore: Johns Hopkins University Press, 1993), 91–110.

Giorgio's access to the estate is extended from garden to the family's private library once he is barred from using the public facility of Ferrara. Micol retreats to Venice, where she completes her degree at the university of that insular city, while Giorgio continues to pine for her, seeking the default company of her brother Alberto and his friend, the robust Giampiero Malnate, a non-Jew brimming with the self-confidence of his Marxist convictions. Within Giorgio's tale of unrequited love, unfolding against the background of the impending Holocaust, the garden represents a dangerous state of withdrawal, a space that, in psychoanalytic terms, suggests the operations of neurotic denial. It takes a stark epiphany to shake Giorgio out of his amorous obsession, and it is the spectacle of Micol, naked by the side of Malnate in their hideaway on the grounds of the estate, that finally frees the infatuated young man from the bonds of erotic entrapment. A series of disastrous occurrences propel the film to its tragic conclusion: Alberto dies of lymphoma; Malnate is killed on the Russian front; and the Finzi-Continis are forced to share the fate of the rest of Ferrara's Jewish population. The garden proves to be a false paradise – neither social privilege nor financial contributions to the Fascist party can save Micol and her family from the ravages of Holocaust history.

In adapting Bassani's novel to the screen, De Sica has made a number of adjustments, in deference both to the requirements of the cinematic medium and to his own authorial agenda as a socially committed director with roots in neorealism. Whereas Bassani's novel, narrated in the first person, is written from a perspective internal to the garden, De Sica's film adopts an external focus, chronicling the events of Holocaust history as they encroach upon the Finzi-Continis' privileged domain from without. While Bassani confines himself to the year 1938–9, relegating the tragic fate of the family in 1942–3 to the novel's prologue and epilogue, De Sica insists on representing those wartime events in all their linear inevitability. The film's determination explicitly to confront the Shoah means that De Sica has resisted the temptation to exploit the 'garden' properties of the cinematic medium – its traditional invitation to pleasurable escape from the world of social and historical engagement. The filmmaker's self-conscious announcement of cinema's need to surmount the garden wall emerges in two scenes strategically set in a movie theatre. On the screen-within-the-screen, we are shown documentary footage of the Nazi-Fascist build-up to war and the devastation of German bombing raids, respectively. In the internal audience of each movie theatre scene there is a Jewish character who suffers anti-

Semitic assaults – by bullying bigots, in one case, and by Fascist police in the second. The boundary between on-screen and off-screen action is thus obliterated – what is happening in the newsreel footage has direct consequences for what occurs among the members of its audience. The cinema cannot serve as a space of refuge from real-world concerns. In other words, the cinema is not a garden. It is, instead, an altar on which the beloved must be sacrificed in the name of historic redemption. De Sica stages the sacrificial scene in the context of prophecy at the end of the Passover service that, according to Jewish tradition, looks ahead eschatologically to the foundation of the Kingdom of God on earth – a promise that is figuratively expressed in the phrase 'Next year in Jerusalem.' In *Il giardino dei Finzi-Contini* this prophetic moment is entrusted to a chalice brought back to Ferrara from Venice by Micol. Adding a pagan twist to the Passover ritual of setting out a cup of wine for Elijah, the prophet who will precede the Messiah at the end of time, the chalice can predict the future. Alberto, self-appointed interpreter of the oracle, consults the vessel to answer a question about the outcome of the impending war. 'It will be long and difficult, but in the end, there will be a total victory for the forces of good.' As he utters this prediction, De Sica's camera cuts to Micol, linking her image to the prophecy of victory through suffering and associating her with the Pascal lamb whose sacrifice makes possible the Passover celebration of collective Jewish survival.

A film that shares with *Il giardino dei Finzi-Contini* a narrative of unhappy love, a female protagonist who is sacrificed to the forces of Holocaust history, an elegiac recall of pre-war glamour, and a dynamic relationship to its literary source (in this case, the short story 'Wanda' by Vasco Pratolini)[17] is Sergio Capogna's *Diario di un italiano* (Diary of an Italian, 1971). Because Pratolini's tale compresses the events of a year-long courtship into four and a half tightly written pages, the screenplay had to undergo an extensive process of *amplificatio* in order to reach feature-film length. Thus, Pratolini's original story of a young man's infatuation with an enigmatic young woman, whose Jewish identity is only disclosed after her suicide in the face of anti-Semitic persecution, required considerable elaboration during the script-writ-

---

17 Vasco Pratolini, *Romanzi* 1, ed. Francesco Paolo Memmo (Milan: Mondadori, 1993), 225–9. The story, first entitled 'Il segreto,' was published in *Il politecnico* 5 (27 October 1945), then in *Mestiere da vagabondo*, 1947, with the title 'Un'altra.' It appeared under the title 'Wanda' in *Diario sentimentale*, 1956.

ing phase. There can be no more powerful index of the film's amplifying operation than the title itself, which gives this small, highly localized Florentine tale the status of exemplarity – one individual's love for a woman named Wanda becomes a chronicle of *italianità* in the hands of Capogna. The film makes this leap from the particular to the general, from the local to the national, by turning an O'Henry-esque narrative into a parable of political awakening with important implications for Italy as a whole.

In its aspiration to tell an 'Italian' story despite its emphatically Florentine setting, the film addresses the need to undertake collective grieving for a covert and festering national loss. *Diario di un italiano* opens in a Jewish cemetery, with the camera trailing a soberly clad and anonymous man into its protected confines. A high-angle shot of this visitor walking among the tombstones comes to settle on a memorial plaque, dedicated to 'the innocent victims of Nazi-Fascist persecution.' With this opening, the film announces its goal of *Trauerarbeit*, and like *Il giardino dei Finzi-Contini*, it will function as a funerary monument to a beloved young woman and, through her, a monument to an Italian body politic whose integrity has been lost.

The film's young male protagonist, Valerio, has been protected from the knowledge of the iniquitous Mussolini regime by his mother, Olga (played by a magisterial Alida Valli), who wants to shield her son from the lethal fate that had met his father, a militant socialist, in a Fascist prison. At a key point midway into the film, the young man finds himself in a small crowd together with Alberto, friend of his mother and late father, as a cadre of Black Shirts hurl insults and throw rocks at the synagogue of Florence. The most energetic and malicious of these assailants actually climbs the high, spiked fence surrounding the building, while the blatant inactivity of two carabinieri assigned to guard the place is the subject of bitter commentary by Alberto. But Valerio professes ignorance of the proceedings, just as he remains oblivious to the meaning of Wanda's 'segreto' (the title under which Pratolini's story was first published in 1945). 'What's happening? I don't understand,' he questions Alberto, who answers by showing Valerio the headlines for that day's newspaper: 'Laws for the Defence of the Race Approved by the Council of Ministers.' The young man's ignorance is emblematic, and this *diario di un italiano* becomes the record of the mass political obliviousness to the mechanisms by which a minority was deprived of all the rights of citizenship and, ultimately, of the right to live at all.

Towards the end of the film, Valerio again finds himself in a group of silent witnesses to anti-Semitic persecution, but this time the generic and symbolic target of the earlier attack has become highly personalized. Wanda's father is being seized by Fascist agents, and it is now that Valerio learns the family's 'segreto.' Returning home to his own distraught mother, Valerio pours out his belated knowledge and gives vent to his sense of failure in Wanda's regard. 'They are Jews, do you understand? That was the secret. I didn't do anything for her, to defend her. I didn't understand her.' Earlier in the film, Wanda had refused to reveal her secret until Valerio had reached the appropriate level of readiness, when his love for her would have led him to plumb the deepest recesses of her identity. Valerio's mother herself will intuit the motives behind Wanda's reticence. 'A Jewish girl would have created a grave danger for you. For this reason she didn't tell you.' Wanda's solicitude for Valerio's safety, her reluctance to impose dangerous knowledge upon him, meant that he had to fathom her truth on his own, that he had to interpret the clues, read the signs, and construct a narrative that would explain her mystery in the context of the larger historical forces that conditioned their lives. 'Why am I blond? I shouldn't be. Don't you know this?' she had once enigmatically asked. In the immediately previous scene, Valerio had recounted in voice-over: 'It was 1938, the Spanish Communists had lost Brunete, a husband had killed his wife, the Government voted on the racial laws, but they were all facts that passed by, far from us, newspaper headlines. For us, what counted was the hours on the Bridge, the walks along the avenues, and her father who refused to meet me.' This passage of narrative exposition, lifted verbatim from Pratolini's text, is rich with meaning for the 'before' and 'after' of Valerio's political awakening. Already in the compilation of news items that the narrator proposes, we encounter a mix of world historical and personal events – the report of domestic bloodshed seems incongruous in the midst of Fascist victories at home and abroad. The deep logic of this juxtaposition between public and private, world-historical and personal, will emerge only at the end of the story, but for now, Valerio is oblivious to the meaning of his own casual and arbitrary way of saying that his story took place in 1938.

Most importantly, Valerio's exposition sets up a false dichotomy between two kinds of narrative emplotments – those of realist-historical fiction, on the one hand, and sentimental romance, on the other. While the first is marked by a linear irreversible movement forward in time, the second is a-temporal, organized by the cycles of seasons, relived every generation in which young love may be thwarted by familial obstacles. But in this particular case, the father's refusal to meet Wanda's fiancé is motivated not by domestic developments, but by events at the level of official history. When Valerio insists that 'your father is against this love,' his logic remains purely within the confines of family melodrama – paternal jealousy, social-class disparity – these are the only genre of obstacles that Valerio could possibly entertain in his ignorance of the historical factors that could militate against such a union in 1938. Within his comfortable cocoon, Valerio cannot conceive of the fact that Wanda is 'other' according to the definitions promulgated by the new government provisions on race, and he persists in seeing her as an extension of his amorous fantasies, as his feminized specular image in the fixed narrative of popular romance. (Significantly, Wanda's alterity was such an important focus of the Pratolini short story that the author had actually chosen to entitle the work 'Un'altra' in the second of its three published forms.)[18] So unaware is Valerio of Wanda's otherness, her exteriority to any easy scenario of sentimental romance in the year 1938, that he woefully misreads her absence of Christian accessories and ostentatiously presents her with a gift of a gold cross on a necklace in order to remedy that lack.

Like Valerio, the film itself remains, for the most part, within the stylistic confines of sentimental romance. Its mood is elegaic, and it abounds in picturesque views of the two lovers enraptured by the beauties of the Arno as filmed from the vantage point of their meeting place on the Ponte Vecchio. From beginning to end, *Diario di un italiano* is accompanied by an obtrusive musical soundtrack that is both mellow and pop, infusing the film with a sense of unremitting nostalgia, lethargy, and loss. Wanda, who works in a clothing store, is herself a fashion plate, and her taste in dress harmonizes perfectly with the cycle of seasons that the film conscientiously records through the mists of winter, the shimmering warmth of summer, or the soft colours of the changing leaves of autumn, all of which are reflected in the omnipresent waters of the Arno. Only at the end do we see how ephemeral and misleading this romantic idyll is, when persecution history intervenes and the waters of the Arno deliver up the body of its desperate suicidal victim.

The cluster of films that emerge in the mid-1970s move the sentimental romance narratives of earlier Italian Holocaust films in the direction

_____

18 See the previous footnote.

of explicit and violent sexuality. These later films serve to radicalize and demystify their predecessors, bringing to the foreground the subli- mated sexual currents of the earlier works and denying the collective redemption that the sacrifice of the female protagonists so consistently promised. Now, the bodies of these women become the literal staging ground for the struggle between dominance and submission, and the outcome of this contest offers no hope for the kind of humanist tran- scendence held out in the films we have considered so far.

This sexualization of the Holocaust in Italian cinema finds its fore- most exponent in Liliana Cavini, whose *Il Portiere di notte* (The Night Porter, 1974) triggered a firestorm of critical controversy. *Il portiere di notte* tells the story of the sado-masochistic love relationship begun in a *Lager* between Max, a Nazi officer, and the young, beautiful, and inno- cent Lucia, interned as the daughter of a socialist. Reunited by chance many years after the war, the two resume their affair, withdrawing into the confines of Max's apartment, where they are held captive by a group of ex-Nazis who ultimately gun them down. As this plot sum- mary suggests, the film's focus is psycho-sexual, and within a Holo- caust context it raises serious questions about the complicity of the victim in her own enslavement, her identification with the oppressor, the interdependence of master and subject, and so on. It could indeed be argued that the *Lager* setting serves as a mere pretext, a laboratory for Cavani to study the workings of human sexuality pushed to the breaking point. 'I felt the need,' the filmmaker explains, 'to analyze the limits of human nature at the limit of credibility, to lead things to the extreme.'[19]

While such an objection to Cavani's use of the Holocaust context is eminently sustainable, I would like to take my analysis in a somewhat different direction: that of social allegory. In so doing, I will read *Il por- tiere di notte* as a study of a society's relationship to a deeply traumatic and disruptive past, in accordance with Cavani's own account of her film's initial inspiration. She attributes the origin of *Il portiere di notte* to an interview conducted with an Auschwitz survivor while the film- maker was doing research for the documentaries *Storia del Terzo Reich* and *La donna nella Resistenza*. In Cavani's words, the woman 'began to

---

19 Quoted in Gaetana Marrone, *The Gaze and The Labyrinth: The Cinema of Liliana Cavani* (Princeton, NJ: Princeton University Press, 2000), 82.

feel guilty for having survived hell, for being the living witness, and therefore [harboring] the bitter memory of something embarrassing that everyone wanted to forget as soon as possible.'[20] The self-silencing of this survivor speaks to the decades-long reticence of Italian culture that is the subject of my current study. Critic Gaetana Marrone sees Cavani's need to revisit this historical trauma as a form of *Trauerarbeit*, the grief-work that the society as a whole has refused to undertake. 'Such an obsessive return to the site of death and horror,' Marrone observes, 'may be ascribed to the symbolic processes of a funerary rite. The *Lager* becomes an object that haunts the survivor from the space of the unconscious, her journey enacting its own ritual of mourning.'[21]

In reading *Il portiere di notte* as social allegory, it is important to note the way in which the film manipulates time frames so that past and present are set in a relationship of uneasy coexistence (what Lawrence Langer will call 'co-temporality').[22] The present-tense narrative of *Il portiere di notte* is set in Vienna in 1957, over a decade after the occurrence of the events that a group of ex-Nazis is seeking to expunge from their personal records. Led by 'Professor' Hans Vogler, and including other officers of an unnamed *Lager*, these war criminals hold regular group-therapy sessions aimed at placating their guilty consciences. The cynical joke here is that their therapeutic process involves not the internal work of moral self-examination and expiation, but merely the destruction of incriminating evidence that would lead them to get caught.[23] 'Memory is not made of vague shadows, but eyes that look you straight in the face and fingers that point accusingly at you,' says Klaus, the group's lead investigator. By redefining guilt as something wholly external and legalistic, and therefore amenable to erasure, the ex-Nazis absolve themselves from ethical responsibility for their deeds. By this definition, once all concrete evidence is disposed of, these men are 'cured' – there is no need for them to come to terms with the past, for it has no power over them, and indeed, in practical terms, no longer exists. But the group fears Max, who is pronounced *un caso speciale* – the

---

20 Quoted in Marrone, ibid., 91.

21 Ibid.

22 Lawrence Langer, *Holocaust Testimonies: The Ruins of Memory* (New Haven: Yale University Press, 1991), 3.

23 On the farcical nature of this 'remedy' see Chris Ravetto, *The Unmaking of Fascist Aesthetics* (Minneapolis: University of Minnesota Press, 2001), 166.

night porter who presides over the threshold between darkness and daytime, between Nazi past and postwar present, and who refuses to close the door between them. The impulse of Max and Lucia to re-enact their *Lager* relationship, to recuperate this traumatic past, is the antidote to the ex-Nazis' campaign of historical erasure. The Holocaust interlude perversely becomes their privileged object of desire, and it is memory itself that serves as their seducer – the go-between that brings Max and Lucia back into each other's arms (or, more appropriately, body locks).

As transgressive as Cavani's decision to sexualize the Holocaust is, this strategy nonetheless partakes of an ancient tradition of allegoresis, intimated by Max's statement that his relationship with Lucia is not romantic, but biblical. Referring specifically to the Gospel episode of Salome's dance, this allusion to Scripture suggests the type of multi-leveled reading that enabled the Church Fathers to neutralize the frank eroticism of Holy Writ through allegory. The pathological sexuality of *Il portiere di notte* is likewise not confined to the literal level of interpretation, but pushes us beyond to the social level, where the Holocaust past must be occluded lest it threaten to destabilize the order of the present.[24]

Of considerable importance to our analysis is the acute cinematic self-consciousness of Cavani's film, which surfaces in Max's own wielding of the movie camera during his flashbacks to the *Lager*. We are told that the protagonist masquerades as a camp physician in order to enhance his access to sensational photo opportunities. Cavani's use of Max as her visual surrogate amounts to a masquerade at one remove that implicates us in her voyeuristic fascination. The filmmaker's own techniques of aestheticizing and spectacularizing the Holocaust are thus made explicit, and nowhere more so than in the several flashbacks in which characters perform for an SS audience within the camp. I am referring to Bert's highly charged ballet of narcissism and homoerotic desire, and Lucia's parody of a Marlene Dietrich routine in which she dons a Nazi uniform (minus shirt and jacket), sings and dances seductively, and is rewarded with the decapitated head of a bothersome fellow prisoner in keeping with Max's 'biblical' scenario.

Cavani's sexualization of the Shoah and her foregrounding of her own voyeuristic investment in it raise uneasy questions about our posi-

---

24 Ravetto comments on this threat to a present-day status quo unpurged of Nazi influence; ibid., 160.

tion as spectators of *Il portiere di notte*.[25] In terms of the social allegory that I am proposing, the efforts of the postwar body politic to repress this traumatic past are analogous to the individual's need to repress the kind of taboo sexual impulses so exuberantly enacted by Lucia and Max. By aestheticizing and spectacularizing those enactments, by making us their prurient witnesses, Cavani forces us to acknowledge the dark and secret recesses of our own erotic fantasies, and our concomitant need to repress them for the maintenance of psychic order and social functioning. In the malevolent activities of the ex-Nazi officers who seek to exorcize the couple's threat to their postwar normalization, we can therefore not help but recognize our own complicity.

Two years after the release of Cavani's film, Lina Wertmüller will add herself to the ranks of women directors who choose Holocaust settings for the staging of a controversial and flamboyant auteurship. Starring Giancarlo Giannini, who served as the male lead in the series of 1970s films that had made Lina Wertmüller the darling of the New York critical establishment, *Pasqualino settebellezze* (Seven Beauties, 1976) represents yet another variation on the themes of gender, power, and sexuality that had pervaded the director's filmography. As in Cavani's *Il portiere di notte*, *Pasqualino settebellezze* will involve a constant oscillation between time frames, but unlike the earlier film, which makes the Holocaust into a perversely desirable past as it erupts into the lugubrious and lifeless present of 1950s Vienna, Wertmüller's story is told from the perspective of an Italian army deserter captured by the Germans and interned in a *Lager* who flashes back to the saga of pre-war misadventures that led him to this perilous pass. The cross-cutting between Pasqualino's vivid escapades as a small-time crook in 1930s Naples and his grim present in the clutches of the Nazi concentrationary machine sets up the conditions of contrast and inversion dear to Wertmüller's

---

25 In an intriguing reading of *Il portiere di notte* from a feminist perspective, Marguerite Waller demonstrates how Cavani's film subverts conventional male and female subject positions, and in so doing destabilizes the binary oppositions on which Fascist power relations are based. 'If binary logic itself and the subjects it produces remain in place, then 'Jews' as well as 'Nazis,' women as well as men, remain burdened with the task of having to represent their positions as stable, coherent, and correct, a task that cannot help but involve them in further representations of difference as opposition and threat.' See 'Signifying the Holocaust: Liliana Cavani's *Portiere di notte*,' in *Feminisms in the Cinema*, ed. Laura Pietropaolo and Ada Testaferri (Bloomington: Indiana University Press, 1995), 213–14.

carnivalized aesthetics.[26] Nowhere is this contrast more pronounced than in the film's episodes of musical montage – sequences of pivotal narrative and psychological importance that dispense with dialogue and depend entirely on a visual track synchronized to a lively and appropriate musical score.

One such scene involves Pasqualino's trial for killing his sister's pimp and dissecting the body for disposal – the crime that earned him the labels of *squartatore* (axe-murderer) and 'the Monster of Naples.' Though Pasqualino had proudly confessed to the deed, since it vindicated the family honour that had been so severely compromised by his sister's prostitution, the lawyer insists on mounting an insanity defence for his client. The attorney presents Pasqualino's choices to him in stark terms – 'either life or dignity' – thus convincing the defendant to commit the very first in a series of concessions he will make at the expense of his own internal code of honour. In fact, we immediately see that Pasqualino's efforts to redeem his family's name have been completely undone by the necessity for his sister to return to the 'workforce' and become his lawyer's mistress in order to pay the legal fees for her brother's defence. In the trial scene, conducted without dialogue to the music of a song sung earlier in the film and whose only lyrics are 'Viv'e campar' (live and survive), Wertmüller presents an eloquent montage of the legal travesty that saves Pasqualino's life but destroys his reputation. Through glances, winks, and triumphant smiles, we see that the lawyer is in cahoots with Don Raffaele, Pasqualino's *camorrista* boss, and that now all eight of Pasqualino's 'women' – his mother and his seven sisters – have become streetwalkers, sporting the dyed blond hair of the trendy, Jean Harlow look. In a series of cross-cuts between Pasqualino's liquid, melancholy eyes and those of the young, innocent Carolina, we sense that this is the sentimental connection that might ultimately vindicate Pasqualino's survival strategy. Instead, the film's final scene will bring the protagonist back to Naples as a camp survivor to find Carolina's eyes now cosmetically enhanced and her body dressed in the garb of the prostitute that all Neapolitan women seem to have donned to welcome the Allied liberation forces.

---

26 See Joan and William Magretta, 'Lina Wertmüller and the Tradition of Italian Carnivalesque Comedy,' *Genre* 12 (Spring 1979), 25–43. On Wertmüller's use of comic
excess, caricature, and the grotesque to shatter audience complacency, see Insdorf,
Indelible Shadows, 73–4.

The amorous reunion that should have justified Pasqualino's ordeal becomes instead a sordid marriage contract aimed only at the propagation of the species. 'Let's get married and start making kids. We haven't much time. I want lots of them, twenty-five, thirty ... We have to become strong because we must defend ourselves. Do you hear them out there? In a few years we'll start killing each other for a glass of water, for a chunk of bread.'[27] In his twisted Darwinism, Pasqualino has completely misunderstood the lesson of the film's most eloquent spokesman for political action in the name of social justice – Pedro, the Spanish anarchist, who advocates the Gospel of the 'new man – man in disorder' as the alternative to a world of subhuman and merely biological survival. Pasqualino's mother, ever the pragmatist, encourages him to repress his Holocaust trauma. 'Don't think about it any more. It's all over. What's been has been ... You're alive, Pasqualino ... alive!' 'Yeah ... I'm alive,'[28] he echoes, but Wertmüller's camera questions this 'vitality' through a double mirror shot that locates Carolina's frontal reflection in the left panel, the mother's in the right, and Pasqualino's image blocked by the frame dividing the two. As the camera moves in to center on this obstructed reflection, it pans to the right to reveal Pasqualino's image in three-quarter view with vacant eyes, and half of his face in ominous shadow.

The second of the musical montage sequences involves Pasqualino's arrival at the *Lager*, whose clichéd visual language – emaciated nude torsos, striped pajamas, squalid barracks, and the inevitable *Arbeit Macht Frei* inscription – undergoes a remarkable stylizing operation in Wertmüller's hands. Shot in the cavernous and chilly expanse of an abandoned paper factory, using pale, washed-out greys and a hazy filter, this horrific montage moves from huddled male bodies to coiled barbed wire to naked cadavers being loaded into trucks, to men swarming over crowded bunks, to corpses hanging from rafters – all inter-cut with extreme close-ups of Pasqualino's disbelieving eyes. As a musical backdrop to this ghoulish spectacle, Wertmüller has chosen 'The Ride of the Valkyries' – perhaps in homage to Fellini's spa scene in *8½* (anticipating Coppola's helicopter attack in *Apocalypse Now*), but surely with the intent to appropriate all the ironic significance of the original Wag-

---

27 *The Screenplays of Lina Wertmüller*, trans. Steven Wagner (New York: Warner Books, 1977), 334.
28 Ibid.

nerian score. This glorification of the myth of Germanic origins, in support of super-race ideology, this paean to heroic exploits and epic warfare could have no more emphatic disproof than the *Lager*. As Wagner's music reaches its crescendo and the visual montage comes to its climax, there emerges out of the mist a massively built woman, Hilde, followed by an entourage of guards and dogs. This latter-day Brünnhilde is no longer the leader of warrior maidens who ride on the clouds and conduct the souls of fallen heroes to Valhalla, but the very earthbound commandant of the camp, loosely modelled on Ilse Koch, the notorious 'Bitch of Buchenwald.' Hilde's grand entrance into her realm is staged as a kind of Infernal Deisis, and she becomes the personification of place, the hyperbolic embodiment of the *universe concentrationnaire*. Wertmüller's adherence to the canons of the comedic grotesque, with its carnivalizing inversion of hierarchies, its satiric overturning of social norms, its parodic rewriting of generic conventions, leads her to reverse the gender roles of the romantic or seduction scenarios we have seen in previous Holocaust representations. Whereas women are the sacrificial victims in *L'oro di Roma*, *Kapò*, *Il giardino dei Finzi-Contini*, and *Il portiere di notte*, Wertmüller's film casts the male protagonist in this role, with a number of twists to the generic formula and all the ironies that attend them. While Pasqualino believes that his womanizing skills, finely honed in the streets of Naples, will ultimately win over the cold heart and equally frigid body of Hilde, it is this very pretence that she turns against him to formulate her grotesquely comic ultimatum: 'Fuck me or die.' Puny, undernourished, and pitifully weak, Pasqualino risks becoming the victim of his own scheme of sexual conquest. By virtue of her power to dictate and enforce the terms of their encounter, Hilde essentially rapes him. Filmed with a series of high- and low-angle shots that further dwarf this already diminished specimen of manhood, Pasqualino must literally scale the heights of Hilde's mountainous body before engaging in hilariously ineffectual attempts to arouse her (and himself). After an interlude in which the commandant mercifully permits him to refuel with a plate of sausage and sauerkraut, Pasqualino succeeds in his sexual mission, only to remain whimpering and spent, in fetal position, as a result of his exertions. Throughout this grotesque scene, Wertmüller mobilizes all the mechanisms of the monstrous feminine, with its connotations of horror, based on atavistic fears of being sucked back into the maternal womb, into the non-differentiation and abjection of the unborn state.[29] Indeed, it is as if this perverse coupling had begotten a freakish offspring, a neonatal Pasqualino reduced to a zero-degree identity, awaiting his new incarnation as *kapò*. In this capacity, he too will become a monster, meting out death sentences to his fellow inmates and discharging the fatal bullet into the bowed head of his best friend, Francesco. For Wertmüller, indeed, the *Lager* can give birth to no possible narrative of human redemption – only survival tales of the worst social Darwinist kind could ever be delivered from its horrid depths.

La linea del fiume (The Line of the River, 1976), by Aldo Scavarda, has double importance for the study of Italian cinematic representations of the Holocaust. It is the first member of the family of films with child protagonists – a family whose progeny will include *La Storia* (History, Luigi Comencini, 1987), *Jona che visse nella balena* (Jonah Who Lived in the Whale, Roberto Faenza, 1993), *La vita è bella* (Life Is Beautiful, Roberto Benigni, 1997), and *Il cielo cade* (The Sky Is Falling, Andrea and Antonio Frazzi, 2000) – and it insists on the link between pre-war Fascist anti-Semitism and the Final Solution. The expository on-screen text, which sets the beginning of the film in the fall of 1943, is eloquent in this regard. 'Fascism, which since '38 had barred Jews from the workplace and schools, declares now that, by law, Jews are enemy aliens. *The way is opened to deportations to Hitler's extermination camps*' (emphasis mine). It is this 'strada aperta alle deportazioni' that the child protagonist, Giacomino Treves, is miraculously able to avoid, thanks to a combination of luck, ingenuity, determination, and the kindness of strangers. The film begins with the round-up of Roman Jews on 16 October 1943, which Giacomino manages to escape by following his mother's instructions in Hebrew, unintelligible to the listening ears of her Nazi captor. During his odyssey through Europe to join his father in London, Giacomino is helped by a series of well-wishers: a hospital orderly who finds the boy unconscious after another Nazi sweep; a priest, Padre Luigi, who places him in the dubious care of Amedeo, a card sharp willing to accompany the boy to Turin; a family who takes him in at Susa, despite the protests of their bratty daughter; the partisans who save him from freezing and starving to death in the mountains; the two

---

29 See Barbara Creed, 'Horror and the Monstrous-Feminine: An Imaginary Abjection,' in *Feminist Film Theory: A Reader*, ed. Sue Thornham (New York: New York University Press, 1999), 251–66.

English aviators who accompany him to France; the doctor who runs a clandestine rescue network in Grenoble; the anti-Fascist proprietors of a cafe in that same city, who offer him cover; the owners of a farm in Normandy who provide a rest cure; the Allied soldiers who find him on the beach during D-Day; the official who leads him to his father in England where the latter serves as the Italian-language announcer for the 'Voice of London' radio broadcast. As this catalogue of rescue efforts suggests, *La linea del fiume* belongs to the genre of the adventure film – it is a loosely constructed series of episodes that trace this child's remarkable odyssey across a continent, traversing the most variegated terrains – cities, mountains, beaches – and amidst the most heterogeneous events, from intimate family meals, to partisan combat, to superpower invasions, and even to spy intrigues in which he plays a pivotal role, before bringing him to safety in the United Kingdom.

The film's production values are of the highest order, featuring the performances of such celebrated actors as Riccardo Cucciola, in the role of the doctor, and Lea Massari, in the role of Giacomino's mother. The director, Aldo Scavarda, comes from a career as a cinematographer working under the likes of Antonioni (*L'avventura*, 1959) and Bertolucci (*Prima della rivoluzione*, 1964). As can be expected, the photography shows the consummate skill derived from such experience. The indoor scenes have the sepia tones that give the film the look of a poignant 'pastness,' while the lighting offers the glow of the great pictorial masters who have inspired the Italian cinematic imagination at its best. Acoustically, the film begins with an original song, 'I tre ponti,' sung by Ornella Vanoni in the style of the rich Roman music-hall tradition. As visual accompaniment to this vocal performance, Scavarda offers shots of *il fiume* – the Tiber in all its picturesque charm, as it flows under arched bridges and along embankments, offering a wealth of optical delights. But intercut with this aestheticized footage are other kinds of visuals that disrupt the a-historical beauty of the river-scape – documentary clips of Nazi occupying forces, stills of signs screaming out 'Jud' and other anti-Semitic utterances, the head of a child in a horrendous mug shot. By combining a-temporal river imagery with historically grounded visual documents in the opening credit sequence, the film hints at the meaning of its enigmatic title.

Midway into the story we discover that *la linea del fiume* is the code name for a network that enables fallen Allied aviators to reach the shores of the Atlantic. The picturesque phrase is thus firmly grounded in history in a way that transforms the elegiac and eternal spectacle of the Tiber in the film's opening shots into a historically dynamic, engagé, and truly progressive image of partisan action. Giacomino's success in following *la linea del fiume* coincides with the macro-historical victory of the Allies in Normandy, announced by his father in his radio newscast at the end of the film.

What gives *La linea del fiume* special prominence in our study is the fact that Giacomino is never reduced to the level of Italian Every Child. He fervently clings to his Jewish identity, despite his awareness of the risks he runs in so doing. Giacomino stubbornly insists on wearing his hat in church, because 'in the house of God it is necessary to keep one's head covered.' He refuses to eat pork even in the presence of Nazis, he proudly admits to Amedeo that he is circumcised, and he announces that he is Jewish whenever the issue of religious identity arises. At one point, the English aviators, anxious for his safety, challenge Giacomino's forthrightness in the presence of the doctor who leads the *linea del fiume* organization, but the child justifies himself as follows: 'I noticed that the doctor is Jewish.' 'How did you manage to figure that out?' asks one of the Englishmen. 'It's hard to explain,' interrupts the doctor. 'Perhaps there is something particular about us.' It is at this juncture that the physician's cherished 'ideals of liberty and justice' give rise to a community in which 'Men won't judge us any more by the colour of our skin or our religion.' Within this Utopian context, a number of healthy and joyous events unfold – Giacomino is given a birthday party, he is taught English by one of the aviators, and all of the men engage in fitness activities for the body and the mind. But as always, Utopia is short-lived. Fearing Nazi capture, the group secretly boards a departing train, and during an Allied bombing raid in which civilians are wounded *en masse*, the doctor feels morally bound to offer his medical services. When asked for his identification papers by an inquisitive Nazi officer, the physician has no choice but to show the tatooed number on his arm – a souvenir of an earlier sojourn in Belsen-Bergen. Witnessing the doctor's subsequent arrest, Giacomino runs to join him, announcing, 'I too am Jewish.'

In the film's final scene, Giacomino's proud and insistent clinging to his religious identity is rewarded on a number of levels. Not only does Second World War history coincide with his personal triumph when he joins his father at the moment of the announcement of the Allied victory in Normandy, but all this is seen as a fulfilment of God's salvational promise in biblical terms. The radio announcement of the 'Voice of London' in fact concludes with an allusion to King George VI's words to the British populace, taken from the Book of Psalms: 'The ancient prophecy has been fulfilled: the Lord will give strength to his people. The Lord will give his people the blessing of peace.'

A Dearth of Films, Offset by the Arrival of the TV Mini-series (the 1980s)

Prima della lunga notte – L'ebreo fascista (Before the Long Night – The Fascist Jew, by Francesco Molé, 1980), based on the novel *Un ebreo nel Fascismo* (A Jew during Fascism) by Luigi Preti (1974), spans the second half of the 1930s, when Mussolini's imperialist agenda and his alliance with Hitler took definitive shape. We experience this history through its effects on the private life of Oberdan (Dan) Rossi, son of a Catholic mother and a father who is both Jewish and a fanatical supporter of the Mussolini regime. At the start of the film, Dan marries Rosa Calzolari in a civil ceremony rife with Fascist bombast, and true to his father's political leanings, the young man later announces his desire to join Mussolini's army in Ethiopia, much to the chagrin of his peace-loving bride. Upon his return from the front, Dan decides to embark on a career in journalism in Bologna, leaving his wife and their two young children behind in Modena. The resulting marital tensions lead Dan into the arms of a co-worker, Elena, who espouses a position of political resistance. Dan's collaboration with the paper is gradually loosened due to the Racial Laws, and he increasingly devotes his time to the writing of fiction. At the end of the film, Dan's novel is accepted by a prestigious publishing house in Florence, but his Jewish identity will require a semi-clandestine, and severely limited, printing run. As a result of this devastating setback, Dan decides to take his own life by leaping off the train as it speeds away from Florence.

The film reveals a hybrid generic identity and a glossy look typical of middle-level Italian film production in those years. The settings are bourgeois, the actors glamorous, and the musical soundtrack bouncy. With the exception of the quiet and introverted Dan, the other characters are portrayed in flamboyant and stereotypical extremes – his father spouts Fascist rhetoric like a wind-up toy, his co-worker Marino, significantly nicknamed Ciclone (Cyclone), is a human dynamo, and his mistress Elena is appropriately bohemian. While the tendency towards caricature, the bourgeois family milieu, and the upbeat music all suggest affinities with a strictly commercial cinema, the film's grim ending and its consciousness-raising function ally it with the more serious, civic-minded strains within the Italian realist tradition.

Accordingly, *Prima della lunga notte* traces the progressive political awakening of Dan, setting this gradual process in sharp contrast to the sudden disillusionment of his arch-Fascist father, who is fired from his job and goes on a suicidal rampage through the streets of the nocturnal city. Dan, instead, loses faith by degrees. When asked to hold forth on his war exploits in Ethiopia, Dan chooses reticence over rhetoric, and a series of brief flashbacks, shot in over-exposed sepia tones, tells us what his family will never know. While his father gushes over the 'titanic enterprise' of Mussolini's Ethiopian campaign and compares it to D'Annunzio's Fiume exploit, Dan quips, 'It's not the plot of a film,' in oblique reference to the heroics of such late 1930s features as *Squadrone bianco* (The White Squadron, Augusto Genina, 1936) or *Luciano Serra pilota* (Luciano Serra Pilot, Goffredo Alessandrini, 1938). The Ethiopian flashbacks indeed show a very different story – Dan sweating and prostrate in his tent, the soothing ministrations of his African concubine, the death of his fellow soldier by a stealthy native wielding a knife meant for him. Dan's doubts are further reinforced by an encounter with a German girl in Paris whose father has been interned in a *Lager* as a socialist, and who brandishes a newspaper with dire headlines about Hitler's treatment of his enemies. 'Are there anti-Semites in Italy?' the girl inquires. 'Not in the sense that you mean,' quibbles Dan. 'There are prejudices.' This spurious distinction will soon break down as the Rome-Berlin axis solidifies. 'Mussolini transformed an old, household dictatorship into a [form of] totalitarianism in the German style,' the voice-over narrator explains. The erosion of Dan's faith in the regime leads him to request a transfer to the literary section of the newspaper rather than remain in a division where he has to espouse political views that he has come to abhor.

It is Elena who formulates the film's moral ultimatum. 'We must react,' she beseeches Dan. 'If not, we will become accomplices of Fascism.' Laughing bitterly, he muses, 'I would be a Fascist Jew' – an oxymoron in light of the Racial Laws of 1938. Over the film's final frames, showing the endless tracks that Dan's suicide train has traversed, the title 'June 1940' appears, and the meaning of the 'long night' heralded by the film's title becomes painfully clear.

A conspicuous subcategory of Italian representations of anti-Semitism and the Final Solution is the TV mini-series, modelled on the highly successful U.S. prototype 'Holocaust' (1978, Marvin Chomsky), whose title brought into common currency the very term popularly ascribed to what scholars prefer to label 'Shoah.' In 1982, Italian television featured *Storia d'amore e d'amicizia* (Story of Love and Friendship, Franco Rossi) in three parts, starring Claudio Amendola as Davide Sonino, a prize-fighter of Jewish descent, and Massimo Bonetti as Cesare Costantini, his dear friend, fellow boxer, and rival for the affections of Sara, played by Barbara De Rossi. Though the love triangle dominates the psychological interactions of the story's protagonists, it never disrupts the friendship between Davide and Cesare, which is strictly governed by the rules of fair play. When the men decide that their romantic rivalry must be resolved, they simply slug it out, and later, when Davide temporarily abandons Sara (now his wife) to pursue a career in America, she has one fling with Cesare before choosing, openly and freely, to return to her husband. In Darwinian terms, the strongest has won, and ethnically it is more appropriate for Sara to remain married to her co-religionist. Cesare, however, never loses his devotion to Sara, and while Davide surpasses his competitor in brute strength, the latter offers the other characters the vision and virtue of his political commitment to the Partisan cause.

The film spans the years between 1935 and 1943, tracing the multiple trajectories of the friendships and love relations, as well as the political-military developments that marked that turbulent period. Set in Rome, in Trastevere for the most part, it involves simple, naive characters, speaking a broadly *romanesco* tongue, while their adventures combine the drama of the boxing world (à la *Rocky*) with the sentimental charms of courtship, the emotional intensities of family life, and the pathos of early death. In historical terms, the film touches on a number of important stages in the deteriorating condition of Italian Jewry under Fascism and the Nazi rule. Davide loses his title as national middle-weight boxing champ and is reduced to illegal work, genteel prostitution, and black marketing. The Nazi scheme to extort 50 kilograms of gold in exchange for Jewish safety, represented so compellingly in Lizzani's *L'oro di Roma* and mentioned in *La linea del fiume*, is re-enacted in *Storia d'amore e d'amicizia* along with the ensuing round-up of ghetto inhabitants on 16 October 1943. The particularities of Roman Jewish life emerge in scenes of ritual observances – in a Bar Mitzvah ceremony, in the wedding of Davide and Sara, and especially in the religiosity of Settimio, Davide's brother-in-law, who is the only devout Jew in the film and who mixes humour with ardor in his orthodoxy.

Of utmost interest is the film's opening voice-over narration. 'I am not Roman, but I like everything about Rome, its merits and its defects,' intones a resonant male speaker. 'When I was younger, I spent so many nights traipsing down these sidewalks and so many days wandering through these neighbourhoods.' The film's opening visuals are set in the present day, with scenes of a *flânerie* through the streets of Rome until the camera arrives at the Teatro di Marcello. 'But I never had occasion to visit the synagogue,' continues the voice-over narrator, 'and I did not know that behind certain famous ruins, there was a neighbourhood that used to be called the ghetto.' Now the camera pans along the expanse of the Teatro di Marcello and past the three remaining columns to its right before zooming to the synagogue dome in the background. 'One day, many years ago, a friend of mine, Rina Sonino, brought me there.' At this point, a woman's voice takes over the narration, and a hand-held camera walks us along a fence erected to keep trespassers from entering a reconstruction zone, but reminding us of the ghetto walls that once prohibited access to this space for other reasons. Now we cut to a long shot of the synagogue at the centre of its own *mise-en-scène*. With Rina Sonino we have found our entrée into this world behind 'certain famous ruins,' just as her narrative has found its way into the forefront of popular historical consciousness with the broadcast of *La storia di amore e di amicizia* on the mass medium par excellence of national television.

Five years later a second Holocaust television mini-series would be aired: *La Storia* (History) directed by Luigi Comencini, whose *Tutti a casa* (analysed earlier in this chapter) included several vignettes related to the fate of Italian Jewry under the Nazi occupation. Comencini's 1987 made-for-TV film is adopted from Elsa Morante's eponymous novel, which chronicles the experiences of Ida Mancuso, a widowed school teacher who is raped by a young German soldier in 1941, gives birth to the extraordinary child Useppe, and is committed to a mental institution after the boy suffers a fatal bout of epilepsy in 1947. Ida's story is one of inexorable decline as she struggles to accommodate the needs of this new and unexpected offspring, while trying to cope with the shifting enthusiasms of her older son, Nino, who quits high school to fight in the Fascist army, then joins the Resistance, only to end up making a fortune in the postwar Black Market before dying in a police ambush. While of great interest, the Nino plot rarely intersects the major storyline, which is that of Ida and Useppe, left homeless after a bomb destroys their neighbourhood of San Lorenzo, forcing them to seek shelter in an abandoned theatre along with a number of other vivid, profoundly humane, but not always savoury, individuals. Once Rome is liberated, Ida's attempts to rebuild her domestic world are thwarted by Nino's delinquency and by Useppe's refusal to adapt to the discipline of public school. His anti-social tendencies develop in tandem with the epileptic disorder that will eventually take his life.

Beneath the surface of *La Storia* lies a powerful and insidious Holocaust narrative. Half-Jewish, on her mother's side, Ida was taught from an early age to hide the dangerous truth of her identity. 'I am Jewish, it is a terrible thing,' her mother confesses to the child Ida in an intimate and picturesque flashback. 'The Jews are a people destined for all eternity to suffer the vindictive hatred of all the other peoples. For this reason I had you baptized, so that no one will know that you have a Jewish mother, and that you are half-Jewish. You must not tell anyone, not even your husband on the day that you get married.' Ida's entire character formation may be traced to this sense of 'original sin' and the necessity of its concealment. Thus, when she notices an anti-Semitic wall poster in the film's opening scene, and is immediately accosted by a drunken young German soldier in search of companionship, Ida automatically assumes her secret is out. The ensuing rape, pregnancy, and birth of Useppe become palpable signs of her guilt – her truth incarnate. As her delivery date approaches, Ida is mysteriously drawn to the ghetto, where she makes contact with the midwife who will ultimately take her in for the birth and post-partum recovery period. The ghetto becomes indeed womb-like – a space of total acceptance, comfort, and nurture – and it is there that Ida will meet Signora Di Segni, an alter-ego for her – the Ida who would live out her ethnicity with openness and pride. As the name suggests, Signora Di Segni is signed by her Jewishness, and it is this that will draw Ida to the woman in the film's heart-rending scene of deportation.

News of the 16 October round-up has reached their shelter the very morning that Ida and Useppe planned to flee the Nazi-occupied city. At the Tiburtine station, two trains, on parallel tracks, await departure – one a passenger vehicle overflowing with travellers bound for the Roman countryside, and one the freight vehicle destined for Auschwitz. This second train, composed of sealed cars with hands gripping the grating of the tiny, elevated windows, and voices pleading for water and air, recalls the scene in *Tutti a casa* when Innocenzi and Ceccarelli witnessed the passage of an identical vehicle through the landscape of northern Italy. In a way, this scene in *La Storia* could be read as the prequel to the episode in that earlier Comencini film, as if the director had felt compelled to visit the origin of the wretched journey so briefly glimpsed, and only dimly understood, by the main characters of *Tutti a casa*. In the comparison between the cursory nod to Nazi-Fascist anti-Semitism in *Tutti a casa* and the fully developed exploration of its significance for the protagonist of this director's 1987 television series, Comencini offers a measure of Italy's increased willingness to confront the Holocaust past.

In the *mise-en-scène* of the two trains waiting on parallel tracks in Rome's Tiburtina station, Ida's life choices are starkly laid out before her. She can continue to dissimulate by taking the passenger train that her paternal, married, and baptized identities allow her to board, or she can accept the consequences of belonging to a persecuted minority. When she spies Signora Di Segni rushing along the tracks to join her family on the deportation train, Ida's instinct is to board with her. The Signora's anguished roll call of her husband's and children's names – Settimio, Esterina, Graziella, Manuele, Angelino – conjures up the world of the large, tightly knit family units that make up the ghetto community to which Ida is irresistibly drawn in her secrecy and solitude. So intense is her impulse to find membership in this community that it leads Ida to confess to the Signora: 'I have never told you, but I too am Jewish.' Ignored by the distraught woman and the Nazi guards, Ida gravitates towards the other vehicle, the 'Aryan' passenger train, where a kindly gentleman makes way for 'questa signora con il pupo in braccio' (this lady with the little kid in her arms).

The meaning of the deportation train, however, is not lost on Useppe, who harbours its dire traces in his young consciousness – traces that are reactivated after the war when he beholds photographs of Nazi atrocities at a newsstand. These images gain a context in the child's mind when he overhears reports by the landlady's husband, a hospital orderly, who has witnessed the condition of Rome's Auschwitz survivors. 'They took away 1056. Only 15 came back. Fifteen in all. I met one who must have been a hunk, [so] tall. His weight was like a child's. He was skin and bones. And when I say skin and bones, I mean skin and bones. He seemed like a child. With his long bones and his eyes so deep in their sockets that you couldn't even see them.' In the recurrence of the term 'bambino' and the focus on sunken eyes, we cannot help but see Useppe's specular relationship to this survivor portrait. No sooner does the child overhear this testimony than he immediately digs out the newspaper wrapping of fruit in the cupboard to find the infamous

Holocaust photographs previously glimpsed at the newsstand. 'Why are you looking at these things? They are ugly, let's tear them up,' Ida implores him. 'Yes, they're ugly,' Giuseppe echoes. 'Let's tear them up.' But it is he who is being torn up by the images – his consciousness has been shattered by the knowledge they bring, and his mind, unable to contain their enormity, turns the horror in on itself through epilepsy.

There is another character who figures prominently in *La Storia*'s Holocaust narrative, and who becomes an occasional foster member of Ida's *ménage*. He is Davide Segre, a Jew from Mantua, who loses his family to deportation, escapes from prison, joins the partisans, violates his personal code of pacifism by brutally killing a young German soldier, and sinks into alcoholism and drug addiction after the war. Davide is, in his own way, a Holocaust victim – committed to anarchist doctrine and given to oratorical performances of his beliefs, in moments both of utter lucidity as well as of drunken stupefaction. This young intellectual cannot tolerate the breech between historical atrocity and his Utopian ideals. Like Useppe's shattered consciousness, Davide's breaks under the pressure, and where the child finds oblivion in the aftermath of his seizures, the man seeks it in the ever-increasing doses of morphine needed to bring him peace.

In filming Elsa Morante's novel, Comencini made a bold and risky decision – that of casting Claudia Cardinale for the part of Ida. Among the reigning divas of the Italian screen during the 1960s and 1970s, Cardinale was perhaps best known for her roles as the sumptuous and extroverted Angelica in Visconti's *Il gattopardo* (The Leopard) and as Claudia, the glamorous muse of Fellini's *8½*, as well as Aida, the ingenuous showgirl of the film that launched her stardom, Valerio Zurlini's *La ragazza con la valigia* (The Girl with the Suitcase, 1961). Within the corpus of Italian Holocaust cinema, we have already seen Cardinale flaunt her sexually flamboyant screen persona in Visconti's *Vaghe stelle dell'Orsa*, where the conventional eroticism of such characters as Angelica and Claudia is revealed to have dark and dangerous undercurrents. By casting Cardinale in the role of the dowdy, repressed, and self-effacing Ida of *La Storia*, Comencini is confronting the actress with a formidable challenge – that of persuading audiences to set aside their memory of her previous incarnations as a sex goddess with the gift of agency. Part of the energy that Cardinale puts into this performance is precisely an energy of suppression – we intuit the effort that goes into the masking of her voluptuous beauty, the restraining of her charismatic personal presence, and the disavowal of her sexual allure. Cardinale's success in bringing Ida to life owes a great deal, I think, to the way in which the actress's denial of her own lusty and vivacious screen persona enacts the character's efforts to conceal the 'original sin' of her identity and protect the child who incarnates that secret.

Gli occhiali d'oro (The Golden Eyeglasses, Giuliano Montaldo, 1987) was the second film to be adapted from a text by Giorgo Bassani, preceded by Vittorio De Sica's highly successful *Il giardino dei Finzi-Contini* of nearly two decades earlier. Like its predecessor, *Gli occhiali d'oro* is set in Ferrara in 1938, the year of the onset of the Racial Laws, and it too recounts a story of unrequited love among Jews for whom affairs of the heart were thwarted by historical circumstance. In *Gli occhiali d'oro*, Davide Lattes, a University of Bologna student, is abandoned by Nora Treves (played by a very self-consciously glamorous Valeria Golino) when the latter decides to become baptized in order to wed a prominent Fascist official. All this occurs against a backdrop of the progressively eroding Italian Jewish condition. First, Davide's thesis adviser, Professor Perugia, is expelled from the faculty in a chilling scene of public degradation, and then the young man is given the lowest possible passing grade on a final exam ('Is this mark for my performance or for my last name?' he snaps). Davide's father is initially sanguine about the fate of Italian Jewry, despite the dire news emanating from Germany. 'Italy, by tradition, is not anti-Semitic,' the elder Lattes assures his disconcerted son. By the end of the film, Davide's parents have relinquished all optimism in the face of persecution history. 'They are isolating us,' admits his mother, while his father, whose increasingly unkempt appearance reflects his declining morale, urges Davide not to be seen in the company of another outcast, the universally reviled Dr Fadigati.

This latter character has been the protagonist of a parallel plot of amorous heartbreak and social ostracism. In Fadigati's case, the alterity is sexual in nature. The doctor, a middle-aged gay man of great dignity and generosity (played by Philippe Noiret), is seduced by Eraldo, a handsome young boxer who unscrupulously avails himself of his lover's financial means to enjoy the luxuries that his own humble upbringing had denied him. Eraldo flaunts the affair before the eyes of all Ferrara, and when he publicly jilts Fadigati, the doctor is shunned by his former friends and patients, sinking further and further into a solitude relieved only by the kind attentions of Davide. Fadigati's story ends in suicide, while the film concludes with the following captions written over its final frames:

Nora died in childbirth in 1940.
Eraldo attempted a boxing career in France without success.
Davide became an internationally acclaimed writer.
The Jews of Ferrara were sent to concentration camps.

We do not need metaphorically to 'put on' the doctor's golden eye-glasses to see the symmetries between these dual narratives of social ostracism, whose protagonists are portrayed as innocent victims of an alterity deemed intolerable to a conformist and authoritarian status quo. The link between the Jewish minority and homosexuality harks back to nineteenth-century pseudo-scientific theories of race that attributed effeminacy, passivity, and perversity to Semitic peoples. The relationship between Judaism and sexual 'otherness,' expressed through parallelism in *Gli occiali d'oro*, will become fused in Ferzan Ozpetek's *La finestra di fronte* (Facing Windows), to be analysed in the second part of this study.

After the Thaw (the 1990s)

Roberto Faenza's *Jona che visse nella balena* (Jonah Who Lived in the Whale, 1993) belongs in the subcategory of Italian Holocaust films – *L'ebreo errante*, *Kapò*, and *Andremo in città* – with a distinctly international bent. This French-Italian co-production, set in Amsterdam and including a cast of non-Italian actors, is based on the eponymous text of Jonah Oberski, a child survivor of the camps. The opening credit sequence is accompanied by a song that recounts the biblical story behind the film's title, and against this backdrop, the voice-over narrator attributes the protagonist's love of these lyrics to a lesson learned at his mother's knee: if Jonah could emerge from the belly of the whale, then 'we never have to be afraid.' The ancient Jonah's three-day ordeal will stretch into three years of internment in the *Lager* for his modern counterpart, but the promise of deliverance that the mother draws from the biblical story will nonetheless be fulfilled in this twentieth-century tale of descent into the belly of the beast.

To heighten the sense of rupture and loss that deportation will bring to the world of the toddler Jonah, Faenza offers an irresistible portrait of prewar family life. The attractive young parents Anna and Max are devoted, fun-loving, and strong, their home is a haven of coziness, and the little boy is simply cherubic. No sooner is this fairytale childhood established than it is threatened by the incursions of anti-Semitism –

Max loses his job and must accept employment as a lowly typist in the publishing firm of his friend Daniel. In a scene that demonstrates the tender and enduring bond between father and son, Max takes Jonah to work and proudly exhibits his secretarial skills by typing out, in large capital letters, the boy's name. Paradise is short-lived, for the family will soon be deported to a series of camps, and over the ensuing three-year period Jonah will lose his father to illness and his mother to pathological depression. After each death, he will claim that he is no longer a child, and can therefore not afford the luxury of grieving.

When Jonah is finally restored to Amsterdam into the care of the publisher Daniel and his wife, who would like to adopt him, the child is in a state of severe traumatic shock. What finally releases him from his torpor is a fleeting glimpse of his father's ghost, busily typing in the room where he had worked before the war. The sighting lasts just a moment, but it prompts Jonah to climb into his father's old chair and to insert a page into the typewriter where he then proceeds to pound out his own name. This climactic scene is rich with meaning for the mourning work that had enabled Jonah Oberski to write his memoirs after ten years of psychoanalysis – mourning work that, by extension, entire cultures must undertake in order to come to terms with historical trauma, according to Eric Santner's formulation.[30] It is through the operations of therapeutic memory, of conjuring up the spectre of his father engaged in the physical process of writing, that Jonah is able to recuperate that past, accept his loss, and retrieve the subjecthood that the Holocaust ordeal had so grievously denied him. In the process of typing out his own name, the boy recovers the identity that his father had conferred upon him in that momentous earlier scene. Importantly, Jonah's act of self-naming, by means of the typewriter, anticipates the authoring of the memoirs that will complete the mourning process begun so auspiciously in the domestic publishing house of his adoptive parents.

Of particular interest is the Zionist subcurrent of *Jona che visse nella balena*, which, unlike the fully realized Exodus journey of *Il grido della terra*, stands as a vain hope constantly thwarted by the course of Holocaust history. Anna saves herself and Jonah from the first Nazi round-up by producing papers that attest to their imminent departure for the Holy Land. At every new stage of the deportation process, the family's hope that this will be followed by the definitive departure for Palestine

---

30 For a fuller discussion of Santner's important study, see chapter 1, pp. 16–17.

only leads them to further disappointment. In one particularly poignant scene, the family is reunited on a truck filled with prisoners singing Hatikva, the Israeli national anthem, and their elation at leaving the first (and most benign) of the camps is underwritten by the belief that their destination is indeed the Jewish homeland. An abrupt cut to three years hence shows otherwise – now the neat bunk beds of the earlier camp have been replaced by the squalid wooden stalls of a new imprisonment, while mother and son appear unrecognizably scrawny and shorn. The Zionist dream has met with yet one more crushing defeat. At the end of the film, as Jonah is seen smiling in his adoptive home against the background music of the Hebrew song taught to the children at the first detention camp, we realize that the promised land is an internal space, conquered through acts of private and public mourning, of confronting traumatic loss and bearing witness to it.

The genre of the television mini-series dedicated to the Jewish plight, inaugurated in 1982 with *Storia di amore e di amicizia*, and revisited in 1987 with *La Storia*, has perhaps its most decisive encounter with Italian Holocaust history in *18.000 giorni fa* (Eighteen Thousand Days Ago, Gabriella Gabrielli) broadcast in 1994. This film broaches a subject heretofore untouched by the cinematic medium: that of the concentration camps established in Italy under Fascism. The existence of two such camps was already well known – Fossoli (in Carpi, near Modena), where prisoners were gathered and held prior to deportation (Primo Levi among them), and the Risiera di San Saba (near Trieste), which served not only as a way station to Auschwitz, but interned many anti-Fascist prisoners as well as Jews, and housed a crematorium. In addition, recent research has revealed a multitude of concentration camps spread throughout Italy.[31] The largest of these facilities, Ferramonti-Tarsia (in Calabria), was the subject of a book-length study by Carlo Spartaco Capogreco published in 1987, and this furnished the reference material on which Gabrielli's *18.000 giorni fa* heavily relied. The film tells the story of Moshe Matoviezksi, a Polish Jew who escapes from Treblinka by jumping aboard an empty train returning to Italy from the Russian front in the winter of 1942. At the Brennero pass, he is rescued

---

31 For a thorough and emotionally laden account of one man's inquiry into this 'buried' history, see Galluccio, *I Lager in Italia*, who reports a total of 200 camps, of various sizes and functions, throughout the country. According to Liliana Picciotto's account, however, current research (as of Fall 2002) reveals the existence of thirty such camps. See 'The Shoah in Italy,' in *Jews in Italy under Fascist and Nazi Rule*, 215.

by Italian soldiers who send him to Ferramonti-Tarsia, where he resides until the camp is liberated by the British Eighth Army on 14 September 1943. The television broadcast of *18.000 mila giorni fa* is introduced by Simon Wiesenthal, whose commentary functions as a paratext – offering a didactic frame that insists on the distinction between Nazi and Fascist concentrationary regimes, and whose lesson will be borne out by a set of written captions that force the spectators to reflect on that distinction. Both the establishing shot of Treblinka and that of Ferramonti-Tarsia identify these locations as *campi di concentramento*, but everything we learn from the film will convince us of the inappropriateness of such common labelling. Treblinka is the place where Moshe's wife and daughter are immediately exterminated, where he is assigned to a gruelling work detail with minimal rations, and where he knows that he is merely 'a beast awaiting slaughter.' Ferramonti is the place where he is able to acquire a new family – he immediately bonds with the orphan girl Blume and eventually falls in love with a fiery refugee from Czechoslovakia named Miriam – and, most importantly, it is the place were he regains his belief in personal agency and the power of human solidarity.

The first index of the benign treatment that Ferramonti will accord its inmates is the ritual roll-call that introduces Moshe into the ranks of internees. Here the filmmaker relies on spectators' prior knowledge of the infamous rite of the Nazi *appel*, which required prisoners to stand outdoors, at attention, for hours in the predawn cold of the Polish winter while they were called out *not* by name, but by the German number to which their identity had been reduced. Failure to respond to one's distinctive number, barked out in a language that was literally foreign to many designees, could result in the direst of punishments. The roll-call in the Italian camp becomes an unwitting spoof of its Nazi counterpart, and the humour points entirely in the direction of Ferramonti's disorderly and endearing humanity. The procedure is conducted indoors and any semblance of military discipline is subverted by the presence of a dog and a rooster in the centre of the barracks and the absence of any required prison garb. Most striking is the fact that the inmates are called by name, with the adjutant Pasquale continually stumbling over difficult-to-pronounce foreign appellations. So confident are the inmates in their right to retain their personal identities that they have no compunctions about correcting Pasquale, who meekly apologizes for his linguistic ineptitude. At the end of the roll-call, one man's comment that 'again today, this torture is over' is laden with irony, given the spectators' knowledge that the Nazi *appel* was a true ordeal, literalizing the metaphor used by the Ferramonti internee, for whom the pain inheres solely in the acoustic distortion of his rightful name.

The film also draws on the audience's prior knowledge of Nazi concentration camp conditions to the benefit of the Italian case through set design. The barracks are clean and bright, containing neat rows of real single beds (not even bunks) complete with mattresses, blankets, and sheets. So comfortable are the accommodations that one woman even remarks upon another's desire to bring her entire family to sojourn there from northern Italy. In terms of social organization, Ferramonti borders on the Utopian – it has a parliament, a tribunal, a school, a newspaper, places of Jewish and Christian worship, and even a soccer league. For this structure to function, however, a strict internal hierarchy has been established, but Moshe's arrival has upset the system, for he has become a favourite of the camp director and therefore inadvertently displaced other inmates whose seniority should accord them the privileges that the newcomer has usurped. Moshe's initial indifference to this complex social structure stems from his dehumanizing experience at Treblinka – he insists that all inmates are merely 'beasts awaiting slaughter.' As he slowly emerges from such defeatism, Moshe becomes an integral part of the community, taking on responsibilities that reflect his burgeoning belief in the efficacy of collective action.

The stark contrast between Nazi and Fascist concentrationary regimes proposed by Wiesenthal in the film's preamble gives way to a further distinction of great import to our study. Among members of the Fascist military of Ferramonti, there is considerable tension between those who administer the camp from within and those who guard its borders. The latter are hardened Black Shirts, a special detail that answers to the local Federale (chief Fascist official), and which has wholeheartedly embraced the regime's penchant for violence and its ideology of racist supremacy. When Moshe is first ushered into the camp, he is greeted by a patrol whose spokesman announces, 'We are not guards, we are a special brigade. We shoot fugitives ... From Jews to anti-Fascists, all the excrement of the world is dumped at Ferramonti.' Later in the film, these same Black Shirts will carry out a systematic and enthusiastic slaughter of all the inmates' pet dogs in a displaced version of what Nazi rule visits upon its human detainees. Throughout the film, the Federale will give voice to Fascist racial policy when he confesses to the local Prefect how impatient he is for the deportations to begin, and when he has the camp director dismissed for being overly protective of the inmates.

It is the director himself who embodies the deeply human and honourable side of Italian official behaviour in wartime. Though a member of the military, his loyalties are to traditional values of justice and decency, rather than to Mussolini's code of gratuitous violence in the name of imperial power. No sooner does Moshe enter Ferramonti than he beholds the spectacle of the camp's director on a joyride with the children interned in the facility. Moshe is told that the director, along with the marshall of the camp are 'good people' who can behave thus 'only because Rome is far away.' It is in the geographic distance between the capital and the remote periphery of Ferramonti, hidden away in Calabria, that the phrase *italiani brava gente* (Italians, good folks) finds its true referent. Far from the centre of power, the director and his minions are free to let their innate humanity emerge in administering the camp, despite the military uniforms that they wear and their assumed loyalty to a vicious, authoritarian regime.

No doubt the best known and most controversial of this recent spate of Italian Holocaust films is Roberto Benigni's *La vita è bella* (Life Is Beautiful, 1997), celebrated by its admirers as a paean to human ingenuity and love in the midst of the ultimate adversity, reviled by its detractors as historically inaccurate and as an immoral appropriation of the Shoah to stage an exercise in comedic virtuosity.[32] The vehemence of audience reactions, both pro and con, is a measure of the film's very audacity in launching an experiment in genre that foregrounds the artistic quest for ever new approaches to the representation of Holocaust history. In other words, the film explicitly engages the problem of how to re-propose the experience of the Shoah to audiences already saturated with documentary and more conventional fictional treatments of the historical record.

Beginning in the southern Tuscan town of Arezzo (near Benigni's birthplace of Castiglion Fiorentino), and set in the year 1939, just after the promulgation of the Racial Laws, the film traces the quixotic fortunes of Guido Orefice, who falls in love with the beauteous Dora, the fiancée of the Fascist functionary Rodolfo. Unhappy with her future

---

32 An extended and in-depth analysis of *Life Is Beautiful* may be found in my *After Fellini: National Cinema in the Postmodern Age* (Baltimore: Johns Hopkins University Press, 2002), 268–84. For a spirited and insightful defence of Benigni's use of humour in *Life Is Beautiful*, see Insdorf, *Indelible Shadows*, 289–92.

bridegroom, and smitten by the extravagant and whimsical romanticism of Guido, she allows herself to be abducted by him at her engagement party. After their night of love, the film cuts abruptly to five years later, as the blissfully married couple and their adorable son Giosuè are deported to the equivalent of Auschwitz. In order to maintain the child's morale amidst the suffering and horror of the *Lager*, Guido invents a game in which childhood stoicism (no crying, no whining for mama or between-meal snacks) will be measured by the accumulation of enough points to eventually win *un carro armato vero* (a real army tank). Guido's rules represent a fictionalized 'translation' of what will truly be needed to survive this ordeal – perseverance, belief, luck, and resistance to the Nazi dehumanization campaign – all of which will be rewarded by the timely arrival of the army tank that will liberate the camp. Guido's gamble with history pays off, and the end of the game indeed coincides with the apparition of *un carro armato vero* from American liberation forces.[33] But Guido's final attempt to keep Giosuè in the mode of the game has cost him his life – in the mayhem of the German retreat, he resorts to playful antics that provoke the anger and the gunfire of his Nazi guard. Unaware of Guido's death, Giosuè greets the tank as verification of his father's claim, and when he is reunited with his mother shortly thereafter, the child is able to utter, in fullest confidence, the heartbreakingly incomplete declaration 'We won.'

Central to Benigni's strategy of Holocaust representation is his film's 'structural schizophrenia.'[34] The generic hybridity of previous Italian films on the Shoah has been taken to hyperbolic extremes in *La vita è bella* – not even the oscillation between the protagonist's carnivalesque past in Naples and his funereal present in Buchenwald as recounted in *Pasqualino settebellezze* can compare, in terms of stylistic dissonance, with the cleavage between the *before* and *after* of deportation in Benigni's work. Wertmüller's back and forth is constant, and devoid of the shock value that accompanies Benigni's radical shift from the romantic comedy of the film's first half to the audacious parable of the second. The film's 'architectural'[35] schizophrenia thus becomes in and of itself a sig-

---

33 Among the liberties that Benigni has taken with the historical record is the substitution of the U.S. army for the true Soviet liberators of Auschwitz.

34 For this phrase, and for his excellent defence of the film, see Maurizio Viano, '*Life Is Beautiful*: Reception, Allegory, and Holocaust Laughter,' *Annali d'Italianistica* 17 (1999), 155–71.

35 Viano uses the term 'architectural allegory' to describe this aspect of Benigni's strategy in *La vita è bella*. See ibid., 163ff.

nifier – both of the violent rupture that deportation brought into seemingly enchanted lives and of Benigni's break with decorum in fashioning his Holocaust comedy.

Part one of *La vita è bella* participates fully in the genre of Italian film comedy, with its caricatures, its gags, and its comfortable promise of a happy ending. Benigni could count on Italian audiences' familiarity with his established screen persona as the physically agile, fantasy-prone, good-hearted, testosterone-driven yet childlike sprite – and his quest to win the affections of whatever female character will be played by his wife, Nicoletta Braschi. These expectations will be thoroughly met by the film's first half, but the genre to which they belong will be unrecognizably transformed after the family's deportation. It is in the disparity between parts one and two that Benigni locates the shock value of the film, and that disparity will gain cumulative weight, in cognitive and moral terms, as the film's second half unfolds.

Giosuè, the product of Guido's and Dora's romance narrative, becomes the living reminder of the enchanted world of the film's first half, and his father's attempt to keep his son alive, by means of the game, becomes the man's way to sustain the innocence and wonder of that earlier, now impossibly inappropriate, narrative genre. The new genre that Benigni invents in part two of his film operates on dual levels of cognition: that of Giosuè's belief in the game – vestige of the marvellous adventures of part one – and our knowledge of the atrocity that Guido's rules cover up. Rather than show us explicit footage of torture, gas chambers, and crematoria – footage that we have seen before and that would cause us to recoil in horror – Benigni asks us to acknowledge the hidden truth by traversing the distance between Guido's fictions and their Holocaust referent each time that the man is forced spontaneously to invent a new gimmick to accommodate Giosue's burgeoning awareness of genocide. In other words, Benigni's strategy for bearing witness is both to refer and to mask, or to refer *through* masking, what Morandino Morandini called 'a horror that ... hidden, is more evident than if it were shown.'[36] In this regard, the film's most wrenching scene is that in which Giosuè confronts his father with reports that Jews are burned in ovens, and their bodies used to make buttons and soap. Guido's tactic is to highlight the absurdity of such behaviour in a just and humane world. By appealing to the child's innate sense of the rightness of things,

36 Morandino Morandini, 'Il bello di Benigni,' *Cineforum* 370 (December 1997), 3.

he is able to talk Giosuè out of believing in reports of such abominations. For the viewing audience, Guido's rhetorical ploy forces us to relinquish our factual knowledge and jadedness as we register, from a position of cognitive innocence, the history surrounding this ghoulish harvest of human bodies.

It is important to note that part one of the film, for all its fairytale trappings, is not without its own polemic thrust. While the Fascists are represented as pompous fools, their propagandistic pageantry is reduced to a series of gags, and the anti-Semitic attacks are limited to the malicious pranks of a few hooligans, we are led to understand in hindsight, from the perspective of part two, the moral link between Mussolini's regime of 1939 and the persecution of Italian Jewry in 1943 to 1944. The casual banter at Dora's engagement party anticipates the genocidal extremes to which Italy's alliance with Nazi Germany will lead. Significantly, it is the elementary-school principal who conducts this discussion, showing the virulent effects of Fascist pedagogy on a nation soon to experience its very worst consequences. The principal formulates the issue of super-race ideology as a math problem. 'A crazy person costs the State 4 marks a day. A crippled person 4.5, an epileptic 3.5. Given that 300,000 people are institutionalized at an average cost of 4 marcs a day, how much would be saved all together if these individuals were to be eliminated? A high-school problem for us. In Germany they pose it to seven-year olds, truly another race.'[37] Part one of the film, then, sets the terms for Benigni's indictment of Fascist Italy as a culture delirious with propaganda, susceptible to racist ideology, and therefore complicitous in the events that will lead to the deportation and extermination of 8529 of its Jewish countrymen.

In the same year that Benigni's audacious Holocaust comedy came out, Francesco Rosi completed his epic adaptation of Primo Levi's *La tregua* (The Truce, published in the United States under the title *The Reawakening*). Though Rosi originally conceived the idea for filming the second of Primo Levi's Holocaust memoirs in 1987, with the approval of the author in the last weeks of his life, it would take another ten years for the necessary funds to be raised and for the project's material obstacles to be overcome. In the interim, the success of *Schindler's List* and the increasingly receptive cultural climate emboldened potential backers to invest in Rosi's ambitious undertaking.

---

37 Roberto Benigni and Vincenzo Cerami, *La vita è bella* (Turin: Einaudi, 1998), 88.

La tregua tells the story of Primo Levi's liberation from Auschwitz in January 1945 and the nine-month odyssey through post–Nazi-occupied Europe on the way back to his hometown of Turin.[38] Levi's journey is anything but linear, involving delays, detours, and even backtracking caused by the vagaries of the railroad system and the bureaucratic incompetence of Soviet authorities. As with all travel narratives, *La tregua*'s progress is multilevelled – psychological, anthropological, and literary developments parallel the geographic meanderings of its protagonist. In Levi's case, the journey from Auschwitz is very much a personal journey into a fully human condition, but it is also the collective journey of a newly liberated Europe in the throes of communal rebirth. Rosi is very much attuned to this choral dimension of Levi's experience, and accordingly he mounts a large-scale production spanning a vast spectrum of locations, from primeval Russian forests to villages and cities spread throughout Mitteleuropa, and involving a cast of thousands to impersonate the rootless masses floating about the Continent in this fluid and undefined post-Nazi world.

While fully international in scope, *La tregua* is also very much obsessed with the quest for *italianità*. Primo's parting words to his dear friend Daniele, who must be hospitalized after the liberation of Auschwitz and cannot immediately join the others on their journey home, are 'See you in Italy.' Thus, from the very start of *La tregua*, Italy becomes a teleology, the privileged object of desire, the reward for Holocaust survival. At each new camp to which he is transferred throughout the many stages of his journey, Primo routinely announces 'I'm Italian,' as if this self-identification could establish the longed-for rootedness so poignantly sought after amidst the ravages of postwar Europe. Primo does manage to experience *italianità* on a microcosmic level in the bedraggled group of countrymen who join him in his wanderings and who hail from locations throughout mainland and insular Italy: Daniele is from Venice, Ferrari from Milan, Cesare from Rome, Unverdorben from Trieste, D'Agata from Sicily.

Contrary to all expectations, the terminal point of Primo's journey is no ending at all, but an agonizing and necessary beginning – that of bearing witness to his ordeal and of giving voice to those who can no longer do so. Thus, Rosi makes the strategic decision to conclude his

---

38 For an in-depth analysis of the film, see my *After Fellini: National Cinema in the Postmodern Age* (Baltimore: Johns Hopkins University Press, 2002), 253–67.

film of Levi's second Holocaust memoir by having Primo recite the opening words of his first volume of testimonial writing – *Se questo è un uomo* (If This Is a Man, published in the United States under the title *Survival in Auschwitz*), The end of the journey coincides with the beginning of its writing, so that the line becomes a circle that revolves ceaselessly around the central and all-encompassing horror of the camps. In this sense, the meaning of Levi's title gains powerful new resonance. The truce, the respite, the lull between hostilities, comes to signify the interval between the release from Auschwitz and the ordeal of bearing witness at home. In Levi's words, 'the months just past, although hard, of wandering on the margins of civilization now seemed to us like a truce, a parenthesis of unlimited availability, a providential but unrepeatable gift of fate.'[39]

For Rosi, the idea of a privileged, but finite period of plenitude and openness had important meta-cinematic application. In terms of Italian film history, that period corresponded to the era of the great postwar movements of neorealism and *cinema politico* when the celluloid medium assumed the role of cultural protagonist, when it occupied a place of pre-eminence in the public arena. Fuelled largely by Marxist thinking, the Second World War Resistance fighters and their postwar successors were deeply beholden to a myth of the Soviet Union as a paragon of social justice and economic fair play. For Rosi, this myth is seen as foundational – it is the basis of the political vision embraced by the Italian Left, which dared to dream of a better world. As such, that myth becomes the object of considerable nostalgia on Rosi's part – a nostalgia expressed throughout *La tregua* in the idealized representation of the Russian characters, Dr Dancenko, Marja Fiodorovna, and especially Galina, and in the recurrent image of the Soviet locomotive, often shot in low angle as it races across the screen to literally drive the narrative to its destination.

If, as I have argued,[40] it took the end of the Cold War to make possible a new Italian historiography that would accommodate the Shoah, then Rosi's film stands at the cusp of these developments. It is both a requiem for the Cold War Italian Left, sustained by the myth of a Soviet Utopia, and an acknowledgment of the Holocaust history that can only be confronted in a post-ideological age. Janus-like, *La tregua*

---

39 Primo Levi, *The Reawakening*, trans. Stuart Woolf (New York: Touchstone, 1995), 206.
40 For a full exposition of this argument, see chapter 1, pp. 18–19.

looks back to a period of Left–Right oppositional thought which allowed no room for the story of Italy's Jews, while simultaneously looking forward to the dissolution of Cold War ideology and the telling of the suppressed history that will emerge full-fledged in the outpouring of films to follow.

PART TWO

Recovered Memory:
Contemporary Italian Holocaust Films
in Depth

1. Davide greets his father, Baron Blau, played by the filmmaker Ricky Tognazzi, in *Canone inverso*. (Webphoto)

2. Jeno and Davide perform the *canone inverso* in competition before a jury that includes the director of the conservatory and their father. (Webphoto)

3. Sophie and Jeno consummate their love on the eve of the concert that will end so tragically for them both in *Canone inverso*. (Webphoto)

4. Wilhelm insists that his family maintain its aristocratic calm, and not leave the dinner table, despite the deafening explosions nearby. (Webphoto)

5. A band of retreating German soldiers, looking for Wilhelm, takes over the Einstein villa in *The Sky Is Falling*. (Photomovie)

6. Katchen tries to protect her daughter Annie from the Nazi assault in *The Sky Is Falling*. (Photomovie)

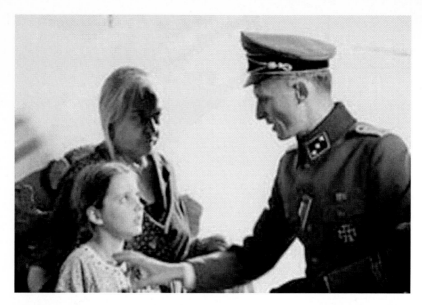

7. The German commander spares Penny the fate of the Einsteins when he notices that she is wearing a necklace adorned with a cross in *The Sky Is Falling*. (Webphoto)

8. Lele and Pietruccio enjoy one of the many constructive games that characterize their childhood friendship in *Unfair Competition*. (Photomovie)

9. Nonno Mattia watches helplessly as the quarrel between Leone and Umberto escalates in *Unfair Competition*. (Webphoto)

10. Leone is stung by Umberto's racial slur in *Unfair Competition*. (Webphoto)

11. Jews from the Spanish 'protected houses' are being led to the train for Auschwitz in *Perlasca*. (Webphoto)

12. Perlasca reads off names of the Jews in his custody to save them from deportation. (Webphoto)

13. Perlasca removes one last child from the train bound for Auschwitz. (Castle Hill Productions)

14. In the flashback to 1943, the young Davide of *Facing Windows* kills his would-be assassin, a fellow baker who is plotting to help in the Nazi round-up of Roman Jews. (Photomovie)

15. Giovanna and Lorenzo finally come together to fulfil their voyeuristic fantasies in *Facing Windows*. (Photomovie)

16. Davide teaches Giovanna a lesson in the art of baking in *Facing Windows*. (Webphoto)

3 The Haunting Strains of Holocaust Memory: Ricky Tognazzi's *Canone inverso* (Making Love)

Direction: Ricky Tognazzi. Subject and Screenplay: Graziano Diana, Simona Izzo, Ricky Tognazzi (based on the eponymous novel by Paolo Maurensig, 1996). Photography: Fabio Cianchetti. Music: Ennio Morricone. Editing: Carla Simoncelli. Costumes: Alfonsina Lettieri. Cast: Hans Matheson (Jeno Varga), Melanie Thierry (Sophie Levi), Lee Williams (Davide Blau), Gabriel Byrne (The Mysterious Violinist), Ricky Tognazzi (Baron Blau in middle age), Peter Vaughn (Baron Blau in old age), Domiziana Giordano (Baroness Blau), Nia Robert (Costanza), Adriano Pappalardo (Wolf), Andy Luotto (Maestro Hirschbaum). Year: 2000. Availability: DVD, *Canone inverso* (Making Love) in English-language original with Italian subtitles, or dubbed into Italian; Cecchi Gori Home Video, distributed through internetbookshop.it.

Synopsis

The film opens in contemporary London, where an unusual violin with a pegbox sculpted in the form of a human head is being sold at an auction. Two audience members, a young woman named Costanza and a silver-haired gentleman, engage in a bidding war, which is won by the latter. When Costanza pays a visit to her competitor for the violin, the story of this unusual instrument and its special meaning for both characters gradually emerges. The woman explains that in 1968, while involved in the democratic uprising of the Prague Spring, she had been sought out by a mysterious stranger who played a haunting tune – a *canone* – on the violin with the anthropomorphic pegbox. Hearing the Soviet troops entering the city to suppress the insurgency, the stranger was reminded of an earlier epoch of military occupation and civilian persecution. The film flashes back to a small town in prewar Bohemia where a young Jewish woman is struggling to survive with her son, born of a romance with an Austrian Jewish soldier who had left behind the distinctive violin. The child, Jeno Varga, shows unusual talent as a violinist from a very early age. Encouraged by his mother and her new husband, a pig farmer named Wolf, to pursue a musical career, Jeno is admitted to the prestigious conservatory of Prague. There he meets and befriends Davide Blau, an Austrian aristocrat of Jewish descent. When Davide is expelled from the conservatory on ethnic grounds, Jeno announces that he too is Jewish and will share the social ostracism of his co-religionist. The two young men withdraw to the Blau family castle in Innsbruck, and it is there that the friendship with Davide unravels. When the trademark violin is revealed to belong to Baron Blau, the suspicion that Jeno is his half-brother leads Davide to viciously turn against his newfound sibling. As the fraternal plot unfolds, so too does a passionate love story between Jeno and a concert pianist of French-Jewish origins, Sophie Levi. Married to a mercenary manager/ husband, Carlo, Sophie is smitten by the romantic and talented Jeno. As reward for graduating first in his class at the conservatory, Jeno has been granted the opportunity to play a *canone* in concert with Sophie, but the performance is interrupted by a Nazi blitz that results in the deportation and internment of the two young people in an unnamed concentration camp. There, Sophie gives birth to a daughter, Costanza, who survives her parents and becomes the film's framing narrator. The old man who bought the violin turns out to be Baron Blau, her grandparent and father of both Davide and the illegitimate Jeno. When Costanza and the baron go to the abandoned and dilapidated Prague conservatory, they find the mysterious stranger who had recounted his story to Costanza in 1968. The man proves to be Davide, finally cured of the madness that had driven him to assume Jeno's identity, out of guilt, after the latter's death. With the meeting in the conservatory, so fraught with memories of musical brotherhood, three generations of the Blau family are brought together, the estranged father–son relationship is remedied, and Costanza is able to bear witness to her parents' story of romantic and artistic passion cut short by Holocaust history.

A compelling example of the Italian need to represent the Shoah at this particular historical juncture is *Canone inverso*, the 1996 novel by Triestine writer Paolo Maurensig, adapted by filmmaker Ricky Tognazzi in

2000. Of the greatest interest to my study is the relationship between novel and film – the adaptive strategy by which Tognazzi has taken a story that is only tangentially concerned with the plight of the Jews in Nazi-occupied Europe, and has made it, instead, a full-fledged Holocaust text. In so doing, he has brought the latencies, half-tones, and ellipses of Maurensig's novel into the foreground of his film, with striking implications for the contemporary Italian engagement with Holocaust history.

In Maurensig's text, Nazism is never named. 'Per la prima volta,' Jeno remarks upon his return to Vienna after leaving Castle Blau, 'mi accorgevo che il mondo era cambiato, era come privato della propria luce. Andando per le strade e per le piazze sentivo aprirsi in me brecce di panico. La gente era diventata folla, ottusa folla, sospinta dallo smarrimento, che si incanalava nella rigida planimetria della città. C'era una smania di aggregarsi. Nessuno voleva restare solo con la propria coscienza ... Mai vista tanta folla in vita mia, mai vista negli occhi della gente una luce così festosa e tragica allo stesso tempo.'[1] (For the first time, I understood the world had changed, that it was deprived of its light. I could not stand to be around people. I did not recognize myself in them, I did not share their ideals, I did not understand them. As I walked in the streets and squares, I was ripped apart by panic. The people had become a crowd, an indistinguishable throng, that funnelled through the rigidly laid-out streets of the city, pushed on by its own bewilderment. There was a terrifying urge to gather together. No one wanted to be alone with his own conscience ... I have never seen such crowds in all my life. I had never seen in the people's eyes a light so joyful and so tragic at the same time).[2]

In his refusal to name the political phenomenon he is describing, Jeno is adopting the rhetorical figure of ellipsis that will characterize Maurensig's entire relationship to the Shoah. Ellipsis is an omission that forces us to supply what is lacking – it is a subtle, even stealthy, form of coercion that makes us collaborators in the completion of meaning.

---

1 Paolo Maurensig, *Canone inverso* (Milano: Oscar Mondadori, 1996), 151-2. All the quotes will be from this edition of the novel, and page numbers will henceforth be included in the body of my text.

2 The English translation comes from *Canone Inverso: A Novel*, trans. Jenny McPhee (New York: Holt, 1999), 178–9. Subsequent page numbers will be included parenthetically in the text.

Elliptical, too, is Maurensig's treatment of the concrete effects of racial persecution within the story. Without labelling them as Jews, Jeno tells us that the director of the Collegium and a number of students were mysteriously rounded up for interrogation, and made to disappear within a few days. 'Il loro nome veniva taciuto all'appello mattutino e cancellato dai registri. Restava una cella vuota con un materasso arrotolato sulla branda. Tutto si svolgeva con tanta rapidità e decisione che finivamo per chiederci se c'erano davvero stati, al Collegium Musicum, quel tale Rosenbaum o Goldmayer o Horowitz, con cui per anni avevamo diviso lo spazio, il cibo, il sapere. Ma era meglio far finta di nulla, meglio convincersi che non erano mai esistiti' (100–1). (Their names ceased to be called at morning attendance and were canceled from the registers. All that remained were their empty cells, their mattresses rolled up on top of the foldout beds. It all took place with such rapidity and decisiveness that in the end we wondered if Rosenbaum or Goldmayer or Horowitz – those with whom we had shared space, food, and knowledge for years – had actually ever been at the Collegium Musicum. But it was better to act as if nothing had happened, better to convince ourselves that they had never existed [117].) It is, of course, the Nazis' own practice of ellipsis, of obliteration, that here Jeno both enacts and subverts, naming the very Jewish classmates whose appellations have been cancelled from the rolls.

The novel's elliptical language is perhaps most noteworthy in its treatment of Sophie Hirschbaum, long-standing object of Jeno's adoration, both as woman and as virtuoso violinist. They had met only once, in a vacation spa where she joined him in playing variations on a popular Hungarian melody as a duet, followed by a fleeting kiss, but Jeno had continued to see in Sophie the apotheosis of all his romantic and aesthetic desires. Though never explicitly labelled Jewish, the surname Hirschbaum could well take its place among the Horowitzes, Goldmayers, and Rosenbaums on the list of those marked for extermination. Attending her final concert in Vienna, 'sentii che Sophie era in pericolo,' Jeno recounts, 'che tutti eravamo in pericolo, che dovevamo fare qualcosa. Tutto sembrava sul punto di sgretolarsi da un momento all'altro. Possibile, mi chiedevo, che nessuno tra i presenti si rendesse conto di ciò che stava per succedere, che non si leggesse su quei volti il minimo turbamento? ... Come facevano, mi chiedevo, a starsene seduti, così tranquillamente ... senza sentire quel che gravava nell'aria?' (153) (I believed Sophie was in danger, that all of us were in danger, and that we had to do something. Everything seemed on the point of falling apart from one minute to the next. Was it possible, I wondered, that no one among those present was aware of what was about to happen, that on their faces there wasn't the least sign of worry? ... How could they, I asked myself, stay peacefully in their seats ... without feeling that which was weighing heavily in the atmosphere? [180-1]). In his use of the relative pronouns *ciò che* and *quel che* and his failure to make explicit their grammatical antecedents, Jeno's ellipsis suggests that the doom that hovers over his story is, in fact, unnamable – it defies the logical structures and civilized practices implicit in the very invention and refinement of human discourse.

Where Maurensig relegates the Holocaust to the interstices and silences of his novel, Tognazzi elevates it to the foreground of his film. Not only is Sophie Jewish (surnamed Levi in the film), but so too are Jeno and his belatedly discovered half-brother (whose name is changed from Kuno to the ethnically appropriate Davide). Much like De Sica's *Garden of the Finzi-Continis*, which makes explicit Bassani's subtle and oblique allusions to the Shoah, Tognazzi's *Canone inverso* abounds in direct, frontal representations of the Nazi threat. Sophie, unlike Micol, is supremely conscious of the fact that privilege cannot protect her from the impending disaster. 'It's just a question of time, Carlo. I'm Jewish,' she tells her manager/husband, who is pushing her to perform in Bohemia despite the Nazi interruption of her last concert in Vienna. 'Your talent will protect you,' he insists.

But events prove otherwise. Nazi zealots deface the posters announcing Sophie's next performance and Jeno is beaten mercilessly for opposing such vandalous acts. In the scene of ostracism from the Collegium Musicum, where Maurensig's reticence forbade his naming the collective object of Nazi genocide, the film's Jeno openly admits to the school's new director that he is Jewish, and we are told that Davide Blau's family prestige does not spare him the fate of his co-religionists. Like the Finzi-Continis, the Blau family retreats to the protected confines of the castle, and when Jeno leaves Innsbruck and returns to Prague, he finds the city festooned with Nazi flags. The threat is such that even Sophie's mercenary husband is alarmed enough to take measures for flight.

From the very start of Tognazzi's film, its Holocaust focus is evidenced in the overt announcement of Jeno's ethnicity. When the boy asks his mother to describe the absent father, she replies: 'He played the violin. He was Jewish, like us.' At that point, the camera cuts to the photograph of a group of Austrian soldiers, one of whom holds a violin poised on his knee. We had already seen close-ups of this violin, with its unusual pegbox sculpted in the form of a human face wearing an expression of barely suppressed horror, in a beautiful, fluid montage during the opening credits of the film, and we will see it again in the photograph that Davide has in his possession, and which reveals to him his transgressive brotherhood with Jeno.

Thus, in the introductory phrases 'He played the violin. He was Jewish like us' Jeno's mother links art with ethnicity, musical genius with 'otherness,' to form a genealogy for her son that is also a destiny. By converting Maurensig's Catholic Jeno into a Jew, and insisting on this identity from the very start, Tognazzi announces that his characters are at risk, and that the entire world they inhabit is on the verge of extinction. Our foreknowledge of the abruptness and violence of the Jews' fate makes Toganzzi's re-evocation of prewar Bohemia (a shift from Maurensig's Hungary) one of great nostalgia and loss. This sense of impending extinction, when generalized to an entire culture, may explain Tognazzi's treatment of the Mitteleuropean setting of the film. Unfairly criticized for being stereotypic and sentimentalized,[3] Tognazzi's prewar Mitteleuropa is not a historically documentable place, but a topos – a sign of a bygone world, rich in cultural variety, combining gypsy, Slavic, Magyar, Jewish, and High German elements – with all the attendant excitement and fascination that such hybridity can bring. To evoke this world is, by definition, to mourn its passing.

Undoubtedly, the most poignant image of that sense of loss is the violin, itself a vestige of an earlier age with its baroque scrolls, elegant volutes, and arabesques. A relic of the seventeenth-century court culture that brought it into being, the violin stubbornly asserts its ancestry despite the ever-changing contexts in which it appears, and the post-baroque scores it is required to play. A perpetual anachronism, obsolete yet ever available for present uses, the violin within the film is a figure for memory – for its recovery, transmission, and centrality to the artistic process. In the case of Jeno's violin, with its anthropomorphic

---

3 For example, Emanuela Martini complains that Tognazzi's treatment of Mitteleuropa partakes of 'this imaginary ... that circulates between Prague, Vienna, Budapest, the Nazi occupation and the Communist one, drowning in soft focus and music. It is in this way that the cinema ends up really doing harm to Mitteleuropean culture.' See the extract from her review of *Canone inverso* published in *Film TV*, 22 February 2000, included in the compilation *Rassegna stampa cinematografica* (Bergamo: S.A.S., 2000), n.p.

pegbox, the baroque form of the instrument undergoes a mutation that proclaims its role in transmitting a unique story – one whose tragic end is prefigured in the horrified expression of its sculpted mask.

Closely linked to the violin's function as a figure for memory, then, is its role in fabulation. Within both novel and film the violin is an instrument of storytelling as much as it is of music. Whoever comes into possession of this violin seems bound, even compelled, to tell a tale. The storytelling process, however, is not sequential like the movements in a concerto or the scenes of an opera. Instead, the narrative is organized within an intricately structured series of Chinese boxes, of stories within stories within stories, whose interrelationships give new meaning to the ever-resonant title of *Canone inverso*.

Maurensig's novel opens in London with the purchase of the coveted violin at an auction at Christie's. The novel's initial narrator, then, is the buyer – a very self-satisfied gentleman who luxuriates in his unusual acquisition, until a knock on the hotel-room door interrupts his reverie. In walks another gentleman who will become the next of the novel's first-person narrators. He too seeks the violin, but arrives at the auction too late to enter the bidding. This gentleman is a writer whose interest in the violin derives from having met Jeno Varga in Vienna, and having heard his saga during a long evening of heavy drinking and conversation. The writer's telling then gives way to Jeno's extended first-person account of his life up until the Second World War, with a brief coda describing Sophie's end in a sanatorium upon her release from a concentration camp. The long section dedicated to Jeno's stay at Castle Blau reads like a Gothic novel, full of eccentric aristocrats, skeletons in closets, and tedious discussions of pop metaphysics. For a brief moment within the Castle Blau section, a fourth voice enters the gallery of first-person narrators – that of Kuno (the film's Davide), recounting the story of his uncle Gustav, whose mysterious disappearance long ago was written off as a suicide. Kuno, instead, believes that the body retrieved from the river, buried, and then robbed from the grave weeks later was not Gustav's at all. According to Kuno, his uncle is alive and well in South America.

Kuno's brief, first-person account of his uncle's mystery is buried in the depths of Jeno's chronicle, which is in turn embedded in the writer's account, which is in its turn enclosed within the outermost frame of the buyer's first-person narration. It is here that the technical meaning of *canone inverso* reveals its logic. The canon, which is a polyphonic musical form, involves the passing of a melody from voice to voice – a process that takes place through the dizzying proliferation of narrative frames in the novel. To add to the appropriateness of the musical metaphor, it is the violin that triggers each level of the telling, driving the urgent impulse to fabulation. The structural implications of the title are further enhanced by the qualifier *inverso*. As I understand it from both Maurensig's and Tognazzi's applications of the term, the title would correspond to the category of the 'mirror canon,' in which the second voice imitates the first in the following ways: upside-down (canon by inversion), backwards (retrograde canon), or both upside-down and backwards (canon by retrograde inversion).[4] For Maurensig, it is the reversibility of the score, its chiastic movement, that makes the *canone inverso* a metaphor for narrative structure. Such reversibility prompts Jeno to compare the progress of his friendship with Kuno to this musical form. 'Ciò che aveva trovato il suo supremo compimento nella folgorazione iniziale, aveva già cominciato da tempo la sua corsa retrograda, il suo conto alla rovescio, o se vogliamo usare un termine musicale: il suo canone inverso' (125) ([That] which had risen to its supreme fulfillment in an original burst of mutual genius, had already, and for some time, begun its descent, its countdown, or, to use a musical term, its *canone inverso* [146]). But it is in the very layering of the narrations that the chiasmus of the *canone inverso* finds its most striking application. At the end of the novel we discover that the outermost narrative voice is that of the mysterious Gustav, returned to the Old World to reclaim his family's musical heirloom. Thus, the object of the innermost narration – the one most deeply buried beneath layers of embedded accounts – becomes the voice of the outermost level. And the source of the innermost mystery – Gustav's disappearance – overlaps with the end of the novel, his re-emergence, and his narrating of the text that we have just read.

The double framing of Maurensig's *Canone inverso* undergoes radical changes in Tognazzi's version – changes that reflect the increased emphasis that the filmmaker accords to Holocaust history and the consequent need to bear witness. Tognazzi replaces Maurensig's second-level narrator, the writer, with a woman named Costanza, fruit of Jeno's love for Sophie that is consummated in the film, but remains abstract and unrequited in the text. Named after one of Davide's ances-

---

4 *The New Harvard Dictionary of Music*, ed. Don Michael Randel (Cambridge, MA: Belknap Press of Harvard University Press, 1986), 128.

tors, whose portrait we see at Castle Blau, Costanza is true to her ety-
mology. She personifies the principle of continuity and the need for
transmission in her quest for familial truth. Tognazzi's Costanza also
serves to give his film a double historical focus. The decision to place
the story in Czechoslovakia rather than in Maurensig's Hungary and
to locate Costanza's first meeting with Jeno/Davide in 1968 sets up a
historical 'canon' of considerable import. The sound of Soviet troops
entering the city to stamp out the democratic stirrings of the Prague
Spring is all too reminiscent, says Jeno/Davide, of the Nazi incursions
of the Second World War. 'Do you hear them?' he asks Costanza.
'They're coming back.'

But the most momentous of Tognazzi's frame-story alterations is
that of substituting Gustav Blau with his brother, making the outermost narrator the old baron himself, father of his two biological sons
Jeno and Davide, as he is father of the narrative he is about to tell. To
further tighten the film's paternal theme, Tognazzi makes Baron Blau
the author of the musical score – a canon – that Jeno and Davide must
sight-read to determine who will become valedictorian of the Collegium Musicum and have the honour of performing in concert with
Sophie Levi. But because the baron had taught his mistress this melody
in her hometown, and she in turn had sung the tune to her baby as a
lullaby, Jeno's thorough knowledge of it since infancy makes his performance of the canon as effortless as it is natural to him. This gives
Jeno, of course, an insuperable advantage over Davide, whose sight-
reading is impeded both by ignorance and by the overwhelming emotional upheaval of his discovery that he has a bastard brother. It is as if
the canon were part of Jeno's genetic make-up, an ancestral memory
that allows him to perform his father's song with a spontaneity and
ease inavailable to the refined Davide, thereby proving himself to be
the baron's 'true' son and heir. In composing this musical score, the
baron has, in effect, scripted the way in which the brothers' sibling
rivalry will play itself out. In fact, the respective father–son relationships are a veritable *canone inverso*, wherein Davide's place as the privileged offspring is usurped by Jeno, who demonstrates a superior
claim to that role.

Another implication of Tognazzi's changes to the identity of Maurensig's multiple narrators is that the film's speakers – the baron, Costanza, and Jeno/Davide – are three generations of the same family,
which brings the theme of genealogy and transmission emphatically to
the forefront of our awareness. This is where the notion of historical

testimony gains special urgency, for Costanza is a child survivor of the Holocaust, giving her narration the status of witness. Furthermore, the filmmaker Ricky Tognazzi plays the part of Baron Blau in the flash-backs, calling attention to the identity of the film as the outermost telling of Maurensig's novel, the newest voice in the *canone*.

We have yet to consider the most obvious interpretation of the *Canone inverso* title, announced early in the film during an exchange between Costanza and Jeno/Davide. 'It makes you turn back,' the man says of this retrograde structure, explicitly linking the musical term to memory. This theme of return through memory conditions all of Tognazzi's generic and formal choices in filming *Canone inverso*. Just as the violin, in material form, is a throwback to an earlier time, so too is the narrative genre a vestige of the past. With its sweeping romanticism, its ambitious interweaving of sexual and artistic passions, its pan-European reach, its blend of personal and public drama, *Canone inverso* recalls the great traditions of the nineteenth-century novel. Tognazzi has been criticized for reverting to antiquated narrative forms and for exploiting their audience appeal in *Canone inverso*.[5] But this, I would argue, is just the point – his generic choice is of a piece with the very purpose of the story. Violin-like, the grand narrative tradition proclaims its source in an earlier era, while asserting its continuing vitality and its power to communicate in new cultural contexts – to reach audiences across the barriers of time and space. One could imagine an adaptation of Maurensig's novel that would be modernist, or even postmodern, in style, using techniques of distancing and estrangement that would require us to step back and judge narrative traditions, in the former case, or, using parody and pastiche, to put the past and present into playful critical dialogue, in the latter. Instead, Tognazzi shuns irony, choosing the path of unabashed sentimentality to immerse himself, and the audience, in the passions of his characters and the turmoil of their historical context. In so doing, he is proclaiming the continued viability of traditional narrative forms, in particular, that of melodrama, whose appropriateness to a story about musicians goes without saying.

Etymologically understood as a theatre piece set to music, *Canone inverso* becomes a melodrama in a double sense, for music dominates

---

5 See, for example, the review by Gian Luigi Rondi, originally published in *Il tempo*, 14 February 2000, and reprinted in the *Rassegna stampa cinematografica* (Bergamo: S.A.S., 2000), of *Canone inverso*.

both the background and the foreground of the spectacle. Throughout the film, Tognazzi uses Ennio Morricone's magisterial score to blur the distinctions between form and content, between diegetic and non-diegetic components. In several blatant instances, music performed by the characters in solo passages swells to become the full-blown orchestral background of the next scene. This happens when Jeno's mother hums the tune of the father's *canone inverso*, which then, in a highly elaborated version, accompanies the spinning of bicycle wheels as his mother commutes to work on the pig farm of Wolf, who will become her husband, and who will ultimately become Jeno's greatest benefactor in furthering his musical career. Debussy's 'Clair de lune,' which Sophie fingers on the piano in an early scene with Jeno, will become the rich orchestral background of all their meetings and will accompany the beautiful love scene in which the sexualized metaphor of the violin as the body of the beloved woman is literalized.

The reverse process also occurs – that is, non-diegetic music becomes diegetic when Jeno, waiting outside Sophie's house in the drenching rain, is about to be welcomed inside, and the music of Dvorak, which he will soon play for her to prove his musical virtuosity, and hence his worthiness for her love, is heard on the soundtrack. This blurring of boundaries between background and foreground, container and contained, enacts, in formal terms, the unifying power of music itself, and explains why Tognazzi's film refuses the distancing techniques of twentieth-century narrative theory. Again and again, Sophie and Jeno assign the epiphanic force of their art to those supreme moments when the performer and the music become one, merging in ecstatic union that momentarily obliterates the pain and solitude of their material condition.

The Utopian properties of music emerge in three of the film's most powerful sequences. The early scene in the conservatory of the student gathering that turns into a jam session of riotous proportions comes to stand for the apotheosis of creative freedom within a repressive regime. A microcosm of the authoritarian state, with its prison-like architecture, its ironclad rules, its physical and didactic rigours, the Collegium inspires its inmates to rebel in the only way they can – through music. But by far the most effective proof of music's liberating power surfaces in Jeno's nascent friendship with Davide. It is through music that the two boys overcome the rigidly patrolled separatism of Collegium life, where confinement to individual cells makes interaction between schoolmates impossible. Rebelling against this stricture,

Jeno breaks the conservatory rules by playing a few strains on his violin after hours, attracting the attention of the school's disciplinarian, who in turn enlists the aid of the curmudgeonly Professor Weigal to track down the culprit. But Jeno is not alone in his musical defiance – the few strains he plays are echoed by someone else. The second player, who answers Jeno *in canone*, turns out to be Davide. As the two boys illicitly leave their rooms, and find each other through their music, they are chased by Weigal and his henchman. In a delightful series of cuts and cross-cuts between the violin-playing boys and their adult hunters, the camera follows all four along multiple storeys of the corridors that encircle the dormitory atrium. A brilliant and witty variation of the archetypal cinematic chase scene, this one is accompanied by the diegetic music of the two violins that perform, appropriately, the Capriccio movement of Paganini's 'La caccia' (The Chase). In this comedic scene, blending action and diegetic music with carefully synchronized camerawork, Tognazzi establishes the cinematic language that will culminate, so tragically, in the episode of Jeno's solo concert with Sophie.

This climactic sequence, in which all the elements of the micro-story are resolved, is interrupted by the macro-story in a way that justifies Tognazzi's recourse to the nineteenth-century narrative tradition. In melodramatic terms, the final concert should provide the comprehensive and satisfying ending to all the longings and tensions of the preceding plot. Jeno's dream, ever since he had heard Sophie's concert on the radio and had played the violin along with the broadcast, was to perform with her on stage. The rift with Davide is resolved when the latter shows up in the balcony of the theatre, smiling and holding Jeno's violin case as a sign of his wish to accept the blood relationship that the instrument represents. Wolf is in the audience, asserting his earned right to paternal pride in Jeno's accomplishments. Maestro Ishbaum, expelled from directorship of the Collegium, is also there to bask in the glory of his student's success.

To further the expectation that this scene will bring formal closure to the film, the climactic concert promises to complete the earlier radio performance that had been interrupted by Nazi hecklers. This final concert scene, then, will be the fulfilment of the previous one, with Jeno on stage instead of accompanying Sophie's faulty radio transmission, and with the hope of finishing the concert left incomplete in Vienna. Tognazzi's invitation to link the two concerts is clinched by the fact that the same diegetic music is featured in both – an original orchestral score by Morricone, entitled 'Concerto romantico interrotto per violino, pianoforte (in canone) e orchestra' (Interrupted Romantic Concerto for Violin, Piano [*in canone*] and Orchestra), heard only one other time in the film – in the auditions to determine which conservatory student would have the honour of performing with Sophie.

Tragically, the relationship between the two concerts is not that of a *canone inverso*. The second concert does not reverse the first – it does not move from the middle of the incomplete piece to the end. Instead, the relationship between the two concerts is one of a simple *canone*, or repetition without change. Like the radio concert, this too is interrupted by the forces of Nazi anti-Semitism. The satisfying grand finale that this concert scene promised in order to resolve all the film's interpersonal relations, according to the grand nineteenth-century literary formula for closure, is not forthcoming. Macro-history takes over the narrative apparatus and blocks the conventional movement of the plot to resolution.

It is in the cinematic language of this scene that Toganzzi's ideology of art most powerfully emerges. Beginning with a shot of the drums, whose rolls set a rhythm of excitement and urgency for the ensuing scene, the camera rises to show a full orchestra, then cuts to a series of disconnected shots – of Sophie's hands racing across the keys; of the balcony where Jeno's classmates gather; of the orchestra conductor; and back to Sophie's hands – before passing finally to Jeno and cutting to Maestro Ishbaum in the audience. Edited to the intense rhythms of Morricone's score, the camerawork shows that almost all the elements of the climactic finale are in place, for Davide will soon appear to complete the gallery of Jeno's listeners. But as Tognazzi cross-cuts between the concert and Davide's frantic car ride towards the theatre, we see that the melodramatic elements of the plot are soon to be obstructed by those of Holocaust history. Davide's car is overtaken by Nazi jeeps and when he arrives at the concert hall, the building is surrounded by German officers shouting orders and herding people to the sound of barking dogs. Morricone's orchestral score continues to dominate the soundtrack, but the Nazi cacophony is disturbingly evident. Back in the theatre, Jeno's triumphant performance proceeds, visualized in cuts between his face in rapt concentration, Sophie's hands on the keys, her face in adoring and tearful appreciation, and the conductor's energetic movements to coordinate it all. Davide finally appears in the balcony to Jeno's grateful acknowledgment. Now the Nazis enter, prompting a series of quick shots of audience members' horrified reactions to the assault. In rapid succession, we see Sophie seized by two officers, Jeno dragged off stage, Davide's balcony invaded by soldiers. The final shot in this wrenching montage shows an officer on stage, in place of the orchestra conductor, filmed from the perspective of the audience members as he 'conducts' them according to the drumbeat of Nazi commands.

If the *canone* is a contrapuntal form, then the counterpoint established in this scene is one between the forces of culture and those of authoritarian repression. This scene is edited contrapuntally – acoustically, through the opposition between Morricone's music and Nazi military cacophany, visually through the cross-cutting between events inside and outside the theatre, between the orderly montage of the concert hall and the disorder of the military siege. In this counterpoint, Tognazzi is enacting the slogan uttered by the boys in their playful romp down the corridors of the Collegium Musicum when they exalted, 'Music is our knife, it is the sword with which we'll conquer the world.' In this paradoxical equation of art with military might, the boys are actually asserting the superior power of the former over the latter. What we learn from the final concert scene is that the real antidote to Nazi oppression is not the operations of an opposing army, but those of culture, of the profoundly civilizing, humanizing, and unifying force of the arts.

'It makes you turn back,' Jeno/Davide had said to Costanza when questioned about the *canone inverso* form. By 'going back' to Maurensig's novel in a way that makes explicit its Holocaust context, Tognazzi's *canone* becomes a figure for the transmission of historical testimony. It is this *canone*, sounded somewhat weakly throughout the Italian postwar period, to which Tognazzi has now added his own distinctive voice.

4 A Childhood Paradise Lost: Andrea and Antonio Frazzi's *Il cielo cade* (The Sky Is Falling)

Dedicated to the memory of Electra Bynoe (1980-2002) and Andrea Frazzi (1944–2006)

Direction: Andrea and Antonio Frazzi. Screenplay: Suso Cecchi D'Amico. Photography: Franco Di Giacomo and Stefano Coletta. Music: Luis Bacalov. Sets: Mario Garbuglia. Costumes: Carlo Diappo. Cast: Isabella Rossellini (Katchen Einstein), Jeroen Krabbé (Wilhelm Einstein), Veronica Niccolai (Penny), Lara Campolli (Baby), Barbara Enrichi (Rosa), Gianna Giachetti (Elsa), Paul Brooke (Mr Pitt). Year: 2000. Availability: DVD, *Il cielo cade* (The Sky Is Falling) in Italian language original with English subtitles, locatable through Amazon.com and Facets.org.

Synopsis

Il cielo cade is based on the eponymous novel (1961) by Lorenza Mazzetti that tells, in fictionalized form, the story of the author's own traumatic experience during the Nazi occupation of Tuscany.[1] At the start of the film, the protagonist Penny and her younger sister Baby, recently orphaned, are handed over to the care of their maternal aunt Katchen, and her Jewish husband, Wilhelm Einstein (cousin of Albert), who live in an elegant villa outside Florence. The estate is an outpost of European high culture, featuring musical soirées, sophisticated dinner table conversations, and the other pleasures of the leisure class that the Einsteins share with their aristocrati-

---

1 Reprinted in Lorenza Mazzetti, *Il cielo cade* (Palermo: Sellerio, 2000).

cally inclined guests, the most flamboyant of whom is a pianist and special devotee of Chopin, Mr Pitt. Snubbed by their adoptive sister Annie, and too young to fraternize with their older step-sibling, Marie, Penny, and Baby are entrusted to the care and companionship of the villa servants – the elderly Elsa and the nubile Rosa – along with the children of the local farming community. When a German platoon requisitions the villa, the commanding officer treats Wilhelm and his household with the respect that befits the family's elevated social status. Meanwhile, the Resistance movement has taken firm root in Tuscany, and Rosa, who is pregnant with the child of Nello, a partisan activist, discovers to her horror that her lover has been arrested by Fascist officials. Wilhelm, convinced of his immunity to Nazi persecution and reassured by the civilized behaviour of the troops occupying the villa, refuses to go into hiding, thus exposing himself and his family to the direst of consequences. During the German troop withdrawal, the endangered man finally agrees to take flight, leaving Katchen, Annie, Marie, Penny, and Baby to face the wrath of a new and ferocious wave of retreating Nazis. Because they are Catholic, Penny and Baby are spared the death meted out to their aunt and cousins, but they are firsthand witnesses of the atrocity. When Wilhelm returns, he commits suicide upon discovering the fate of his wife and daughters. The liberation of the area by British forces coincides with the rustic and hurried funeral rites of the Einstein family.

'Let's recount History again,' said Andrea and Antonio Frazzi of their film *Il cielo cade*, 'but this time through the stupefied eyes of an eight-year-old child. The gaze of a child is always something that puts History up against a wall – a child is a privileged observer and narrator because ingenuous, direct ... and on the road to transformation.'[2] By recalling the Second World War past, and especially the effects of the Shoah, through the sensibility of a young girl, the Frazzi brothers join ranks with a host of other authors, both literary and cinematic, who choose not only to narrate the events from a *tabula rasa* perspective, but also to make a commentary on the generation of those born in the 1930s who, though not responsible for Fascism, were the immediate stewards

2 Quoted in Raffaella Antonutti and Paolo Finn, '*Quando il cielo cade,*' *Cinemasessanta* 41 (September–October 2000), 24–5.

of its legacy. The testimony of these adults, in their compulsion to revisit their childhood memories of historical trauma, constitutes what I call 'generational witness.' Such narratives bear the special representational burden of not only dredging up and working through the horrors of the wartime past, but also of accounting for a subsequent postwar history that failed to enact the social rebirth heralded by the Resistance movement in the throes of the liberation.

As in the eponymous novel by Lorenza Mazzetti on which the film is based, *Il cielo cade* makes Penny the focalizer of the story, filtering its occurrences through her enchanted childhood eyes. From the very start of the film, the Frazzi brothers privilege the child's point-of-view in a camera movement that focuses on the entrance to the villa from a high-angle perspective, and then lowers itself to the ground, just as the young boys Zefferino and Pierino climb down from a tree, revealing that the camera had indeed appropriated their vantage point. From the very outset, then, we are alerted to one of the film's most distinctive stylistic traits – the use of low-angle shots to simulate the child's-eye view of experience. Though *Il cielo cade* is not consistently shot this way, lest it descend into mannerism by calling constant attention to the film's own artifice, the striking moments of low-angle perception (certain kitchen scenes, the arrival and departure of German convoys, the final Nazi rampage through the villa in search of Wilhelm, for example) serve firmly to ensconce us in the perceiving consciousness of the child.

Within this focalizing regime, the Frazzi brothers create a spellbinding world of childhood wonder. Released from the formality and elitism of the villa routine, Penny and Baby are allowed to play with the children of the peasants who work the land. Together they form a classless Utopia, linguistically characterized by a highly inflected Tuscan vernacular, and accompanied musically by melodies of whimsical lightness and grace. The dispensation to frequent the peasant children allows Penny and Baby to give vent to their creative fantasy, rather than to submit to the stiff parlor games and culturally improving music lessons of the villa. Most importantly, it allows them frequent forays into the lush natural surroundings of the villa, and gives the Frazzis' camera the pretext to luxuriate in the trademark landscapes of Tuscany. In literary terms, of course, the children have discovered an Edenic world in which the primal unity between the human, the natural, and the divine has remained miraculously intact. Mazzetti's novel makes the identity of this pre-Fallen state explicit in the Adam-and-Eve games that the children include in their repertory of play. In creating this Edenic space within their film, the Frazzis make use of the Florentine countryside to the greatest possible advantage, exploiting the privileged place that Tuscany holds in the Italian (as well as the Anglo-American) collective imaginary.

What complicates Mazzetti's appropriation of the Edenic myth is the fact that it is not limited to the world of childhood innocence. Wilhelm, in his own way, is just as naive, just as much of a fantast, as are the young inhabitants of the garden. The earthly paradise of the children's brigade finds its adult equivalent in the enchanted castle of high cultural refinements and old world civility over which Wilhelm presides. Though the autocratic ruler of his little realm, Wilhelm is nonetheless an enlightened monarch, the philosopher king, beloved by his family and friends, revered by his dependents. Wilhelm's blind faith in humanistic values – those of aesthetic order, personal dignity, and human justice – leads him to assume a position of intransigence to and disbelief in the onslaughts of history. Convinced that his values put him above and beyond the petty skirmishes of the historical arena, particularly those of his anti-Semitic German countrymen who could not possibly unleash their violence against so upright and decent a family, Wilhelm remains inert in the face of the Holocaust threat. When the parish priest urges him to flee with his family, Wilhelm replies, 'I have done nothing wrong,' and to Penny's tearful urgings that he take protective action, he responds, 'I won't escape because of respect for myself and human dignity.' It is this naive belief in the workings of justice, this withdrawal into the abstract fortress of his ideals, that puts Wilhelm and his family at such mortal risk. Unwilling to leave the false paradise of his humanist faith, Wilhelm invites the most horrific of historical incursions. This aristocratic aloofness from history, this reluctance to take corrective action in the face of the encroaching threat recalls the stance of the Finzi-Contini family, which also chose to remain within the garden of historical denial.[3] Though the Ferrarese family's paralysis seemed to derive more from fatalistic surrender than from blind belief in social justice, both the Finzi-Continis' and the Einsteins' passivity bespeak an elitist reluctance to enter the messiness of the concrete historical arena.

---

3 For a detailed analysis of this syndrome, see my chapter on *Il giardino dei Finzi-Contini* in *Filmmaking by the Book*, 91–110.

Perhaps the most striking visual manifestation of Wilhelm's cultural ideals is the magnificent villa, whose Renaissance architecture is a triumph of balance, restraint, symmetry, and reason. Filmed frontally in a number of scenes, the classical facade says everything we need to know about the order and hierarchy of life within its walls. The interior scenes are always shot making full use of the perspectives offered by the infinite regress of rooms, the classically proportioned corridors, and the framing of doorways and windows. Of particular interest is the episode in which the bishop is received by Wilhelm on the occasion of the First Communion rites over which the prelate presides. In this scene, the Frazzis set up a visual counterpoint between the classical balance of villa architecture and the off-kilter perspective of Penny and Baby, under the spell of the irrational belief that it is they who must save their uncle from perdition. Filmed from the interior of the entrance hall looking out, the scene begins with the theatrical opening of the front door by two servants, one of whom warns the other not to step on the red carpet that they are rolling out for the bishop's arrival. Taking advantage of the Renaissance balance of this space, the camera remains centred on an elegant vista, composed according to the rules of one-point perspective, leading towards the doorway that frames the exterior as if it were indeed a painting. Entering from this doorway are two rows of people – darkly dressed peasants and girls clad in bridal white for their First Communion – who file into the hall, standing on either side of the carpet to keep it pristine for the bishop's tread. Next, we see the villa inhabitants, Wilhelm, his family, and guests, who march in from the opposite direction, filmed from a lateral angle, as they take their place in the receiving lines. Finally, the car arrives, emerging from the vanishing point at the centre for the frame. But rather than stop in front of the door, the automobile comically disappears to the right, causing the two lines of observers in the hall to lean precariously over the carpet to get a view of the outdoors, just as we too strain to see the whereabouts of the bishop's conveyance. Now the vehicle backs up and returns to our view, disgorging the prelate and his retinue, who are then ushered into the villa, where Wilhelm makes his ceremonial introductions.

The geometric rigour of the camera-work, reflecting that of the villa's classical architecture, has not remained unchallenged throughout the scene. It has been disrupted by several shots that reflect the child protagonists' skewed perspective on events, and that anticipate the way in which Baby will upset the orderliness of the bishop's visit. Cutting away to Penny and Baby's conversation with one of the First Communicants, the scene adds fuel to the young girls' rescue fantasy. 'Your uncle has to kiss the ring if he wants to be saved. It's the ring that works miracles,' the catechistically wise young girl informs them. With this agenda in mind, Penny and Baby witness the churchman's arrival in the anxious hope that their uncle will acknowledge the cleric's spiritual authority over him. Wilhelm's failure to do so leads Baby to compensate by kissing the bishop's ring with such vehemence and desperation that the solemnity of the scene is totally undone. The camera's appropriation of this agitated, off-centre perspective ultimately comes to dominate the classically balanced viewpoint of the scene's opening shots, just as the girls' anxiety about their uncle's welfare has succeeded in disturbing the calm of villa life as a whole.

The drama of the children who believe that they are responsible for their uncle's safety, and who feel helpless to avert the tragedy that looms before them, brings into high relief a tendency within the neorealist tradition that the Frazzi brothers develop to create a film language of special appropriateness to Holocaust representation. Gilles Deleuze argued that the originality of neorealism resided in its abandonment of the conventional 'movement image,' according to which sensory-motor stimuli lead to action on screen, giving viewers a vicarious sense of agency. Neorealism replaced this regime with the 'time image,' which puts the movement image in crisis by preventing characters from translating sensory-motor stimuli into effectual action, reducing them to the status of passive bystanders who witness events without being able to affect their course. In Deleuze's words:

> What defines neorealism is this build-up of purely optical situations (and sound ones) which are fundamentally distinct from the sensory-motor situations of the action image in the old realism ... The character has become a kind of viewer. He shifts, runs and becomes animated in vain, the situation he is in outstrips his motor capacities on all sides, and makes him see and hear what is no longer subject to the rules of a response or an action. He records rather than reacts. He is prey to a vision, pursued by it or pursuing it, rather than engaged in an action.[4]

Children, with their inherent sense of motor inadequacy, become perfect vehicles for the neorealist impression of impotence before real-

---

4 Gilles Deleuze, *The Time Image*, trans. Hugh Tomlinson and Robert Galeta (Minneapolis: University of Minnesota Press, 1997), 2–3. Hereafter, page references to Deleuze will be included, parenthetically, in the body of the text.

world demands. 'The role of the child in neorealism has been pointed out, notably in De Sica,' Deleuze continues. 'This is because, in the adult world, the child is affected by a certain motor helplessness, but one which makes him all the more capable of seeing and hearing' (3).

Penny's delusions of agency – her plan to write to Mussolini to complain of Nello's arrest, her intent to hold a tea party for the German general and beg him to spare Wilhelm – only heighten the pathos of the child's agonizing helplessness within this particularly dire historical context. In Deleuze's terms, Penny becomes a pure instrument of perception, a vehicle for the registering of experience 'in a visual and sound nakedness, crudeness, and brutality which make it unbearable, giving it the pace of a dream or nightmare' (3). Significantly, the episode that marks the girl's most extravagant attempt to intervene on her uncle's behalf – the tea party for the German general – is immediately followed by a brief shot of Penny waking up from a nightmare. In this succession of scenes, the second serves to call into question the first in a way that reveals how the child's sense of helplessness, in its most acute form, is experienced as the suspension of reality itself.

If neorealism signals the crisis of the movement image and its replacement with the optical-sound image, by relegating characters to the level of childlike impotence, then *Il cielo cade* indicates the special pertinence of this neorealist tendency to the problem of Holocaust representation. Through Penny, the neorealist denial of effectual action in response to sensory-motor situations is taken to its absolute extreme: the child becomes a set of perceiving eyes, ears, and affections (and nothing more) whose desire to intervene must be dissipated in fantasy, dream, or prayer. We, watching her dilemma through the medium of film, thus undergo a second order of disempowerment, becoming 'meta-bystanders' whose sense of impotence and frustration before the events of Holocaust history are magnified and refracted through the gaze of the child observer within the story.

Our identification with the child as helpless bystander coalesces in the scene in which Penny spies on the priest's conversation with Wilhelm concerning the Nazi deportation of Italian Jews. The fact that the clergyman has asked for an audience with Wilhelm is itself remarkable, given the chilly relations between the two men, and Penny at first had been asked to convey the news to her uncle, before the priest thought better of it and decided to confront the imperiled man himself. Primed for the importance of this encounter, we, through Penny, spy on the conversation, shot with two distinct planes in focus – that of the room in which the men converse, framed by a doorway, half ajar, surrounded by black on the right and left foreground, against which we see the girl's head in medium close-up as she watches and listens to the proceedings. The inner room thus becomes a screen-within-the-screen, configured as a rectangle twice as high as it is wide, flanked by the eavesdropping child, whose very act of surveillance becomes as much an object of representation as the embedded scene that she is observing. The priest's report is the only direct reference to the Shoah that the film will provide, and no sooner is it communicated than Wilhelm insists on his invulnerability to the Nazi threat. 'I've heard that all the Jews are being taken away,' the priest announces. 'They put them in sealed wagons and take them to Germany. It happened in Rome and now it's happening in Florence.' Wilhelm's refusal to acknowledge the pertinence of this news to his own case rests on his humanist faith in justice and right action in the world. In Wilhelm's mind, what happens in 'cities' – in Florence and Rome – belongs to the realm of history, contingency, time, while he lives in splendid immunity in the Eden of his provincial estate. It is significant that after his dialogue with the priest, Wilhelm remains in the hermetic enclosure of his study, while the clergyman exits into the corridor, which is teeming with German soldiers who have requisitioned the villa. In the hall, he finds Penny, whom he exhorts to pray for Wilhelm. 'He's in real danger,' the priest reports, 'and not just his soul.' The camera shoots this exchange in deep focus so that the spectacle of German soldiers at the end of the corridor reinforces the priest's dire admonition. As the scene ends, Penny turns towards the door of her uncle's study, and in so doing, looks into the camera, her gaze alighting on us as the second-order witnesses to her uncle's impending doom.

With the priest's injunction, the child's agony now becomes acute, for she has been made to feel accountable for her uncle's rescue, and the sense of impotence that normally accompanies the childhood condition is magnified a thousand-fold before the enormity of the task. Penny's anguish, which reaches apocalyptic proportions at this point, is the dead-serious realization of the seemingly humorous fantasy that she had woven in an earlier scene of the film. 'I dreamt I was in heaven with mother,' Penny had narrated in voice-over as she wrote in her school notebook. 'I saw the Virgin Mary, tried to touch her and tripped instead and grabbed onto her veil. I looked up and saw that the Madonna was bald like Mussolini. Everything began to tremble. Mama said to hold my hands up to keep the sky from falling.' Little did Penny know that this hilarious dream, improvised to satisfy an in-class assignment, would take on the status of prophecy.

The agony of the childhood perspective reaches its climax in the scene of the 'Final Solution' for Katchen and her daughters. Penny and Baby, huddled against the protective folds of Elsa's skirts and guarded by the vicious Nazi commander, witness the massacre of their aunt and cousins in the next room indirectly, through glimpses in a shattered mirror. The editing of the scene is lightning fast, involving intercuts between close-ups of Penny's sobbing face, and shots of what she sees reflected in the mirrored room next door. On the sound track, we hear the Nazi command to 'get it over with,' followed by the victims' screams, the rat-tat-tat of automatic weapon fire, and Penny's cries of horror. Like the child narrator, we experience the carnage indirectly, in three separate mirror shots: first we behold the glass cracked by a bullet hole; then we witness Katchen and her daughters on the ground; and finally we catch a glimpse of the woman in her death throes, reaching towards someone else (perhaps Penny) as a gun is pointed at her head. We hear, but do not see, the firing of this fatal bullet, for the camera has shifted once again to a reaction shot of Penny. The choice to film this carnage indirectly serves to ensconce us in the child's perspective, to insist that this trauma be experienced in a refracted, mediated form that calls attention to the very process of witnessing. In fact, the spatial relationship between Penny and the victims in the next room is ambiguous – we don't know how close she is to them, and we are unsure if Katchen's final reaching out to Penny is an optical illusion produced by the mirror or not. Our disorientation as viewers, then, only intensifies the impression of horrific unreality to which the childhood perspective can lead, when taken to such extremes of helplessness and frustration. In other words, with the slain Katchen, Annie, and Marie reflected in the shattered glass, the sky has indeed fallen, and the world has turned nightmarishly upside down. In the funereal postscript to the massacre, Wilhelm's suicide takes place entirely off-screen, heralded only by the sound of a single gunshot from the 'salon of death.' Such reticence is precisely in keeping with Wilhelm's own values of dignity and self-respect, and the Frazzis choose to preserve his privacy in committing this final, desperate act of contrition.

Those critics who fault *Il cielo cade* for its restraint have failed to understand the filmmakers' strategy of indirection.[5] In this scene, the shattered mirror through which we experience the slaughter in frag-

---

5 'Mai uno spunto originale o un rischio' (never an original departure or risk) comments Fabrizio Liberti in his review of the film for *Cineforum* 40 (August–September 2000), 50.

mentary and oblique form is the child's traumatized perception of the event. It is through the mechanism of refraction that Penny's consciousness becomes the Frazzis' privileged object of representation, making the perceptual screen itself the film's referent, or to vary McLuhan's classic formula, the focalization is the message.

The foregrounding of the child's gaze of helplessness on which Deleuze bases his theory of neorealism is not the only way in which the Frazzis' film aligns itself with the great tradition of postwar Italian cinema. Far more obvious is the subject matter itself – that of war, occupation, and liberation – which Rossellini recounted in the foundational films of the movement. (Nor is it possible to overlook the casting of Isabella Rossellini as a gesture of homage to her father's achievement.) But perhaps most important for our purposes is the liberation scene on which the film ends, for this was the event that marked the zero-degree moment of postwar Italian history, the blank slate on which a new Italian identity would be founded according to the neorealist ideals of social justice and political rebirth.

No film offered a more celebratory or foundational representation of this scene than *Paisà*, whose Roman episode featured documentary footage of the triumphal entry of Allied soldiers into the newly liberated city. The cheering crowds, rumbling tanks, and exhausted but euphoric soldiers who emerge from their vehicles to accept the adulation of the populace marked this as a time of collective redemption and as a prelude to Italy's fresh start. Francesco Rosi echoes this celebratory representation in *Tre fratelli* (Three Brothers, 1981) when Rocco, the middle son, gazes upon his dead mother and flashes back to a memory of her embracing the Allied soldier who liberated their town. By associating this memory with the dead mother and the demise of the rural world that she embodied, Rosi suggests that the vitalizing promise of the postwar rebirth has met with terrible disappointment. The Tavianis' *La notte di San Lorenzo* (Night of the Shooting Stars, 1982) subjects the liberation scene to withering critique by staging three illusory versions of the event: one the auditory hoax perpetrated by the broadcast of a recording of 'The Battle Hymn of the Republic'; one the delirium of a dying girl, shot because she mistook Nazi soldiers for a contingent of Sicilian-American liberators; and one the encounter between two GI's and two little Italian girls, who come away with a Hershey Bar and a balloon made from an inflated condom, respectively.

The liberation scene of *Il cielo cade* is likewise fraught with irony, but it is devoid of the humour that leavened the Tavianis' demystifying portrayal of the event. As in *La notte di San Lorenzo*, where the true liberation was preceded by a series of illusory ones, the characters in *Il cielo cade* are fooled into rejoicing too soon. When Katchen and the girls hear the sounds of cheering in the air, they rush to the front door to find that what they take to be liberators are really retreating Nazi troops. Unlike the civilized German general of the earlier platoon that had occupied the villa, this is a band of vicious, cold-blooded executioners. The true liberation takes place too late to save the Einsteins, whose four rustic coffins are loaded onto an oxcart on the way to their burial place when the Allied troops finally arrive. The soldiers' apparition is anything but the triumphal moment that should accompany such a climactic event – the Italians are not at all sure who the troops are, and it is only Baby who greets them festively, prey as she is to an illusion that serves as a powerful critique of liberation mythology. In Baby's mind, the Scottish soldier, ridiculously attired in short pants and metal headgear, could be none other than Don Quixote wearing Mambrino's helmet. 'Everything he came across, he with great ease adapted to his extravagant notions of chivalry,' Cervantes recounts of his incorrigibly befuddled hero. The relevance of this comment to an Italy prone to romanticizing liberation history is not hard to see. In a reversal of Baby's tendency imaginatively to inflate and embellish experience, the Scottish soldier dismisses the tragedy of the Einsteins' plight with the reductive and patronizing remark 'It's just a farmer's funeral.'

The outsider's underestimation of the victims' social class stands for a much more cataclysmic failure of understanding – it is the indifference that macro-history shows to the micro-events of personal lives. The clash of perspectives could not be more violent at this point, because for us in the audience, as for the mourners on screen, the annihilation of the Einsteins signals a loss of immeasurable proportions. Penny and Baby have been doubly orphaned, and all of us have been expelled yet again from paradise. Both the adults' humanist Utopia and the children's enchanted garden have given way to the forces of Holocaust history.

At the meta-level of the film's relationship to its own expressive possibilities, *Il cielo cade* enacts the story's fall from a personal and cultural state of grace. The film medium's conventional invitation to pleasurable escape (implicit in the epithet 'factory of dreams'), means that the cinema is admirably equipped to represent the twin paradises of Penny's childhood enchantment and of Wilhelm's aristocratic realm. *Il cielo cade*, however, cannot linger in these Edenic spaces, but must put them in jeopardy and, like Bassani and De Sica in *Il giardino dei Finzi-Contini*, must display the beauty and refinement of this world on the verge of extinction. It is the eccentric Mr Pitt who gives voice to the filmmakers' desire to memorialize Wilhelm and his paradise lost. Objecting to a radio broadcast of Chopin's last composition, 'dictated on his deathbed,' Mr Pitt asks, 'How can you play them [those notes] if you're not aware of that?' As the sentimental pianist proceeds to perform the piece with full awareness of Chopin's meaning, the other guests of the villa drift in to contemplate the relevance of this swan song to their own imperiled state. 'There is nostalgia, so much nostalgia for his past that will no longer return,' Mr Pitt explains as he plays the melody. 'No one can forget this music. You feel it here.' Lorenza Mazzetti's written memoir may be seen as a version of Mr Pitt's fully conscious performance of Chopin's final work, just as the Frazzis' adaptation in turn renders Mazzetti's elegy in filmic terms. It is through the superimposition of adult knowledge on childhood experience, put to the service of a postwar Italy that must remain mindful of its past, that generational witness strives to keep the sky from falling.

5 The Alter-Biography of the Other-in-Our-Midst: Ettore Scola's *Concorrenza sleale* (Unfair Competition)[1]

Direction: Ettore Scola. Subject: Furio Scarpelli. Screenplay: Ettore Scola, Silvia Scola, Furio Scarpelli, Giacomo Scarpelli. Costumes: Odette Nicoletti. Sets: Luciano Ricceri. Music: Armando Trovajoli. Editing: Raimondo Crociani. Photography: Franco Di Giacomo. Cast: Diego Abatantuono (Umberto Melchiorri), Walter Dragonetti (Pietruccio), Anita Zagaria (Margherita), Elio Germano (Paolo), Gérard Depardieu (Zio Angelo), Augusto Fornari (Zio Peppino), Sergio Castellitto (Leone Della Rocca), Simone Ascani (Lele), Antonella Attili (Giuditta), Gioia Spaziani (Susanna), Jean Claude Braily (Nonno Mattia), Claude Rich (Count Treuberg), Claudio Bigagli (Commissioner Solopaca), Sabrina Impacciatore (Matilde), Rolando Ravello (Ignazietto). Year: 2001. Availability: DVD, *Concorrenza sleale* (Unfair Competition) in Italian-language original with English subtitles, distributed under the title *Concurrence Déloyale* by Christal Films.

Synopsis

Set in the Via Ottaviano neighbourhood of Rome in 1938, *Concorrenza sleale* tells the story of two merchants, Umberto Melchiorri and Leone Della Rocca, whose businesses are adjacent to one another and who are engaged in a fierce rivalry to win over each other's clientele. The Melchiorri family, having relocated from Milan several decades earlier, runs an elegant men's shop (*sartoria*) for clothes made-to-order. The Della Roccas are newcomers,

1 This is a revised version of an essay that originally appeared in *Incontri con il cinema italiano*, ed. Antonio Vitti (Caltanisetta: Salvatore Sciascia, 2003), 79–94.

having moved next door two years prior to the time of the story, and their business (*merceria*) features ready-made clothing at bargain prices. The 'disloyal competition' of the title involves what Umberto considers to be Leone's unsavoury advertising practices, aimed at undercutting his rival's carriage trade. While these gentlemen engage in their petty skirmishes, their respective children forge powerful bonds: Susanna Della Rocca (a conservatory student and aspiring pianist) and Paolo Melchiorri (architecture student) are in love, and their younger siblings, the eight-year-old Lele and Pietruccio, are classmates and best friends. Things turn ugly when the commercial rivalry gives way to name-calling, and Umberto hurls an anti-Semitic insult at Leone. In an audience with the Fascist police commissioner Solopaca, however, Umberto refuses to lodge a complaint against his rival on the basis of ethicity, and later he stands up for his Jewish neighbour when the commissioner tries to minimize the gravity of a vandalous assault on Leone's shop window. The condition of Italian Jews begins to deteriorate with the promulgation of the Racial Laws of 17 November 1938, and when Leone is forced to give up the *merceria*, he offers to sell his stock to his erstwhile rival. At the film's conclusion, the Melchiorri family watches helplessly as the Della Roccas are carted off to the ghetto in a scene which looks ahead to a future of far more dire dislocations.

'Non sanno raccontare l'Italia' (they don't know how to tell the story of Italy), Ettore Scola said of the current generation of filmmakers during a round-table discussion of his work at the 38th Mostra Internazionale del Nuovo Cinema in Pesaro on 29 June 2002. Scola argued that because of their reliance on thinly veiled autobiography, today's Italian filmmakers are unable to create a cinema that uses personal fictions to stand for the larger, national story. In Scola's judgment, current filmmakers are so narcissistically engaged in holding up a mirror to the sophisticated, hip world of thirty-somethings as they struggle with problems in the workplace and in love that they are unable to bring an incisive critical intelligence to bear on their representation of the contemporary Italian scene. Prime examples of this self-congratulatory tendency can be found in the lucrative film corpus of Gabriele Muccino (*Ecco fatto*, 1998; *Come te nessuno mai*, 1999; *L'ultimo bacio*, 2000; *Ricorditi di me*, 2002) or in the highly polished and witty *Casomai* (2002) of Alessandro D'Alatri. For Scola, coming from an earlier generation of filmmakers who felt compelled to measure themselves against the great postwar neorealists, such bourgeois introversion is regrettable, if not irreversible. 'Raccontare l'Italia' means the invention of fictions that connect the plight of the individual to that of the larger social whole in an ideologically progressive way, so that imaginative identification with the former enables spectators to critically analyse, and perhaps even intervene in, the latter. We could call them micro-histories, or we could use the rhetorical label synecdoche, or, in Georg Lukács's terms, we could consider these the narratives of 'maintaining characters' whose concrete experiences express the movements and conflicts of the great historical processes that condition their lives.[2] Through the mechanisms of dramatic plotting, or even humorous *divertissement*, these *racconti* are able to lead us beyond the particularities of their characters' stories to the level of collective enlightenment and activist engagement in the workings of macro-history. 'Raccontare l'Italia' means, for instance, that the plight of Antonio and Bruno Ricci in *Ladri di biciclette* (Bicycle Thief, 1948) necessarily invites a generalized reflection on an Italy whose institutions have failed to address the predicament of those excluded from the ranks of social privilege. 'Raccontare l'Italia,' to give another example, means that the odyssey of Marcello in *La dolce vita* (1959) lays bare the moral and cultural bankruptcy of an Italy in the throes of 'Il Boom.'

For Ettore Scola, 'raccontare l'Italia' means telling not a displaced version of the author's own story, but telling the story of the other, or of *the others*, so that the very imaginative process by which autobiographism is renounced in favour of *alter*-biographism reflects the push towards social accountability. Among contemporary films, Scola singles out Pasquale Scimeca's *Placido Rizzotto* (2000) and Marco Tullio Giordana's *I cento passi* (The One Hundred Steps, 2000) to exemplify the kind of stories of *the other* – of individuals remote from the filmmakers' own authorial subjectivity – that can serve as models for the construction of the utopian Italy to which neorealism and the entire postwar realist cinema aspired.[3]

In *Concorrenza sleale*, a film that represents one of his own recent efforts to 'raccontare l'Italia,' Scola turns autobiography into historical

---

2 See Georg Lukács, *The Historical Novel*, trans. Hannah and Stanley Mitchell (London: Merlin, 1962), 43.

3 See the interview with Scola in Lino Miccichè, 'Il cinema non cambia il mondo ma può farci riflettere,' in *Trevico-Cinecittà: L'avventuroso viaggio di Ettore Scola*, ed. Vito Zagarrio (Venice: Marsilio, 2002), 20-1.

testimony, the story of the self into the alter-biography of the other-in-our-midst, by exploring the effects of the 1938 Racial Laws on the personal lives of two families located in the heart of Rome. It is no mere coincidence that *Concorrenza sleale* revisits the historical event that played such an important part in Scola's 1977 masterpiece *Una giornata particolare* (A Special Day) – Hitler's visit to Italy in May 1938 to consolidate the Rome–Berlin axis. By converging on the same event from the perspectives of the several groups disempowered and persecuted by Fascist ideology, these films form a diptych that examines and indicts Mussolini's domestic policy from the margins. Banished from the festivities of that 'special day' are the socially disenfranchised housewife Antonietta and the homosexual Gabriele, in *Una giornata particolare*, while the racist consequences of the Hitler–Mussolini alliance divest Leone Della Rocca of all the rights and privileges of citizenship to which Italian Jews had been entitled from the time of the Risorgimento, in *Concorrenza sleale*. Both films trace the moral awakening of unthinking patriots Antonietta Tiberi and Umberto Melchiorri as they come to identify with those on whose exclusion Fascist identity depends: their respective co-protagonists Gabriele and Leone. Appropriately, both stories unfold in small, highly circumscribed spaces – the apartment complex, perfect analogue to Foucault's panopticon in *Una giornata particolare*,[4] and one block of Via Ottaviano, reconstructed in Cinecittà to emphasize the self-enclosure of the social sphere in *Concorrenza sleale*. Finally, in both films the micro-stories serve to critique and reverse events that occur on the macro-level, calling into question the authority and credibility of history in its official guise. The domestic romance of Antonietta and Gabriele in *Una giornata particolare* violates the social and political underpinnings of the Hitler–Mussolini union on the streets of Rome, while in *Concorrenza sleale*, a bond develops between Umberto and Leone in opposition to the Racial Laws promulgated by the regime to honour the publicly touted 'friendship' between Il Duce and Der Führer.

This diptych of films represents Scola's struggle to come to terms with the significance of 6 May 1938 not only for the course of Italian national history but also for his own childhood involvement in the festivities surrounding Hitler's visit on 'that special day.' 'I too contributed in some way,' Scola confessed, 'to convince Hitler that Italy had

---

4 For this connection, I am grateful to Lawrence Tooley, my former student at the University of Texas. On the panopticon, see Michel Foucault, *Discipline and Punish: The Birth of the Prison*, trans. Alan Sheridan (New York: Random House, 1977), 195–228.

reached the highest level of military efficiency. When the Chancellor of
the Third Reich came to visit Rome, I was, in fact, a *figlio della lupa* [lit-
erally, wolf cub], the lowest rank of the Fascist military, required of
every Italian citizen from two to seven years of age. I too participated in
the great parade in honour of our guest, in Via dell'Impero.'[5]

This autobiographical impulse towards self-expiation, implicit in
Una giornata particolare, is made explicit and ironic in *Concorrenza sleale*
through the character of Pietruccio Melchiorri, the narrator and focalizer (and future director) of the film. It is through Pietruccio's voice-over
narration – the auditory transcription of his diary – that the exposition
of the story unfolds, and it is his commentary that provides the continuity, transitions, and motivations behind the narrative as a whole. Significantly, Pietruccio is a cartoonist, who illustrates his diary with a series
of wry vignettes, prophetic of the caricaturist's art that Scola will display to such good advantage in the pages of the humour magazine
Marc'Aurelio. Eight years old at the time of the story's events (Scola
would have been seven in 1938), Pietruccio is a witness to the persecution of the family of his best friend, Lele Della Rocca, who is Jewish. Just
as important as the voice-over commentary in establishing Pietruccio's
role as narrator and focalizer is the final image of *Concorrenza sleale* – the
spectacle of the boy who stands alone in the street after the eviction of
Lele and his family from the neighbourhood. As the cart transporting
the Della Roccas, and all their belongings prepares to leave, there follows a montage of gazes that pairs each member of the exiled family
with their counterparts in the family that is entitled to stay. With rigorous symmetry, the camera offers a series of matched close-ups, beginning with the exchange of glances between the respective older siblings,
then the exchange between the mothers, then between the fathers, and,
finally, between the two young boys. As the cart disappears through the
gate leading outside the confines of the neighbourhood walls, the Della
Roccas' expulsion from this haven of *italianità* into the segregated
recesses of the ghetto foreshadows the Final Solution for over one thousand of Rome's Jewish population. Now the camera returns to Pietruccio, and it remains rivetted on the figure of the child for an
uncomfortably long time as he stands in solitude, bereft of his bosom
buddy, in the deserted street that had been the scene of so much neighbourhood life, and of the many childhood games that had made of the

---

5 Quoted in Pier Marco Santi and Rossano Vittori, *I film di Ettore Scola* (Rome: Gremese,
  1987), 132.

Pietruccio–Lele friendship a true Utopia. In filming this final sequence, Scola made the strategic decision not to conclude with a freeze-frame of the young boy, but instead to let the camera remain running while the child actor stood awkwardly awaiting a nod and a smile from the director to signal that the scene was over and he could leave the set. Since Scola did not give such a signal, the boy simply stood still in puzzled expectation for the several minutes that the camera continued to roll, creating the sense of considerable disquiet on which the film necessarily ends.[6] Had Scola chosen to conclude with a neat freeze-frame of Pietruccio sombre and alone, such a technique would have conferred a sense of formal closure on the film, whose final stillness would have consigned the pathos of Lele's departure to a fixed and immutable past. Instead, by allowing the child actor to fidget and sigh, restlessly, through the completion of the credits, *Concorrenza sleale* spills over the boundaries of its official end, foregoing the slickness of a finished product, and insisting that the issues raised by the film are on-going and unresolved.

Scola's impromptu decision to fixate on the figure of the companionless child radically departs from the film's original ending, in which Umberto and his anti-Fascist brother Angelo were to recede against the auditory background of Mussolini's announcement that Italy has entered the war. By choosing to linger on the boy, *Concorrenza sleale* shifts its generational focus from that of the adult enablers of Fascist power to that of the children who inherited its moral and political consequences. The Italy personified by the solitary image of Pietruccio is therefore a desolate entity, left alone with this heritage to understand, to reject, to supersede, and, most importantly, to remember. In the solitude of Pietruccio, figure of the author, Scola is telling us that the task of his generation is to bear witness, by every appropriate means, to what Primo Levi would call 'il fatto centrale ... la macchia, del nostro secolo' (the central fact ... the stain, of our century).[7] In so doing, Scola follows in the footsteps of his great maestro, Vittorio De Sica, who took upon himself the moral obligation of representing the plight of Italian Jews as a continuation of the neorealist mandate. Speaking of his motivations for adapting Giorgio Bassani's *Giardino dei Finzi-Contini* to the screen, De Sica explained: 'After the disaster of Sunflower [a Carlo Ponti enterprise starring Sophia Loren and Marcello Mastroianni], I wanted to

---

6 Scola recounted this anecdote at the round table devoted to his cinema in Pesaro on 29 June 2002.

7 Primo Levi, *I sommersi e i salvati* (Turin: Einaudi, 1991), 10.

make a true De Sica film, produced just as I wanted it. I accepted this
subject because I intimately feel the Jewish problem. I myself feel
shame because we all are guilty of the death of millions of Jews ... I
wanted, out of conscience, to make this film and I am glad I made it.'[8]
For De Sica, representing the Italian Holocaust offered a path of return
to an earlier self, a way of atoning for the commercial lapses of his later
career and of making 'a true De Sica film ... out of conscience' in the
great postwar cinematic tradition of historical accountability and civic
engagement.

While De Sica adapts *Il giardino dei Finzi-Contini* according to the canons of romantic realism dictated by Bassani's novel, Scola chooses to
use the means best suited to his authorial temperament and experience:
that of the *commedia all'italiana*. As in the case of Benigni's *La vita è bella*,
the application of so incongruous a genre to Holocaust subject matter
has momentous formal and historiographic implications.[9] Genre and
subject matter are reciprocally transfigured by the encounter, which
brings the *commedia all'italiana* to a new phase of its development, and
which, in turn, brings Holocaust representation to new areas of reflection and insight.

Highly conscious of his own role in the evolution of the comedic
genre, Scola offers the following genealogy of his art:

Italian film comedy was the slightly degenerate offspring of neorealism, a
sort of mildly reactionary reaction, in that it was born as an appeasing
'witness' to an Italy that was plump, consoled, and provincial, maintaining scarce contacts with reality. A cinema of science fiction (or of 'conscience fiction'). Then Italian film comedy grew up, it entered into closer
contact with reality, it dug deeper, it became uneasy, [transformed] from
being consolatory into something often provocative. It is in this direction
that I believe I have worked, toward an Italian film comedy in which,
behind the inheritance of neorealism, and the charms of satire, there
appeared a civil apologue.[10]

In choosing to represent Fascist anti-Semitism according to the canons
of Italian film comedy, Scola advances his agenda for generic progress.

8 Charles Thomas Samuels, *Encountering Directors* (New York: Putnam, 1972), 159.
9 For a detailed analysis of the use of comedic structures in representing the Shoah, see
   my chapter on Benigni's *Life Is Beautiful* in *After Fellini*.
10 Quoted in Roberto Ellero, *Ettore Scola* (Florence: La Nuova Italia, 1988), 6.

Treating 'a theme absolutely unpalatable to the mass public – a theme that would have raised unresolved questions about our embarrassing recent past,'[11] Scola's film brings the *commedia all'italiana* into alignment with the traditional goals of the Italian cinema of commitment: to awaken the public consciousness with regard to current problems, or problems of a past whose legacy has never been adequately addressed.

Within the narrative of *Concorrenza sleale*, Scola marks the passage of the film from conventional comedy to one that subverts the complacency of its generic codes by extending its confines to include subjects that are disturbing and even taboo (as was homosexuality in the 1970s of *A Special Day*). To this end, the first part of *Concorrenza sleale* presents a world of benign comedic events – a sit-com in period setting. It is the morning run of the trolley car, slow and quaint, that takes us into the space of the Via Ottaviano neighbourhood with its walls and gate, giving the impression of a closed, insulated world, a *hortus conclusus*, immune to the assaults of history. Within the confines of this set, daily life begins to stir, and Scola reconstructs those stirrings with a precision of detail that verges on the philological. This meticulous recreation of a bygone world is suffused with nostalgia for a past of security, innocence, and community, the *Italietta del ventennio* (the dear little Italy of the twenty-year Fascist regime). True to the requirements of conventional comedy, there are gags, *lazzi*, quips – little accidents that really do not hurt, such as the piano teacher's regular fainting sessions, which end as soon as the pastry tray arrives. The competition between the two shopkeepers seems itself to be one extended gag – the adult version of the games played by Umberto's and Leone's sons. Infact, the rivalry between the fathers is reduced to a quarrel over publicity slogans to sell beach-wear (who has the right to use the advertising concept *tutti al mare* – everyone to the shore). It is the younger generation, Pietruccio and Lele, who reveal the childishness of their fathers' behaviour when they label the shopkeepers' war a 'battle of the seas' in a clever variation on the actual children's game the boys will play later in the film: 'battleship.' True to *commedia all'italiana* tradition, Scola casts in the leading roles two renowned film actors, Diego Abatantuono and Sergio Castellitto, making the competition between Umberto and Leone a face-off between two *maschere* (established screen personae) whose familiarity will provide a ready source of comic pleasure for viewing audiences.

---

11 This quote, cited already in my Introduction, is from the review of *Concorrenza sleale* by Finn in *Cinemasessanta* 42 (March–April), 22.

Thus, everything seems to be proceeding according to the norms of conventional comedy, and our expectations are set for a resolution to the commercial rivalry that will permit the fathers to put aside their childishness and to follow the example of maturity, wisdom, and solidarity of their eight-year-old sons. While this resolution will ultimately come about, it will do so against a historical background that will completely undermine the complacency and stability that we expect of the standard happy ending. The turning point, from routine comedy to something generically quite different, occurs when Umberto, in a quarrel with Leone, strikes below the proverbial belt of comic repartee. While exchanging insults permissible within the norms of their business rivalry, Umberto breaks frame by referring to the 'race' of Leone. 'A Jew is always a Jew,' Umberto concludes, shattering not only the composure of his rival, but the comic hilarity of the film itself. It is as if this line had found its way into the wrong movie, hailing from an elsewhere completely foreign to the universe of *commedia all'italiana*.

With this racist slur, Holocaust history enters the protected borders of the neighbourhood, and in fact we discover that this day is indeed 6 May 1938, climax of the festivities accompanying the Hitler–Mussolini pact, with all its consequences for a future of genocide and war. To make this scene even more disruptive of our comic pleasure, Scola shows us the exchange of gazes between fathers and their sons – the latter, witnesses to the shame of the generation that accepted Fascism. Surrounding this turning point in the film, a number of previously quaint details recur, now as dire premonitions of the catastrophe to come. The windows of the trolley car that so innocently led us into the neighbourhood at the beginning of *Concorrenza sleale* are now festooned with Nazi flags, and the Fascist parade that filled the street with all its tackiness in the film's early moments now leaves the broken glass of Leone's shop window in its wake – a chilling, if highly localized, *Kristallnacht all'italiana*.

The second half of the film requires us to reread the comedic codes of the first half from the critical distance afforded by hindsight. This doubling of perspectives, of course, is the prime ingredient of irony – a device made explicit in the rantings and ravings of the anti-Fascist school teacher Angelo as he marks a student paper brimming with pro-Mussolini sentiment. Assigning the student a grade of zero for the ideological content of the essay, Angelo fulminates, 'Where did irony end up? ... Irony is dead.' Within the comedic structures of *Concorrenza sleale*, instead, irony is alive and well, thanks to the boys, who see the absurdity of their fathers' behaviour and who are aware that their own childhood games are, in fact, mere play, while their elders take seriously the silly antics of their rivalry. But a larger irony surrounds the entire comedic structure of *Concorrenza sleale*, when seen in the context of the macro-history that threatens to swallow it up. The happy ending of the generational plot – fathers come to imitate the exemplary behaviour of their sons – emerges as futile in the face of the larger historical forces at work. Comedic games, even when conducted on the various levels of awareness productive of irony, are nonetheless games, whose outcomes hold only in the realm of play. At the level of Holocaust history, the rules are ironclad, the outcomes are horrific, and the line between imaginary and real is subject to systematic violation. In other words, the happy ending decreed by the canons of conventional comedy is not forthcoming in *Concorrenza sleale* because the year is 1938, the place is Italy, and Leone is Jewish. It is this thwarting of expectations, this clash of generic codes between comedy and historical realism, that constitutes Scola's way of bearing witness to the onslaughts of Fascist anti-Semitism.

In keeping with the codes of Italian film comedy, *Concorrenza sleale* is populated with stock characters who cover the spectrum of possible responses to the ideology of the regime. There is the token intellectual, Angelo, played by a self-deprecating Gérard Depardieu, who chides Umberto, and by extension the bulk of the Italian citizenry, for their uncritical allegiance to Mussolini. We learn through dialogue that Angelo's Jewish colleague, Elio Carpi, commits suicide after being expelled from the faculty. Ignazietto, Umberto's errand boy, is anti-Fascist by intuition rather than by intellect, having spent time in an Italian prison and rubbed shoulders with a number of Resistance activists. Ignazietto's Fascist counterpart in instinctual partisanship is Matilde, also an employee of Umberto, and also an unthinking conduit of ideology. Matilde's political sympathies amount to a form of fan worship. In her eyes, the regime's leaders are celebrities, inspiring the kind of adoration that Fellini's Gradisca reserves for Gary Cooper and the ocean liner *Rex* in *Amarcord*. For Matilde, the greatest compliment a woman can pay a man is to confer upon him the status of Fascist stardom. In admiring the transformation of Umberto's brother-in-law Peppino from failed ballroom dancer into ardent Black Shirt, Matilde enthuses: 'Peppino has certainly become a handsome man, he resembles a bit Ciano' (Mussolini's son-in-law). The object of her admiration, Peppino, has indeed traded his loser image for the ersatz glamour of Il Duce's palace guard, strutting around in a tight black uniform and spouting Fascist slogans with fanfare and authority. Several steps above Peppino in the regime's hierarchy is Commissioner Solopaca, played by an impeccable Claudio Bigagli, whose caricature of Fascist swagger puts the finishing touches on Scola's satire of the regime.

Though its treatment of the Jewish characters is also stereotypical, *Concorrenza sleale* works against the negativity of ethnic stereotyping in two ways. First, Scola offers an unequivocally positive and constructive image of Italian Jewish life by emphasizing its strong sense of family solidarity and its love of musical culture, both of which converge in the scene of Nonna Eugenia's eightieth birthday party. Packed with members of the extended family, the Della Rocca living room presents a microcosm of festive Italian Jewry as the celebrants partake of the ever-present pastries and listen to the piano and violin duet of Susanna and her grandmother. When Nonno Mattia complains about the solemnity of the music, the two women strike up a lively melody, whose Magyar strains reinforce the stereotype of Jewish provenance from a generic Mitteleuropean 'elsewhere.' Pietruccio's voice-over commentary, 'I had never seen a grandmother who plays the violin,' only serves to emphasize the stereotype of a close-knit, extended family unit, bound by a love of culture that crosses generational lines. Family solidarity is also a factor in the Della Rocca's business success, and becomes a point of invidious comparison for Umberto, who gripes that his own wife and children provide no help in the workplace. While Umberto's comments turn this into an ethnic slur ('These guys are a herd, they're tightly-knit, they're merciless ...'), Scola clearly represents the family collaboration in the shop in a positive light, providing material for cheerful banter between Leone, his father Mattia, and his wife Giuditta, who lend a helping hand. Treuberg, a family friend who sought refuge in Italy from pogroms in Lithuania, and runs a tiny watch-repair shop, is also portrayed sympathetically as the northern European Jew full of wry humour and indomitable love for his host country.

The second way in which the film neutralizes the dangers of ethnic stereotyping is through the character of Pietruccio, whose bond with Lele gives him access to the world of a Jewish family in a way that attenuates the perceived threat of difference. Pietruccio is a permanent fixture in Lele's house, which emerges as every bit as bourgeois and familiar as the Christian domicile downstairs. When Umberto finally sets foot in this unknown terrain at the end of the film, he marvels to find how similar it is to his own – 'What a lovely house,' he remarks, in surprise and relief. Like the Melchiorris, the Della Roccas too have a maid (though they are forced to dismiss her owing to the injunctions against Jews having Aryan servants). In fact, the two households are presented as being so similar as to be specular doubles of each other, complete with older children who study the arts (piano in the case of Susanna, architecture in the case of Paolo) and who, of course, are in love.

Given this warm, respectful, and comfortable representation of Italian Jewry, the gradual subtraction of the Della Roccas' rights to citizenship becomes all the more gratuitous and absurd. The confiscation of the radio is revealed to be especially harsh in light of Giuditta's love of opera and her despair at the prospect of missing next Saturday's broadcast of *La Bohème*. Reduced to listening to the radio of the concierge, Giuditta is shown in rapturous concentration, even singing along to the music of act 1. The carting off of their own instrument, foreshadowing the final eviction of the Della Rocca family itself, becomes a scene of funereal loss, and the line of Jewish neighbours at the police station, all of whom must reliquish this medium of access to the outside world, reveals the first step in the forced ghettoization process that will lead inexorably to the *Lager*.

The loss of the radio and the teary dismissal of the servant Chiaretta (accompanied by the maid's wonderfully ironic line, 'Can I help it if I was born Christian?') are nothing compared to the next blow to which the Della Rocca family must submit: Susanna is expelled from the conservatory and Lele is banned from grade school. This development leads to one of the most wrenching images of the film – the spectacle of Lele, meticulously dressed for the day, with his book bag on his lap, sitting alone on his carefully made bed waiting, in vain, for Chiaretta to accompany him to the school in which he is no longer welcome.

Despite this shattering series of deprivations, Lele continues to inhabit the childhood Utopia he shares with Pietruccio. The film abounds in concrete details of the activities that fill their leisure and that contribute to the construction of a world doubly lost, both because it recalls everyone's memory of bygone childhood, but also because it marks the end of the prewar era, evoked with such precision and charm. The film presents a veritable inventory of childhood games, including hopscotch, erector sets, battleship, trading cards, not to mention boyish pranks involving caps placed on the tram tacks, makeshift telephones constructed out of discarded tubing, shared prepubescent fantasies about a female shopkeeper's sexy stockings, and the stray kitten named Fang adopted by both boys. Most significant for its allusion to 1930s pop culture is Pietruccio's addiction to the serialized stories of the magazine *L'avventuroso*. In a scene at the newstand, Pietruccio's escapist reading of 'Cino and Franco and the Cannibals of the Cliffs' is juxtaposed with the front page of the *Giornale d'Italia* that Lele reads with consternation. The date is 15 July 1938, and the headlines announce 'The Provisions on Race' – the official counterpart to the racist brainwashing taking place at the level of popular culture for the consumption of Italian youth. In their common tendency to demonize the 'other,' the relationship between *giornalino* (adventure magazine for children) and *giornale* (newspaper) is clear, recalling the propagandistic comic book read by Antonietta as she cleaned up the breakfast dishes in *A Special Day*. Entitled 'In the Realm of the Pygmies,' this text served as both a manifesto of the Fascist right to conquer Africa on the grounds of racial superiority, but also, more importantly, as a sedative that put Antonietta to sleep. The implication is that such pop cultural propaganda had a soporific effect on the collective consciousness, inducing a state of torpor in which its powers of suggestion could take the firmest possible hold.

In a related scene, Fascist commissioner Solopaca interrupts his audience with Umberto and Leone to engage in the task of censorship. Newly arrived on his desk is a book about interracial romance entitled *Amore nero* (Black Love), which prompts Solopaca's outbursts on the unacceptability of such a publication 'in a country that has an empire in Africa.' Later, in the same office, the camera will linger on the magazine *Difesa della razza* (Defence of the Race), displayed prominently on Solopaca's desk. But it is also in this office that Umberto evidences the first signs of his moral awakening with respect to the imminent campaign against the Jews. When asked by Solopaca if he had other grounds for reporting Leone to Fascist authorities, beyond those pertaining to commercial rivalry, Umberto hesitates. Without ever naming the racist rationale behind his inquiry, Solopaca makes the following request, couched in bureaucratic jargon of the most turgid and obscurantist sort: 'In the case that there were other causes such as, for example, having different ethnic origins, it would be the obligation of this office to protect with sword drawn, whichever of the two of you were of unequivocal, absolute, and, I might add, historical *italianità.*'

Mystified by this torrent of verbiage, Umberto is slow to answer. But as soon as Solopaca hands him the document for filing a formal complaint, Umberto realizes the gravity of what he is being asked to do, and refuses to collaborate. Now the camera slowly closes in on Umberto's expression of profound disquiet as he replies, 'No, I don't believe that I have anything to add in this regard.' Such a comment, offered so soon after the scuffle in which Umberto had used Leone's Jewishness as a weapon against him, suggests an immediate desire to atone for this affront to his neighbour. In Solopaca's office, Umberto understands the virulence of the racial slur that he had used so spontaneously and impulsively in a moment of rage. Further evidence of Umberto's moral awakening emerges in his spat with Matilde for mistreating a Jewish client, in his resentment of Peppino for rejoicing over the job possibilities liberated by the firing of Jews, and in his support of Leone's father, Mattia, who denounces anti-Semitic vandalism as the work of 'scoundrels.' But it is his refusal to profit from Leone's misfortune, and hence from the *concorrenza sleale* imposed by an anti-Semitic regime, that marks Umberto's achievement of full human empathy for the man whom he had previously considered to be so irreconcilably 'other.'

Towards the end of the film, when Umberto pays a visit to the ailing Leone, their sons eavesdrop on the conversation. 'They're laughing, they're chatting,' Pietruccio announces. 'It seems they've grown up,' Lele concludes. The same could be said of the *commedia all'italiana*, which has progressed to maturity in the hands of a filmmaker willing to confront 'a passage, little frequented, and hardly edifying, of our History.'[12] In so doing, Scola offers a powerful example to contemporary filmmakers, mired in the narcissism and intimism of thinly veiled autobiography, of the need to *raccontare l'Italia* by telling the story of 'the other,' both in the present tense and in the past that continues to haunt us.

---

12 See Scola's preface to the published screenplay of *Concorrenza sleale*, 5.

6 The Holocaust Rescue Narrative and the End of Ideology: Alberto Negrin's *Perlasca, un eroe italiano* (Perlasca: The Courage of a Just Man)

Direction: Alberto Negrin. Screenplay: Stefano Rulli and Sandro Petraglia (with the collaboration of Enrico Deaglio, author of *La banalità del bene*). Music: Ennio Morricone. Photography: Stefano Ricciotti. Editing: Antonio Siciliano. Costumes: Ágnes Gyarmathy. Sets: Giantito Burchiellaro. Cast: Luca Zingaretti (Giorgio Perlasca), Amanda Sandrelli (Magda Levi), Jerome Anger (Zoltán Farkas), Franco Castellano (Adam), Lorenzo Lavia (Daniel), Cristiane Filangieri (Eva), Giuliana Lojodice (Mme Tourné). Year: 2002. Availability: DVD, Italian original with English subtitles. Castle Hill Productions.

Synopsis

Giorgio Perlasca, a businessman working in Budapest in 1944, runs afoul of the Hungarian government and seeks refuge in the embassy of Spain, where he is welcomed as a veteran of the Italian contingent that Mussolini had sent to fight on behalf of Franco during the Spanish Civil War. When Angel Sanz Briz, the Spanish ambassador to Hungary, flees to Switzerland, Perlasca takes over the running of the diplomatic mission, pretending to be the Consul, and thereby maintaining the 'safe houses' where thousands of Jews are living under the protection of Franco's neutral government. Perlasca attributes his fictitious power to protect this endangered minority to the fact that Sephardic Jews (making up the bulk of the Hungarian Judaic population) are of Iberian origin, and therefore entitled to Spanish citizenship, thanks to an obscure law passed in 1924 under the then-dictator Manuel Primo de Rivera. After many harrowing turns of events in which Perlasca contrives the most ingenious stratagems for rescuing himself and his charges from disaster, Budapest is liberated by Soviet troops, and the fake Spanish consul is free to reclaim his Italian birthright.

This is a story about rescue, but it is also about the rescue of a story. In 1990 Italian television broadcast an interview with Giorgio Perlasca about his activities towards the end of the Second World War in Budapest, where he managed to save the lives of 5200 Hungarian Jews through a series of intrigues and diplomatic sleights of hand. Two years after the airing of the TV interview, journalist Enrico Deaglio published his superb book-length study of Perlasca, entitled *La banalità del bene* (The Banality of Goodness) in an ironic recall of Hannah Arendt's landmark work on the psychological 'normalcy' of Adolf Eichmann. In 1997 Perlasca's own memoir, entitled *L'impostore* (The Imposter) went to press, and in 2002 Alberto Negrin's mini-series, *Perlasca un eroe italiano*, was broadcast on the RAI UNO television channel to a record-breaking audience of eleven and a half million viewers on two successive evenings in January. Negrin's film may be seen as the composite, audiovisual adaptation of the two written texts – Deaglio's and Perlasca's own – becoming the climactic version of the story that will consolidate it in Italian collective memory.

Not only does Negrin's film exemplify Italy's recent willingness to confront Holocaust history, but it adds another element to that difficult confrontation. Giorgio Perlasca was an ardent Fascist – he fought in the Ethiopian campaign and he answered the call of Il Duce to combat on behalf of Franco in the Civil War in Spain (hence his privileged access to the Spanish embassy of Budapest). In proposing Perlasca as *un eroe italiano*, the film invites viewers to consider this man's strange yoking of Fascism and heroic humanitarianism, with all of the challenges that such a coupling poses for a study of postwar national identity. The way in which Perlasca's story calls into question the ideological givens of Italian culture during the Cold War period explains why his narrative could not emerge until the thaw of the 1990s. In reviews of Perlasca's written memoir and Negrin's film, the issue of political partisanship took on paramount importance, eliciting a wide array of responses, from that of James Southall, who sees the protagonist as 'a converted Fascist,' to Simonetta Robiony, who argues that he was a 'fascist who had never renounced his ideology' and therefore 'a difficult figure to locate.'[1] Apologists for Perlasca's right-wing leanings argue that he was a Fascist idealist whose enthusiasm waned when the moral and civil renewal of Italy heralded by Mussolini failed to materialize. In the film, Perlasca's idealism comes to verge on libertarianism when he explains that he fought in the Spanish Civil War against a movement that advocated the burning of churches and forbade all freedom of worship. Perhaps most indicative of the post–Cold War context that allowed Perlasca's story to emerge is the insistence that this Italian hero's actions transcend ideology. The actor who plays Perlasca, Luca Zingaretti, is eloquent in this regard. Comparing his current role to the one that made him famous, the role of the Sicilian detective Montalbano in the series of TV adaptations of Andrea Camilleri's enormously popular novels, Zingaretti claims that 'Montalbano and Perlasca are two very different characters – all they have in common is their way of reasoning with their heads and their hearts. Therefore, both are free to think and to act on the basis of what they feel, without taking account of ideology.'[2]

The subtitle of the film, *un eroe italiano*, then suggests that interpretations of Second World War heroism need no longer pass through the filter of ideology in the post-1990 cultural context. But it is the second element of the subtitle, the adjective *italiano* that lies at the heart of *Perlasca*. *Italianità, latinità, mediterraneità* all enter importantly into the representation of this historical chapter, as do the clichés about Hungarian culture and Nazi barbarity. For Zingaretti, Perlasca's story has the virtue of challenging stereotypes, and the actor is particularly gratified by the fact that this drama takes place on an international stage. Zingaretti relishes the chance to 'enact the part of an Italian who has done great things abroad, instead of being known always and only for pizza and mandolins.'[3] The dismissal of culinary and romantic stereotypes, however, does not mean the wholesale rejection of *italianità* as a behavioural

---

1 James Southall, 'Perlasca,' at http://in www.movie-wave.net/titles/perlasca.html and Simona Ribiony, 'Il fascista Perlasca eroe per 5000 ebrei,' *La stampa*, 24 January 2002, reprinted at http://culturitalia.uibk.ac.at/gmerz/ESERCIZ/TEMI/ARTind/ Perlasca.htm, 2.

2 Adele de Gennaro, 'Perlasca – un eroe italiano,' at http://www.televisione.it/ articoli/2002/01/24/251316/phP, 2.

3 See Gabriella Sassone's interview with Luca Zingaretti for Tamtamcinema at http:// www.tamtamcinema.com/persona.asp?ID=348&lang=ita, 1.

category. On the contrary, the actor attributes Perlasca's heroism to gifts inherent in the Italian national character – an inclination towards theatricality, a knack for improvisation, a facility with words, an intuitive grasp of individual and group psychology. Perlasca operates, according to Zingaretti, 'with something that is in the Italian character, disguising himself [*travestendosi*], being an actor.'[4] The term *travestendosi* is revealing on several levels, literally referring to Perlasca's masquerade, but also to Zingaretti's work of impersonation. The idea of 'dressing up as another' well explains Perlasca's exchange of identities from Italian businessman to Spanish diplomat, with all of the trappings of the embassy dignitary that the imposter so enthusiastically embraces – the sartorial finery, the chauffeur-driven car, the pageantry of the Spanish flag, the rhetorical pretense of authority. The ease with which Perlasca changes nationalities can also be explained by the cultural affinities between Italy and Spain – affinities revealed by the linguistic closeness that requires only the most minor changes of spelling and pronunciation in order for Giorgio to become Jorge.

Perlasca's flair for theatricality, his ability to masquerade as another, finds its equivalent in Zingaretti's own impassioned performance of his role. The actor, short and squat, had to overcome his physical unlikeness to the tall, lean Perlasca through a prodigious effort of psychological identification. 'Although I do not resemble Perlasca in height or physical type,' Zingaretti explains, 'my esteem and appreciation of him convinced me to stick exclusively to the importance of the man's story. I was able to play the figure of the hero who had, nevertheless duped the world, by means of a deep work [*un profondo lavoro*] on myself.'[5] The 'work' of becoming Perlasca, of getting into character, also involved an intricate game of intertextuality, given the fact that Zingaretti was already firmly entrenched in the popular imaginary as Montalbano. The image of the solitary, politically progressive, temperamentally gruff Sicilian detective in the popular TV series could not help but leave its residue in the minds of the viewers who formed the record-breaking audience of *Perlasca*. Zingaretti could count on a carry-over of audience sympathy from Montalbano to Perlasca, but the actor would have the daunting task of replacing the Sicilian detective's persona with the

---

4 See 'Perlasca,' at http://www.rai.it/RAInet/cinema, 1.
5 See Daniel Della Seta's interview with Luca Zingaretti in 'Quell'eroe un po' guascone che imbrogliò i nazisti,' at http://www.shalom.it/2.02/P.html.

right-wing political idealism, seductive charm, and gregariousness of the Northern Italian businessman turned bogus diplomat.

We would be remiss, however, to overlook the influence of the film that obviously served as a model and a point of comparison: Steven Spielberg's ground-breaking *Schindler's List*. The parallels between the two films' protagonists are many and significant – both were card-carrying supporters of anti-Semitic regimes, both were businessmen working in Nazi-occupied, or pro-Nazi Eastern Europe, both ran formidable risks in their rescue efforts, both operated in tandem with Jewish partners (Isaac Stern in the case of Schindler, Zoltán Farkas in the case of Perlasca), and both compiled lists. Schindler's compulsive chant 'more, more' as Isaac Stern types the names of the saved, finds its equivalent in Perlasca's frantic solicitation of names for his roll-call at the train station of Budapest. As businessmen, both Schindler and Perlasca have an ethic of accumulation, but in the context of Holocaust rescue, their inventories consist of living persons in a radical reversal of the Nazi policy of human merchandizing. Given the striking similarities between these two sagas, it is a distinct mark of pride for the Italians that their hero can claim mathematical superiority over his German counterpart: Perlasca saved 5200 to Schindler's 1000.[6]

It is Enrico Deaglio, writer of *La banalità del bene*, who best formulates the meaning of Perlasca for a redefinition of *italianità* in the post–Cold War era. 'We must discuss if Perlasca was the greatest Italian hero of the war, if he was greater than Schindler, why he did it, why only he did it, how does politics enter into what he did. [We need to discuss] how much we Italians succeed, more than others, in being human, when we succeed. [We need to discuss] how much we succeed in making fun of uniforms, of authorities, how much taste we have for risk.'[7] In Deaglio's pointed question, 'perchè solo lui lo fece' (why only he did it) lies Perlasca's paradoxical relationship to the cherished collective image of *italiani, brava gente* (Italians, good folks). 'Humans of a humanity that doesn't even have to be elaborated by the brain,' Deaglio explains, 'but that comes from the gut, suddenly, in the face of a humiliation or an abuse suffered by others, despite orders, uniforms, ideologies – [Ital-

---

6 See, for example, Giorgio Vincenzo Bonatesta's review at http://www.itismaglie.it/html/pdidattici/Perlasca, 2.

7 Enrico Deaglio, 'Perlasca, l'uomo che sfidò Hitler,' *L'unità*, 19 January 2002, reproduced at http://www.ilportoritrovato.net/html/perlasca.html, 2.

ians are] endowed with an innate theatricality, and psychological intuition' (14-15).

In his disregard for authority, his delight in defying official protocols,
his willingness to take mortal risks, and his disinterested humanitarianism, Perlasca's *italianità* distinguishes him from the passive, cowardly, or
corrupt members of the diplomatic circles in Budapest. Of all the characters in the story, Zoltán Farkas is the one who best serves as a foil for Perlasca. In his memoirs, Perlasca dedicates an entire chapter to Farkas,
which reads as an affectionate epitaph for this unfortunate friend and
collaborator, eventual victim of a fatal fall in his rash attempt to flee the
Russian liberators of Budapest. As a lawyer and consultant to the Spanish embassy, Farkas was a stickler for the rules who could not counte-
nance the diplomatic imbroglios so dear to Perlasca. 'But if he was a
luminary of the law,' Perlasca wrote of Farkas, 'I was a stubborn-head
who looked only at the utility of the things for which I answered. In an
epoch in which the words justice and right no longer had any value, we
must be sure that what we want to do, to say, or to propose be useful to
our goal, and if we judge that it is, I couldn't care less if there is an international law that forbids it.'[8] Despite his legal scruples, and the 'uncer-
tainties proper to the cultured man that he was,'[9] Perlasca's Farkas
emerges as man of vigour with a record for heroism in the war against
the Bolsheviks and the stamina to waltz all night at the Hungaria Hotel.

The film's Farkas, by contrast, is a man of tragic inertia. His inactivity
makes him an on-screen observer, or focalizer, of Perlasca's escapades.
It is through Farkas's astonished eyes that we witness the Italian's
impulsive, death-defying feats of rescue. Impeccably dressed in a fash-
ionable overcoat, stylish hat, and rimless glasses (cinematic trademark
of the intellectual), Farkas becomes a fixture in any number of scenes –
the motionless, statuary opposite of the perpetually moving Perlasca.
Farkas's refined, inactive 'Hungarianess' becomes the inverse measure
of Perlasca's activist *italianità*. In two important scenes the film makes
explicit the opposition embodied by the fake Spanish consul and his
sidekick. 'You think the right way. Or rather, you do much more,' Far-
gas muses over cocktails in the Grand Hotel. 'I myself would like to
have done what you've done, but I'm not able to ... It's almost as if I had
rheumatism of the soul. You are different ...' Towards the end of the
film, Farkas attributes a specifically Jewish ancestry to his inaction. 'I'm

---

8 Giorgio Perlasca, *L'impostore* (Bologna: Il Mulino, 1997), 133.
9 Ibid., 129.

a *kibbitzer,*' he confesses to Perlasca. 'One of those who are seen in cafes sitting next to the card players. The others play but the *kibbitzer* doesn't play. He watches the others play. Yes, it's true, I'm patient, I'm obstinate, I tolerate, like all the children of Abraham. But what strength is mine? What strength? It's a passive strength, inert.'

The decision to exaggerate Farkas's immobility and to make it the anguished object of the character's self-consciousness in order to highlight, by contrast, Perlasca's frenetic activism is but one of an array of strategies employed by the filmmaker in adapting this story to the screen.[10] Foremost among those strategies is the invention of a cast of characters who benefit from Perlasca's heroism and who, in their interrelationships, bring forth behaviours in him that serve to illustrate the depth and range of his humanitarianism. A few of these characters, such as Magda, Lily, Sarah, and Ben, come from the biographical record, but they are developed in ways that diverge significantly from the written sources. The film desexualizes Lily and hints, if anything, at her mother Magda as a potential love interest for Perlasca.[11] Magda and Lily come under Perlasca's protection early in the film, functioning as a surrogate family unit for the protagonist until the very end, when the woman's husband is miraculously restored to Budapest. In another episode from the memoirs significantly modified in the film, twin children being ushered towards the deportation trains catch Perlasca's eye and he snatches them from the clutches of Adolf Eichmann. In the film, these two children become Ben and Sarah, the former rendered mute by the horror of witnessing his parents' murder at the hand of the Nazis, the latter portrayed as compulsively talkative to compensate for her brother's silence. By the film's end, these orphans will be taken in by the young couple Daniel and Anna, to form a new, instant family unit.

10 As important as the director are the two renowned screenwriters, Stefano Rulli and Sandro Petraglia, in the shaping of this filmic representation. To avoid the unwieldiness of such phrases as 'the filmmaker and the scriptwriters' or 'Negrin, Petraglia, and Rulli,' I will use the name Negrin alone, or the term filmmaker, to signify the collective authorial process that went into the adaptation of Perlasca's story to the screen.
11 Lily is highly eroticized in the memoirs, where Perlasca describes her wearing a sweater 'che lasciava capire come la piccola avesse già iniziato lo sviluppo: era molto graziosa.' *L'impostore*, 91. In his text, Perlasca tells the story of how this child had offered to sleep with him in exchange for saving her mother's life. The Italian's reaction was to slap the child, but only later did he learn that Lily had no real understanding of the meaning of her proposition.

In their final scene together, Perlasca is able to elicit an embrace from the little boy, who had refused physical contact with anyone but his sister until then.

The character of Daniel, the young adoptive father, reflects the film-maker's aim to offer a representative sampling of Hungarian Jewry and the problems involved in organizing its members into a community capable of surviving the genocidal threat. Daniel first appears on screen as a Chasidic Jew, pledged to non-violence, and sporting the required yarmulka, sidelocks, and beard. Gradually, Daniel's orthodoxy gives way to the pragmatic demands of the war zone, prompting him to accept the need for arms, and to cut his hair to avoid unwanted Nazi attentions. In further relaxation of his behavioural standards, Daniel resorts to theft, to bearing arms, to lovemaking with his fiancée Anna, and to slaying the man who attempts to rape her. Adam, the father of Anna, is richly developed in the film, and his death, once he has assured the safety of his daughter, elicits the second of Perlasca's *pietà* scenes. Coming upon Adam's body on the street outside the safe house, Perlasca gathers him in his arms to grieve, just as he had done with the lifeless form of the child Gyorgy, found in a Nazi charnel house together with his slain parents in an earlier scene. The *pietà* pose sharply contrasts with Perlasca's memory of Gyorgy in a flashback featuring the boy astride the shoulders of the man who had succeeded in cheering him up in the aftermath of trauma.

Within the broad spectrum of Hungarian Jewry entrusted to Perlasca's care, there is an especially vivid character who sets himself in opposition to the aristocratically aloof Farkas, on the one hand, and the religiously motivated non-violent Daniel, on the other. I am referring to Ferenc, the brash, unruly, anarchic hooligan who swaggers into a safe house with two henchmen and lays claim to a large quantity of bread. Unfazed, Perlasca displays the same tough-guy bravado as the intruder, and succeeds not only in subduing Ferenc, but in channelling the young man's ferocity for the common good. Towards the end of the film, when Ferenc is gravely wounded and Perlasca saves his life by insisting that the reluctant, ill-equipped Dr Balazs perform surgery on him, we discover the source of the Italian's affinity for this young man. 'Seeing you and your friends reminds me of myself as a youth wanting to change the world to make it become more beautiful, more humane.' In his impulse to project onto Ferenc his own juvenile idealism, Perlasca is able to elicit from the young man those behaviours that will help promote the humanitarian agenda of the mature self.

With another carefully developed set of minor characters, Negrin leads us inside the film's most horrific episode of Nazi cruelty. In this scene, the filmmaker has taken a fact from the historical record involving the survival of a young woman from a mass execution, and constructed a subplot that personalizes the enormity of the event. The woman, unnamed in Perlasca's memoir, becomes the film's Eva, married to Sandor, an acquaintance of Perlasca through his earlier business activities in Budapest. Though Eva is gentile, her marriage to a Jewish man has compromised her safety and the situation is rendered even more critical by her state of advanced pregnancy at the time. We learn eventually that Eva lost the child due to prenatal malnutrition, but the most harrowing of her trials is yet to come. She and Sandor are among the victims of a nefarious Nazi strategy for slaughter on the shores of the Danube involving the lining up of people, tied together two by two, so that when they reach the bank of the river, one is shot in the head, dragging the other with him or her to drown. To add to the ghoulishness of this scene, the Nazis coerce a violinist into playing soulful tunes throughout the proceedings until his services are no longer needed and he too is dispatched into the Danube. The romantic myth of Budapest charm on the shores of its landmark river could not have a more diabolical inversion than this. But the carnage in the scene is not total – Sandor has been able to save his wife by secretly untying their bonds and offering to take the Nazi bullet himself.

The Sandor-Eva subplot offers perhaps the most poignant example of Negrin's technique in dramatizing Perlasca's story. Taking a nameless and faceless individual from the historical record, he has created a full-fledged character whose few screen appearances suggest the rich narrative wellsprings of all the people whose lives were touched by Perlasca. In highly synthetic, distilled form, we are given glimpses into a marital relationship that had to overcome dreadful difficulties to end in a gesture of self-sacrifice that changes the Nazi massacre on the shores of the Danube from one of abstract horror into one of excruciating personal loss.

From a generic point of view, the cleverest of the film's fictional portraits is that of the beautiful countess who reveals herself, by the end of the film, to be a Jew willing to return to her origins and share the fate of her people. In her glamorous, aristocratic guise, the countess exchanges pleasantries with Perlasca when he makes the rounds of Budapest social circles required by his diplomatic station. Though the memoir mentions several luxury venues – the Hungaria and Ritz hotels, the Arizona night club – the film consolidates them into one

Grand Hotel, with obvious meta-cinematic intent. In so doing, *Perlasca* taps into the Hollywood myth of Budapest so brilliantly propagated by the Hungarian refugee community in the United States, for whom the city became the place of remembered enchantment. Not only is the elegant setting of the Grand Hotel redolent of Hollywood Golden Age cinema, but so too is the arch dialogue between the countess and Perlasca, laced with hidden political understandings and erotic double entendres. In this witty repartee, the countess reveals herself to be Perlasca's intellectual and cultural equal, as well as a potential partner in romance. What we learn by the end of the film is that Perlasca and the countess are linked by far more than their shared adherence to the canons of film noir glamour – they are both imposters, poseurs masquerading as members of a social and political elite in order to hide identities seriously at risk.

Into this atmosphere so redolent of spy movies and noir mystique there enters another character who seems to come straight from central casting – the cold-blooded German commander Bleiber, the most recent in a long line of Nazi caricatures from Roberto Rossellini's Bergmann to Steven Spielberg's Amon Goetz. 'I'm fascinated by irony, it's the salvation of the world,' he quips, and indeed all of Bleiber's dialogue will be delivered with an ironic edge whose malignant sharpness is accentuated by the use of extreme close-ups of his sneering facial expressions. Needless to say, Bleiber himself will not be spared the filmmaker's irony when a Russian soldier casually lights a match on the heel of the Nazi's boot as his corpse dangles from a gibbet, recalling the German's own earlier gesture of contempt for the body of a young Jewish woman whose shoe was similarly used for match-striking purposes.

The spy movie and film noir are not the only cinematic traditions to which *Perlasca* owes a debt. In its opening moments the film promises to be a swashbuckling adventure movie with an action hero able to run, jump, leap, and perform all the gymnastics of a Harrison Ford if not a Harold Lloyd. In an attempt to evade his Nazi pursuers by stealing away from Budapest on a train, Perlasca hides under a boxcar, then exploits the chaos of an Allied bombing raid to dash away from a suspicious Hungarian guard. During this sequence, a caption appears on screen announcing that the setting is Budapest, 1944, adding a documentary ingredient to the film's generic mix. This element of historical authenticity is reinforced by the use of newsreel footage at various points, beginning with the opening frames in which Perlasca's face is superimposed on shots of wartime devastation. Later, documentary footage will be inserted to illustrate the Soviet military advance towards Budapest.

In addition to the hybrid generic codes that Negrin will use in adapting Deaglio's and Perlasca's texts to the screen, cinematic techniques of montage and *mise-en-scène* will be employed to tell the story in medium-specific ways. Perlasca's initial efforts to escape Budapest amidst a flock of sheep being loaded onto cattle cars anticipates and literalizes the metaphors conventionally applied to the extermination of European Jewry. Editing will dramatize the efficacy of Perlasca's attempts to bribe military personnel into tolerating his rescue efforts. At the freight station where 'his' Jews were being loaded onto deportation trains, Perlasca confronts Lieutenant Steiner, the commanding officer, with the comment that there is perhaps a 'language problem' whose solution may lie in the wads of money he proceeds to pull out of his suit pockets. The film editor, as if in keeping with Perlasca's own impatience, does not linger on Steiner's reaction to the bribe, but cuts crisply to the resulting scene of rescue. The 'language problem' to which Perlasca refers in this encounter could well be generalized to the Nazi genocidal machine as a whole, which defied all avenues of diplomatic recourse and required instead the creative and unorthodox methods of a Giorgio Perlasca. The 'language problem' becomes even more dire in another scene in which Perlasca seeks to free his charges from the ferocity of the Hungarian militia. When Perlasca opens his briefcase full of money, the commanding officer reveals himself to be not only unreceptive to the bribe, but morally outraged by it. Looming over Perlasca with a knife poised to slit his throat, the intransigent officer is offered double the amount in the briefcase before a neat cut takes us to the scene of the prisoners' release. The efficacy of Perlasca's answer to the 'language problem' – his generous greasing of palms – is translated cinematically into editing cuts that take us instantly from cause to effect. Such cuts are frequent enough in the film to form a kind of 'styleme' – a technical formula whose every occurrence reminds us of earlier ones as the film builds up its own internal memory of the Perlascan bribery approach to the rescue operation.

At the meta-textual level, it would be no exaggeration to say that Negrin's film is about the 'language problem' of adapting Perlasca's memoir to the screen. Examples of the filmmaker's techniques of generic mixing, *amplificatio*, editing, and *mise-en-scène* have been brought forth to illustrate the adaptive process. But perhaps the final and most powerful strategy may be found in the appropriation of that quintessentially cinematic answer to the 'language problem,' the gaze. In two scenes of wordless communication between Perlasca and his beneficiaries, the gaze is used to its greatest possible linguistic advantage. Midway into the film, the news that Sanz Briz is abandoning Budapest and that Perlasca can have safe passage to Switzerland is received sombrely by those entrusted to the embassy's care. The monumental inner stairway of the building serves as the staging area for the ceremony of Sanz Briz's departure, shot from an upper landing where Perlasca stands, looking down at the door from which the ambassador takes his leave. No sooner does this dignitary disappear than the throng of Jews turns around to face Perlasca, in whose hands their fate now lies. An old woman, the very one whom Perlasca had saved when she wanted to linger over her husband's slain corpse in an earlier scene, makes her way through the crowd to confront him with the most momentous of questions: 'What have you decided? Are you leaving too?' During this encounter, the camera alternates between shots and counter-shots, but since Perlasca stands a step above the woman, her viewpoint endows him with the visual authority of the low-angle perspective, just as the reverse shot emphasizes her sense of powerlessness. The old woman does not wait for an answer, but solemnly continues her ascent of the stairs, followed by all the other embassy wards who file by Perlasca, repeating the woman's query with their mute glances of interrogation. At the end of the scene, a slow zoom onto Perlasca's face registers the impact of this procession of gazes, and when he finally turns his head to the left, to follow the last of the suppliants upstairs with his eyes, we know what his choice will be.

Similarly wordless is a scene toward the end of the film in which the mute gaze of Jewish survivors conveys a very different kind of message. This particular group is alive thanks to Perlasca's success in thwarting plans to burn down the ghetto of Budapest. When the rabbi emerges from the gate of the ghetto, leading his congregation to safety, Perlasca is there to monitor the scene. His expression is sober – we see none of the jubilant triumphalism that such an event would lead us to expect. There follows a series of shots and counter-shots between Perlasca and the rabbi, the latter shown either in close-up or surrounded by his community as he removes the bar blocking the ghetto entrance. The gazes are those of concern and relief on the part of Perlasca and grateful acknowledgment on the part of his beneficiaries. This dialogue of glances may well be considered the answer to the earlier visual exchange between Perlasca and his dependents on the steps of the

Spanish embassy. In these paired scenes of 'dialogic gazing' the film-maker has found another styleme, a purely cinematic means for expressing Perlasca's profound sense of ethical accountability – his willingness to be his brother's keeper.

In 1989, the state of Israel conferred upon Giorgio Perlasca the title of 'Just Man among Just Men,' and in Jerusalem a tree was planted in his name. Towards the end of Negrin's film, a voice-over commentary by the adult Lily endows this title with the sanctity of an ancient Hebrew source.

> And ever since the first time I saw him in action, I thought that he was one of the 36 just men from the bible story that my father told when I was little. In any given moment of history, there are always 36 just men. Thanks to them God does not destroy the world. No one knows who they are and they themselves do not know who they are. However, they know how to recognize the suffering of others and they take that suffering upon themselves.

Thanks to Giorgio Perlasca, Italy too is represented in the ranks of this tiny minority. But any sense of collective national pride that might follow from such an honour is quickly curtailed by Deaglio's nagging question: 'perché solo lui lo fece?' Deaglio's query, cast in the *passato remoto*, prompts us to pose a related question in the present tense. It is the question that has been hovering over this entire study and that leaves it necessarily open-ended. If the end of ideology made it possible for Perlasca's story to be told, is the singularity of his, and other such cases, all that we can ask of our post-ideological age (and here the spectre of Marx[12] is speaking).

A Brief Flash-Back

A year before the January 2002 broadcast of *Perlasca*, another made-for-TV film in two instalments featured a kindred Italian Holocaust rescue narrative. *Senza confini* (Without Borders, Fabrizio Costa, 2001) tells the story of Giovanni Palatucci, a high-level police officer stationed in Fiume (Istria) who is credited with saving the lives of over five thousand Jews before being deported to Dachau where he died, in January

---

12 I am indebted to Jacques Derrida's *Specters of Marx*, trans. Peggy Kamuf (New York: Routledge, 1994) for this conceit.

1945, on the eve of the liberation of the camp. Like Perlasca, Palatucci belonged to 'the other side' – he was a Fascist government functionary committed to fulfilling his official duties with the highest standards of professionalism. But when obeying orders meant implementing the Racial Laws and coercing Jews into forced labour squads under the Mussolini regime, or facilitating deportations under the Nazi command, Palatucci did everything in his power to thwart the anti-Semitic measures he was expected to enact. Among his rescue activities, Palatucci welcomed Jews from northern and central Europe into Fiume, hid them in the countryside, launched a refugee ship bound for Palestine, and provided false passports for fugitives seeking sanctuary in Allied liberated Italy. In this last regard, Palatucci benefited from the considerable influence of his uncle, Father Ferdinando Palatucci, who managed a displaced-persons camp in the region of Campania and who generously received the tidal wave of Jewish escapees being sent by his nephew from Fiume.

Though a made-for-TV film, *Senza confini* exhibits the highest production values – an excellent cast, led by the restrained but extremely compelling performance of Sebastiano Somma, whose southern Italian accent becomes a phonic signifier of goodness, a period setting recreated with consummate skill, and a number of details that add cultural, as well as moral 'thickness' to the film's texture. The Prefect Piazza, played by an impeccable Omero Antonutti, is delirious with D'Annunzianismo – his office is bedecked with portraits of The Poet, whose look he emulates and whose bombast he obviously adores ('This is the balcony where D'Annunzio incited his legionnaires,' he effuses while leading Palatucci on a palace tour).

Fiume's identity as a border culture, heterogeneous, contested, and strategic, offers the film its ideological matrix. Palatucci's humanitarianism operates 'senza confini' – it crosses, ignores, or undermines borders that subject their 'confinati,' especially those branded with the stigma of alterity, to the injustices of a dominant regime. 'We must be without borders' Palatucci urges Alida Magris, an Italian of Fiume who boycotts a group singing an Austrian anthem. 'We must overcome hatred.' Implicitly equating borders with intolerance, the film argues that territoriality, if not nationalism itself, is among the prime deterrents to solidarity and world peace. Where Fiume could serve as a model for harmonious coexistence among culturally and ethnically diverse populations, it has instead become a staging ground for the most malevolent imperialist struggles. In the final tally, the signifier *confini* transcends its own narrowly geographic signified to include all the artificial boundary lines that obstruct the path to human concord.

It is no coincidence that the popular press greeted both Palatucci and Perlasca as 'Italian Oskar Schindlers.' Spielberg's film served not only to bring the Holocaust into mainstream commercial cinema, but it laid the ground rules for what we might call the 'rescue subgenre.' The Schindlerian model places at centre stage the stereotypical 'good Nazi,' heretofore a secondary character, such as Rudolph Stassen in *Il monastero di Santa Chiara* or the one-handed Karl of *Kapò*. Such a politically ambiguous hero offers multiple dividends for the rescue saga. His insider status affords him privileged access to information, and power, while providing obvious cover for his subversive operations, and it also implies a narrative of conversion from Nazi or Fascist allegiance to active and audacious opposition.

All three works appropriate the conventions of forties spy films to great advantage. Though *Senza confini* and *Perlasca* do not adopt the austere black and white photography of Spielberg's film, they do emulate the shadowy cinematography and sepia tones so redolent of that literally dark time. Elite social settings, elegant costumes, evocative period music, a charming, physically prepossessing hero, glamorous, sexually available women, suspense-filled episodes of political intrigue, fast-paced dramatic developments, arch dialogue – all these elements provide a veneer of generic familiarity and allure for subject matter whose documentary basis might otherwise discourage the mass spectatorship to which these films so successfully appealed.

7 The Present through the Eyes of the Past: Ferzan Ozpetek's *La finestra di fronte* (Facing Windows)

Direction: Ferzan Ozpetek. Screenplay: Gianni Romoli, Ferzan Ozpetek. Photography: Gianfilippo Corticelli. Editing: Patrizio Marone. Music: Andrea Guerra. Sets: Andrea Crisanti. Costumes: Catia Dottori. Cast: Giovanna Mezzogiorno (Giovanna), Filippo Nigro (Filippo), Massimo Girotti (Davide Veroli), Raoul Bova (Lorenzo), Serra Yilmaz (Eminé). Year: 2003. Availability: DVD, *La finestra di fronte* (Facing Windows) in Italian-language original with English subtitles, distributed through Amazon.com and Facets.org.

Synopsis

Set in contemporary Rome, *La finestra di fronte* tells the story of a young couple, Giovanna and Filippo, parents of two small children and struggling to live within a marriage where practical concerns and everyday routine have taken the place of passion. Giovanna has a dreary job as the accountant of a poultry firm and Filippo does maintenance work on trucks during the night shift. To help make ends meet, Giovanna bakes cakes and pies to be sold at a neighbourhood pub. The woman's one respite from the drudgery of her life is to watch the handsome young man, Lorenzo, living in the apartment across the way. The action of the film begins when Giovanna and Filippo happen upon an old man wandering lost through the streets of Rome. Against Giovanna's wishes, Filippo takes the old man home to their apartment. Despite herself, Giovanna grows fond of the elderly gentleman and when he wanders off one day, she is helped in her quest to find him by Lorenzo. The plight of the missing man soon comes to form a bond between

Giovanna and her neighbour, and the story that emerges of a transgressive love on the old gentleman's part, buried in the distant past, serves to express and facilitate the young people's own adulterous longings. To complicate the contemporary love story, Lorenzo is about to be transferred to a bank position in Ischia, and his infatuation with Giovanna makes his imminent departure highly problematic for them both. The couple arranges to meet in Lorenzo's apartment to consummate their love, but when Giovanna looks out from his window into hers, reversing the direction of her own voyeuristic curiosity, the spell is broken. Meanwhile, the quest for the mysterious old man continues and Giovanna is able to track him down through an antiquated love letter that she has found among his belongings. Back in his own home, the elderly gentleman reveals to Giovanna that he is Davide Veroli, concentration camp survivor, rescuer of many families within the ghetto of Rome, and in the postwar period owner of a famous pastry shop. During the 16 October 1943 round-up of the Roman Jewish community, Davide had been forced to choose the latter of two mutually exclusive options – either to save his lover, Simone, or to warn the majority of ghetto dwellers of the impending Nazi raid – in order to expiate his perceived sin of sexual deviance. The horror of this experience has permanently damaged the psyche of the old man and this is what sent him wandering the streets of Rome at the start of the film. It is Giovanna's affection for Davide that enables him to bear witness to his Holocaust ordeal, and to experience the cathartic effects of the testimonial process. Thus liberated, he can perform a therapeutic role for Giovanna, encouraging her to pursue the art of *pasticceria* for which she has demonstrated considerable talent. The young woman takes this lesson to heart, choosing her family over her forbidden love for Lorenzo, but radically altering the status quo by leaving her job in accounting to develop her vocational dream.

'Roma, 1943.' With this caption, Ozpetek plunges us into a world that is both historically grounded and phantasmagoric, objectively true yet filtered through the traumatized memory of a disturbed old man. Only later will we learn the precise month and day of this initial scene, as well as its location on the map of Rome. But for now all we know is that two men are engaged in an exchange of intense and suspicious glances in a bakery enshrouded in shadows. The scene's focalizer, the younger of the two men, makes a desperate attempt to escape this space, but is blocked by the older man who grabs a knife during the ensuing scuffle.

Wresting the weapon from him, the younger man overcomes and kills his assailant before disappearing into the night, leaving a bloody hand print on a wall flanking the street along which he flees. In a breathtaking lap dissolve, the gory stain modulates into a pale blemish on the same wall in the film's narrative present, some sixty years later.

It would be no exaggeration to read into this lap dissolve the key to the historical hermeneutics of *La finestra di fronte*. Though faint and barely decipherable, the past marks the present in ways that invite our most attentive and impassioned work of analysis. In fact, one of the salient interpretive processes required of us as viewers of *La finestra di fronte* is that of retro-reading – we must constantly return to this *incipit* with the help of the knowledge provided by subsequent revelations of the old man's troubled past. Only later do we realize that in witnessing the film's opening scene, captioned 'Roma, 1943,' we are inside the consciousness of this gentleman, whose mental composure is shattered by his memories of that historical moment. In fact, no sooner is this flashback complete than we meet the aged and decrepit Davide Veroli, wandering deranged through the streets of present-day Rome. When the young married couple take Davide into their home and into their lives, the film establishes the second of the two temporal planes on which it will operate – a present-tense plot involving Giovanna's own struggle for selfhood at home and at work begins to unfold against the backdrop of a fragmented and mysterious Holocaust past. The two narratives mirror and reinforce each other, so that by the end of the film, Davide succeeds in exorcizing the ghosts that haunt him, while Giovanna is able to make a series of life-defining decisions with serenity and courage.

Contemporary Italy, as represented in *La finestra di fronte*, is utterly devoid of historical memory. Giovanna, in dialogue with Sara, Davide's caretaker and the beneficiary of his wartime rescue efforts, admits to her ignorance of what happened on that fatal day in 1943 and her historical obliviousness exemplifies that of an entire generation, living in the eternal present of contemporary media culture. Ozpetek's decision to cast Giovanna Mezzogiorno in this role is strategic, given the actress's association with such recent film ventures as Michele Placido's *Del perduto amore* (1998), Sergio Rubini's *L'amore ritorna* (2003), and Gabriele Muccini's enormously successful *L'ultimo bacio* (2001). The 'star discourse' associated with Massimo Girotti's performance as Davide is equally revealing of Ozpetek's meta-cinematic intent, for this actor may be seen as the veritable personification of postwar Italian film history, 'a living icon' according to scriptwriter Gianni Romoli, 'the Memory of Italian cinema.'[1] Given the fact that Girotti's career spans six decades and includes every genre produced by the film industry of those years, I am tempted to see his character's psychopathology in *La finestra di fronte* as a symptom of the Italian cinema's troubled relationship to the Shoah. Indeed, the disturbances of Davide's mind caused by the fragmentary recall of traumatic events may be seen as the unhealthy effect that repression of this excruciating chapter of Second World War history has had, in general, on Italian collective identity. Davide's success in coming to terms with his past – a success facilitated by his bond with Giovanna – points to the need for Italian cinema to confront this anguished episode in national history. Giovanna's internalization of Davide's example, and her decision to live out the lesson of his suffering, suggests that the current generation has much to gain from a cinema that dares to acknowledge and mourn a traumatic past.

But Davide's model is not one of surrender to historical inevitability – on the contrary, it is one that insists on the necessity of conscious and morally responsible choices. In the film's opening flashback, the bloody handprint that modulates into a faint blur on a wall in contemporary Rome also marks the place of decision. When the young Davide stopped here and leaned against the wall, he was in the throes of the tragic choice over whether to save Simone or the bulk of his co-religionists in the ghetto of Rome. The street map makes literal the moral crossroads at which Davide finds himself, and the term *crisis*, meaning literally *decision*, is painfully appropriate to the young man's dilemma at this point. Davide's meaning for Giovanna, then, is the necessity of choice as she faces her own crisis of identity within marriage, household, and workplace. 'You can still choose, you can still change,' Davide says to his young interlocutor in the film's present tense. 'Don't simply content yourself with surviving. You must demand to live in a better world, not just dream about it' (177). Davide's example, then, endows Giovanna with agency. In his absence at the end of the film, Giovanna mourns Davide in the therapeutic and salubrious way that Freud advocated in 'Mourning and Melancholia' – through a remem-

---

1 See the essay 'Work in Progress' in the front matter of the published screenplay, Gianni Romoli and Ferzan Ozpetek, *La finestra di fronte* (Milan: Idea Books, 2003), 38. Page references to the screenplay and the front matter will henceforth be included in the body of this text. The translations are mine. On Girotti as a personification of Italian film history, see also Stefano Lusardi, 'Il dolce è la vita,' *Ciak*, March 2003, 92.

bering that enables her to ultimately detach herself and form new bonds and passions, to take her life forward.

Ozpetek's decision to make Italian cinema itself accountable to Holocaust history through the representative figure of Massimo Girotti means that the filmmaker must mobilize specifically cinematic techniques to bring past and present into alignment. He does so not only through the lap dissolve described above, but also through camera movements that simulate time travel in sophisticated and powerful ways.[2] Seated at a table in a cafe that Davide had obviously frequented in his youth, the old man is exquisitely receptive to the undercurrents of transgressive, adulterous desire linking the two young people, Giovanna and Lorenzo, who have watched over him during his nocturnal odyssey. At a certain point, as Giovanna and Lorenzo engage in small talk, Davide hallucinates the presence of his beloved, the young Simone, at the table with them. As the camera circles the table, simulating Lorenzo's and Giovanna's mutual attraction for one another, Davide journeys back to the time of his own infatuation with Simone. The boundaries between past and present dissolve in the hallucinating mind of the old man, for whom time travel is expressed by the slightest lateral movement in space as the camera glides between the members of the desiring young couple and between Davide and the object of his own passion of sixty years prior.

Mistaking this vision for reality, the elderly Davide gets up to follow his phantomatic lover. In so doing, he encounters another hallucinated figure – that of a young mother who implores Davide for help in rescuing her daughter from the Nazi round-up. Indifferent to the woman's desperate plea, Davide continues to trail after his ghostly lover, until he reaches the sealed door of Simone's shop, where the old man collapses in grief. This mysterious scene will only make sense from the perspective of the ending, when Davide explains to Giovanna that he had placed the welfare of the majority of the ghetto Jews ahead of that of his lover in order to expiate his sin of homosexuality in their eyes. As a result, Simone had died in Auschwitz. With the benefit of this knowledge, we can retroactively interpret the scene of Davide's hallucination as a wish-fulfilment fantasy in which his real-life decision to sacrifice his lover to the welfare of the community is reversed.

Like the beautiful camerawork that included the Simone of 1943 at

---

2 On these devices see Emilio Cozzi, 'L'ombra del passato che ritorna,' *Cineforum* 43 (April 2003), 37.

the table of Giovanna and Lorenzo of 2003, another seamless lateral movement will be used to turn time into space in the poignant scene of the dance. Giovanna and Davide are standing at the window debating about the relationship between passion and domesticity when the latter invites the young woman to dance with him. The camera glides smoothly from the present-tense window to one that looks onto a social gathering of the early 1940s. The young Davide is dancing with Giovanna (another example of slippage between past and present), but his eyes are riveted on someone of far greater importance to him. When the young Simone returns his gaze we realize that Davide's desires are homoerotic, and we understand, in retrospect, why the lovers must exchange secret messages hidden in the crevice of a fountain. This scene also serves to double the 'otherness' of Davide, who is not only victimized as a Jew in Nazi-occupied Italy, but is ostracized within his own community for the so-called *colpa omosessuale.*

As in Ettore Scola's *Una giornata particolare, La finestra di fronte* establishes a profound understanding between a female protagonist and a male homosexual victim of the regime, and in each film windows serve as important signifiers of political and emotional consciousness. Once Antonietta Tiberi manages to overcome the sexist stereotypes inherent in Fascist thought, she comes to closely identify with Gabriele as a social outcast. In *La finestra di fronte*, Giovanna is powerfully drawn to Davide the very moment that she first beholds him. The spectacle of the dignified old man lost on the bridge strikes her with the force of an epiphany, exerting an uncanny influence over her that she first tries to resist. An intense bond of identification develops between the two, based not only on a shared penchant for pastry-making, but also on a common inclination towards forbidden love ending in renunciation, self-sacrifice, and sublimation.

Up to this point in our analysis, *La finestra di fronte* appears to be a full-fledged Holocaust film that directly confronts problems of historical trauma and its effects on the Italian collective psyche as it struggles to come to terms with the past. But to limit our interpretation of *La finestra di fronte* to its Holocaust narrative would be to commit a figure-ground error of considerable proportions. The primary focus of Ozpetek's film is the voyeurism and the wish-fulfilment fantasy of adulterous passion that link Giovanna and Lorenzo in the contemporary plot. To use a cinematic metaphor, Ozpetek represents this relationship in close-up, and relegates the Holocaust story to the deep recesses of the narrative space. When Davide flashes back to the past in moments of lucid memory or delirious recall, it is as if Ozpetek's entire film had undergone the process of rack focus – the technique by which image sharpness shifts between foreground and background to call the viewer's attention to a different focal plane in mid-shot. Because the 'back' story remains relatively underdeveloped, from the perspective of Holocaust studies, it could be argued that Ozpetek uses 16 October 1943 as a mere plot device, as a pretext to bring Lorenzo and Giovanna together around the figure of an old man profoundly damaged by a traumatic past. In defence of Ozpetek's choice, we could claim that any number of other wrenching episodes from Italian Second World War history could have been selected to illustrate Davide's moral conflict – we could imagine, for example, a Resistance scenario in which it would behoove the protagonist to make an agonizing choice between personal happiness and the common good. The decision to set the 'back story' in the Roman ghetto of 1943 reflects, I would argue, Italy's current compulsion to represent this repressed chapter of its wartime past – in short, to engage in the task of belated mourning.

The film's governing image, that of the window, is rich with promise for our study of Italian cinema and Holocaust memory. In addition to its implications for vision, imagination, and desire (which we will explore in the following pages), the window also signifies historical consciousness – a view onto a world that is not only spatially, but temporally distanced from the story's here and now. And finally, the window offers important analogies to the movie screen (as Alfred Hitchcock knew only too well),[3] making the actors simultaneously agents and spectators of their own stories, with obvious repercussions for our own voyeuristic engagement in the medium of film.

Most obviously, the window within the screen serves as a sign of authorial self-consciousness, inscribing the filmmaker's awareness of the mechanisms of vision that underwrite his art. 'A window in a film,' writes Francesco Pitassio, 'refers, then, to a representation: pictorial, theatrical, cinematographic. To have us see something limited by the frame of the window underlines the existence of another frame: that of the matte. The window, then, can be a reflexive device through which the arts of the diopter are enunciated as such.'[4] The window represented on screen thus calls attention to the 'windowness' of the film

---

3 In fact, Hitchcock's film *Rear Window* was distributed in Italy under the title *La finestra di fronte*.
4 Francesco Pitassio, 'Finestre superficiali,' *Cineforum* 41 (August–September 2001), 7.

itself: its confinement of the images to the limits of the frame, and the pre-eminence of the gaze as our means of gaining access, in Peeping Tom fashion, into the 'houses' of other peoples' lives. The implied illicitness of our gaze, however, does not prevent the spectacle from presenting itself as something *to be looked at*. 'The window suggests, then, the primacy of the look,' continues Pitassio, 'but also someone who looks and something that is disposed and equipped for him to do so. A machinery desired and fulfilled. A spectacle. In other words, a fetish constituted by and for the spectator-fetishist.'[5]

From its earliest scenes, *La finestra di fronte* presents Giovanna as a voyeur, whose visual obsession with the young man in the apartment across the street is made explicit by the wisecracks and incitements of her prying friend/neighbour/co-worker Eminé. 'Come on, he's almost naked! Come before he closes the shutters!' (60), Eminé urges Giovanna as the protagonist unpacks the groceries in the cramped kitchen that bespeaks the dreary life from which she longs to escape. Given her financially straitened circumstances, her ungainfully employed husband, the demands made by two young children, and the drudgery of a job in a poultry factory, Giovanna is given to displacing all of her unrealized desires onto the imagined world so tantalizingly glimpsed through the *finestra di fronte*. In watching Lorenzo through the window, Giovanna is constructing her own film, supplying the continuity between the visual fragments offered by fleeting glimpses of him from window to window, inferring the information that is withheld from her limited vantage point, and prompting her imagination to perform the guesswork that so much 'off-screen' activity invites.[6] At the same time, she is the prime consumer of the film she creates, enjoying all of the pleasures of scopophilia that Laura Mulvey's theory accords to viewers of mainstream cinema.[7] In a reversal of Mulvey's gender alignments, Lorenzo is filmed as the traditionally feminized bearer of the gaze – he becomes a visual icon, frozen within the limits of the window frame, the passive and inert object of Giovanna's desire.[8] In this regard, it is signif-

---

5 Ibid.

6 See Cozzi, 'L'ombra del passato che ritorna,' 38. On the 'potenzialità narrativa' that windows within the *mise-en-scène* imply, see Adriano Piccardi, 'La merlettaia e il canarino,' *Cineforum* 41 (August–September 2001), 4.

7 For this canonical essay, see Laura Mulvey, 'Visual Pleasure and Narrative Cinema,' *Screen* 16:3 (1975), 6–18.

8 In directing this role, Ozpetek had to continually remind the actor that 'he was the only "feminine" character in the film.' See Romoli, 'Work in Progress,' 38.

icant that Ozpetek chose for the role of Lorenzo Raoul Bova, an actor whose screen persona as 'sex symbol *da calendario* (pin-up), incarnation of extraordinary fantasies'[9] was firmly ensconced in the Italian film-going imaginary. Thus, Bova's presence on screen would automatically trigger, at the level of the 'meta-performance' (the way in which the performance brings our prior knowledge of the actor's career to bear on our interpretation of the current role), the very fetishized viewing practices that the character Giovanna experiences in watching her neighbour within the fiction of *La finestra di fronte*. The irony, of course, is that the actress Giovanna Mezzogiorno is herself an icon for the Italian film-going public – an icon, if not of sheer beauty, at least of feminine fascination and charisma. To heighten our awareness of this irony, the character has retained the actress's first name, blurring the distinction between performer and performance that the role of the bedraggled housewife would seem to require of the glamorous and rising young star.

Giovanna's nightly ritual of voyeurism, her 'Lorenzo Show,' begins, appropriately, once she has completed her evening chores and has earned the right to separate herself from the world of domestic drudgery. Having finished washing the dishes and tidying up the kitchen, Giovanna turns off the light, smokes a cigarette, and proceeds to enjoy the spectacle of the *finestra di fronte*. When that spectacle involves another woman, such as the seduction scene that Giovanna witnesses with considerable interest, the dynamic becomes a powerful mix of jealously and identification.

Giovanna's voyeurism is by no means unilateral, however. Midway into the film, we learn that Lorenzo, in turn, has been spying on her, that he too has been engaged in a game of spectatorship that has made him the intimate witness of her daily routine. 'All I know is that you leave home every morning at 8 to take the children to school, and you are always with a friend with children of colour,' Lorenzo confesses. 'I know that in the evenings, after washing the dishes, you linger a while alone in the kitchen to smoke. And you put out your cigarette under the faucet. I also know that often, during the night, you wander through the house and you approach the window and look outside ... but I don't know what you see' (128). This final comment can be read in two diametrically opposed ways: either Lorenzo is being obtuse to the point of imbecility, or he is being disingenuous and coy, knowing exactly what it is that she sees. In the second case, Lorenzo's act of surveillance would

---

9 See Cozzi, 'L'ombra del passato che ritorna,' 38.

become a kind of second-order watching and therefore a confirmation of his desirability in her eyes.

The narcissistic underpinnings of romantic passion, where the lover's idealized self-image is mirrored in the eyes of the beloved, find their cinematic equivalent in one of the film's most striking visual effects. I speak of Ozpetek's penchant for shooting through glass – a technique that allows the camera simultaneously to film what lies on either side of the window pane, so that one image is superimposed upon the other. This happens repeatedly when Giovanna is filmed frontally, from outside her kitchen window as she watches Lorenzo, and his image appears over hers, or is relegated to one of the corners of the frame.

It is Eminé who calls attention to the *finestra di fronte* as a screen for the projection of romantic desire, just as it is she who encourages Giovanna to cross the line between fantasy and lived experience. 'But you've been creating a *telenovela* (soap opera) about him for months!' (123), Eminé comments halfway into the film. And later she succinctly advises Giovanna to 'get laid' (157). Following this sage counsel, Giovanna indeed agrees to a tryst with Lorenzo, but the decision to meet in his apartment – to literally occupy the space on the other side of the *finestra di fronte* – is disastrous. At a strategic point in their love-making, Lorenzo mentions the window and it is as if the spell were broken. Giovanna's passionate writhing gives way to a mood of profound self-reflection as she gets up to approach *la finestra*. The act of looking out at her own kitchen window has momentous consequences for her, and from the vantage point of Lorenzo's apartment, Giovanna beholds a very different kind of spectacle from the *telenovela* of her earlier fantasy. Instead, what she sees are quiet, unremarkable scenes of domestic life, a neorealist film for the new millennium. First, the kitchen window is illuminated as Filippo comes home from the night shift, grabs a bottle of water, and, momentarily obscured by the exterior wall, reappears in the bedroom window. Now Eminé and the two children materialize in the kitchen and Filippo gathers his young son in his arms. All that is lacking to complete this scene is Giovanna. And then, for a breathtaking moment, Giovanna too appears, dressed in her nightclothes looking back at the *finestra di fronte* from which the 'real' Giovanna observes her. In the young woman's very impulse to project herself back into the domestic scene, in her inclination to reinstate herself into the family unit, we see her renunciation of adulterous love. It is the vantage point on the other side of the *finestra di fronte* that enables her to see herself through an alternative consciousness – not that of a Lorenzo caught in the throes of romantic desire, but that of Davide, whose lover did not live long enough for their passion to mature into something else. 'It must be beautiful to see that love grow from a beginning that was only passion,' the old man had observed, ' ... to help it to change, to protect it from the passage of time' (116).

In this wistful comment, together with his subsequent insistence that 'You can still choose,' we find the key to the meaning of Davide's example for Giovanna. Up until now, she has been able to envision only one alternative to the frustration of an unfulfilling marriage and a dreary job – that of romantic escape. The *finestra di fronte* offered the only imaginable remedy to her plight – the Madame Bovary antidote to domestic unhappiness or, in Eminé's more vernacular idiom, the *telenovela* answer to ennui. Locked into the binary opposition between dreary personal routine and the imagined erotic idyll, Giovanna remained at an emotional impasse until Davide entered her life. At first, the old man seemed to facilitate the *telenovela* scenario, bringing Giovanna and Lorenzo together from behind their respective windows to collaborate in the solution of his mystery. And that mystery was one that lent expression to their own unspoken passions, for the love letter of Davide to Simone that Giovanna found among the old man's belongings contained phrases entirely appropriate to the contemporary romance. When Giovanna recites the letter aloud to Lorenzo on the park bench, it reads as a possible text for their own love, as if Davide were scripting their encounter from a place far back in the past. But the old man's influence on Giovanna grows into something very different by the middle of the film, when his perspective allows her to step outside the *telenovela* plot and entertain an entirely different set of personal options. The true *finestra di fronte* – the alternative aperture through which Giovanna learns to envision her life – is that offered by Davide as the result of his historic and personal perspective.[10] 'It must be beautiful to see that love grow from a beginning that was only passion,' Davide had said, and with this comment he had reminded Giovanna that the evolution of romantic love into everyday affection is a luxury that Holocaust history denied him. Looking back at her kitchen window from the

---

10 'Giovanna must not be content to [merely] survive,' writes Valerio Guslandi. 'She must understand that she can make choices and go beyond appearances, observing things from a different angle.' See 'Doppio colpo di fulmine, *La finestra di fronte*,' *Ciak*, April 2003, 10.

finestra di fronte, the scenes that Giovanna conjures up are precisely those moments of domestic intimacy that develop, under normal conditions, in the aftermath of passionate beginnings.

But Davide's lesson is not about resignation – it is about agency and choice, and this lesson has much to do with alternative objects of the film's much touted theme of *passione*. 'Don't permit anyone to put himself between you and your passion' (153), Davide admonishes her, and here, out of context, the referent could easily be the amorous one. In Davide's experience, however, *passione* can also apply to the realm of *vocation*, understood in the etymological sense of 'a calling.' As such, baking comes to assume, by synecdoche, an entire category of artisanal activity whose meanings invite symbolic as well as culture-specific interpretations. The prestige of the term *pasticcere* may indeed be lost on non-European audiences, for whom the activity of baking does not hark back to a long tradition of guild-controlled craftsmanship. The translation 'pastry chef' rather than 'baker' better renders the true status of the *pasticcere* who has undergone rigorous training over a period of years as apprentice before acceding to the ranks of *maestro*. Giovanna's decision to resign from her job as accountant in a poultry factory, represented by rooms full of dangling chicken carcasses, and to enter into the world of gorgeous pastry confections displayed in Davide's kitchen, is clearly a decision to move up the 'food chain' of human activity. Davide's insistence 'You can still choose' is thus not just about changing work addresses, but about ascending into a realm of creative endeavour involving the higher gifts of craftsmanship and self-expression.

There is, of course, more than this to Ozpetek's choice of baking as the foundation of Davide's bond with Giovanna. Any number of other arts or crafts could have filled the bill: jewellery making, ceramics, or even the cinematically appropriate activities of painting and photography. But the symbolic richness of baking, in which the sweetness of love is literalized, could not be more apt to Davide's case. Indeed, the sublimation theory of art as the re-channeling of frustrated amorous passion is made explicit when Davide answers Giovanna's query 'Simone is dead, right?' with the comment 'In every dessert that I make there is a little of that love for him' (153). In some primitive, even ritualistic way, then, the art of pastry-making offers Davide not only a means to express his affection for Simone, but also literally to feed others with it. Giovanna, in fact, will be so fully nourished by Davide's practice of the baker's art that she will be inspired to make her own life-shaping decision in accordance with his.

As the heir to Davide's trade secrets, Giovanna is not the only one to undergo a process of radical personal change. Through his encounter with Giovanna, Davide has finally come to terms with his tormented past. By giving this young life the strength to change its negative course, Davide has in some measure expiated his guilt over the death of Simone. By the end of the film, we learn the destination of Davide's deranged wandering in the opening scenes: the old man was looking for his secret meeting place with Simone in the mad hope of finding him there and of belatedly receiving his pardon. (Psychologists would call this closure.) As long as his agonizing search went on, 'I was not yet able to die' (176), Davide tells Giovanna. Thanks to the young woman's intervention in his life, thanks to her willingness both to let him bear witness and to live out his legacy, Davide can finally lay to rest the unquiet ghost of Simone, and therefore can finally come to rest himself. The film's concluding scene is set, significantly, in the secret place where the lovers left their messages in 1943, and there Giovanna walks alone, dictating a letter, in voice-over, to the memory of the old man. The camera lingers on Giovanna's eyes, in extreme close-up, for an inordinately long time, and we realize that her *occhi* are now our *finestra di fronte*.[11]

With this ending, the titular image has completed its transformation, beginning as the aperture onto a *telenovela* world of romantic escape and progressing on to an alternative vision of experience, filtered through a consciousness scarred by historical and personal trauma. It is significant that while the first *finestra di fronte* involved physical vision, and allowed for the narcissistic self-mirroring of reflective glass, the second *finestra di fronte* remains metaphoric. In order to appropriate the perspective of Davide, to see through the window of his eyes, Giovanna had to go beyond narcissistic self-reflection to entertain a perspective that was truly other. Only in this way could she gain the strength to make a free and conscious choice outside the limits of the *telenovela* plot.

With the final incarnation of the window image, Ozpetek turns his film back on us. As Giovanna looks into the camera her eyes become windows for our alternative glance at the world. We too can still choose, Ozpetek is saying, and his own film has chosen to be that other kind of *finestra di fronte* – the kind that signifies, not romantic escape, but the passionate vocation for creativity and responsibility that is Davide and Giovanna's legacy to us.

---

11 See Cozzi, 'L'ombra del passato che ritorna,' 38.

Postscript – A Glimpse at 2004: *Il servo ungherese* (The Hungarian Servant) and *La fuga degli innocenti* (The Flight of the Innocents)

A film that partakes of the internationalizing impulse of much Italian Holocaust cinema[1] is Massimo Piesco and Giorgio Molteni's *Il servo ungherese* (2004), whose very title announces its eastern European focus. The story takes place in the Teufelwald concentration camp, and it foregrounds the relationship between the commanding officer, Major August Dailermann, his wife Franziska, and the Hungarian prisoner who becomes their personal servant, Miklos Cohen. Dailermann, indifferent to the genocidal activities of the camp, happily leaves its management to the young and fiendish Lieutenant, Tross, preferring to spend his time listening to opera music and bickering with his wife. Franziska, in turn, despises her husband's musical tastes, complains bitterly of her boredom, and spares no opportunity to remind August of her nostalgia for the glamorous social scene left behind in Berlin. When the learned and refined Miklos enters their service, Franziska's character undergoes a marked change. In the edifying company of Miklos, her longing for high-cultural improvement begins to take shape, and when he identifies one of the paintings retrieved from the deportees' belongings as a genuine Kokoshka, the servant's interpretation of the work has a profound impact on Franziska's evolving sense of self. The painting, is in fact, a woman's portrait and it inspires Franziska to

---

1 Here I am referring to two subcategories of trans-Italian films made by Italians – those that include Italian characters and are, at least partially, set in Italy – *Il grido della terra, Pasqualino settebellezze, La linea del fiume, La tregua, Perlasca,* and *Senza confini* – and those that are absolutely devoid of Italian characters and are impervious to the question of *italianità* – *L'ebreo errante, Kapò, Andremo in città, Portiere di notte, Jona che visse nella balena,* and *Canone inverso.*

have her own likeness portrayed by an artist recruited from among the inmates of Teufelwald. When seven volunteers step forward, Miklos convinces Franziska to allow all of them to audition for the honour of capturing her essence on canvas. Dailermann, jealous of his wife's artistic patronage, commissions Tross to create its musical counterpart, and a small orchestra, complete with an operatic soprano, takes its place next to Franziska's atelier. The woman's conversionary process reaches its culmination when she learns that Teufelwald is not really an industrial centre at all, but a 'factory of corpses,' and that her patronage amounts to a stay of execution for the artists in residence. This revelation opens her to Miklos's appeals for help in his rescue campaign, and that very evening Franziska confronts her husband with the horrific truth that she has learned. August is profoundly shaken by his wife's humanitarian stance, which causes him, in turn, to question the dictates of the Reich. In a dramatic gesture of solicitude, Dailermann orders a special meal for his musicians and Franziska's painters, who celebrate this gift of food and drink with a spontaneous concert of thanks. But the aesthetic vacation from atrocity is short lived – Dailermann's request for a transfer has been granted, and the direction of the camp will devolve to the ambitious and blood-thirsty Tross. Franziska's joy in her imminent return to Berlin overrides her newfound social conscience, and she scoffs not only at Miklos's plea to remember the prisoners' plight, but even at her husband's own query, 'Don't you want to know what will happen to them?' – proof that Dailermann has undergone a genuine conversion, whereas hers has been a mere pose, a temporary ploy to combat her boredom at Teufelwald.

'You have no values, you are empty,' August had said to Franziska early in the film in response to her litany of complaints. From the very start, then, Franziska is presented as a blank canvas, an empty vessel waiting to be filled with the meaning that *il servo ungherese* is so well equipped to supply. His pedagogy begins with a line from the Greek poet Simonides: 'as beasts we live' – and he proceeds to guide Franziska to an interpretation of the Kokoshka portrait that transcends physical appearances to fathom the hidden truths of the soul. When Franziska asks to have her own portrait painted, it is in the hope that her interior meaning will materialize on the canvas and that she will emerge as more than just a beautiful shell of a woman, more than a mere decorative covering for a vast spiritual void.

Like *Canone inverso*, *Il servo ungherese* sets up culture as the most powerful antidote to the forces of Nazi oppression, and Jewish artistic accomplishments form the basis of the film's argument against German super-race ideology. Even the ghoulish Tross admits that 'these Jews can do much more than just transact business,' and Franziska objects to her husband's defence of genocide in the interests of purifying the Fatherland when she asks, 'How can you say this when we both know they have the capacity to make our nation great?' It is, of course, Miklos who gives voice to the film's central philosophical premise when he encourages the seven portrait painters to persist in the belief that prolonging their activity may indeed stave off death. 'One can also stand up to those who mistreat us,' Miklos claims, 'by opposing civilization to barbarity, sensitivity to brutality, culture to uncouthness.'

Such a formulation goes far towards justifying the film's own aestheticizing tendencies, for *Il servo ungherese* is indeed 'delirious with aestheticism' (to use Pasolini's apt term)[2] – it revels in the operatic soundtrack that is diegetically required by August's musical tastes, it luxuriates in Franziska's highly manicured beauty and her magnificent wardrobe, and it delights in the Nazi chic of the set design. The self-conscious artifice of *Il servo ungherese* extends to the dialogue, delivered with a mannered *gravitas* that borders on the absurd, and punctuated by pedantic philosophical pronouncements that would seem tongue-in-cheek were it not for the absolute earnestness and virtue of the protagonist himself in uttering these lines. We see the risky extremes to which the film's aestheticism can lead in the scene of Franziska's dance to the music of Bizet's 'Habañera.' The Jewish prisoners, justifiably eager to exploit the lady's narcissism and her hunger for high culture, encourage Franziska to enact Carmen's seductive movements of stereotypical 'gypsy' abandon. Like the Jewish prisoners who play along with the performance in the illusion of its life-saving potential, the movie camera becomes an accomplice of Franziska's dance, using film techniques – a montage of extreme close-ups of discrete body movements – that reveal its own prostration before her beauty.

In the face of the film's extravagant aestheticism, two possible readings emerge – one veering towards parody, the other towards personification allegory. Foremost among the parodic elements are the caricaturized treatment of the film's main characters – Dailermann and Tross are descendents of a long line of Nazi villains whose Italian pater-

---

2 Pasolini applies this description to Antonioni's vision in *Il deserto rosso*. See the ground-breaking essay 'Cinema di poesia,' in *Empirismo eretico* (Milan: Garzanti, 1981), 181.

nity may be easily traced to the figure of Bergmann in *Roma città aperta*, and whose most recent incarnations include Bleiber in *Perlasca* and the executioner of Katchen and her daughters in *Il cielo cade*. The gorgeous, alluring Aryan goddess Franziska harks back to the divas of vintage Hollywood cinema, and in particular Marlene Dietrich, while Miklos is doubly stereotyped as a Jewish intellectual endowed with the cosmopolitanism of prewar Budapest.

Parody would also explain the heavy-handed dialogue, the excessive artifice of the virtuoso set designs, the lack of in-depth character development, and the predictability of the film's narrative structure. But to limit our reading of *Il servo ungherese* to Nazi kitsch would be to commit a category error of considerable proportions. For one thing, the film lacks the playfulness and the dialogic relationship between past and present artistic practice that are prime ingredients of parody. More important, to consign this film to the category of the parodic would be to dismiss the obvious seriousness of its didactic intent. Instead, if we read the film's aesthetic exuberance as a sign of its aspiration to play out the very idea of art that it counterposes to Nazi injustice, then we are moving to the level of allegory, and the film becomes a collective Psychomachia, a war of personified ideas, an extended exercise in prosopopeia with Miklos as the embodiment of European high culture and Tross as the incarnation of Nazi barbarism in the battle for the Dailermanns' soul. *Il servo ungherese* thus becomes an admirable attempt to allegorize the opposition between art and brute force that *Canone inverso* had so successfully entrusted to the mechanisms of melodrama.

Sharing in the international scope of *Il servo ungherese*, but heavily invested in the question of *italianità*, is Leone Pompucci's made-for-TV mini-series *La fuga degli innocenti* (2004). The film tells the story of a group of Jewish children from Poland, Austria, and Germany who converge on Zagreb and from there are led on a perilous journey to Slovenia (Ljubljana) and Italy (vicinity of Modena), before reaching safety in Switzerland. Loosely based on a true historical episode, *La fuga degli innocenti* embroiders the record with forays into sentimental romance, spy-film intrigue, and comedy in order to engage the sympathies of the broadest possible TV audience. Using intertitles to provide spatio-temporal markers (Vienna 1941, Dresden 1941, Berlin 1941), the film introduces three distinct groups of children who will be sent off to Zagreb under the custody of the Italian rescue network Delasem. Directing and funding this effort is attorney Diego Levi, played by a magisterial Max von Sydow, who persuades the Fascist Minister of the Interior to guarantee safe asylum for these imperiled children. Developing in tandem with the rescue narrative is the persecution plot, led by the vicious Colonel Kreig, who cuddles his own small daughter while setting out methodically to track down and exterminate the twenty-four children who have eluded Nazi grasp. Of utmost interest is the fact that every sequence of the persecution plot includes a Nazi character who is filming the proceedings – shooting a 16-mm documentary of the 'German side' of the story. This detail comes to the foreground each time that *La fuga degli innocenti* cross-cuts to the Nazi pursuit and we see these events in black and white after a transition from colour footage that included the internalized documentary filmmaker within the frame. Pompucci's insistence on this technique is rich with promise, for it reveals both the Third Reich's mania for documenting its heinous workings and his own film's insistence on using the medium to expose and denounce those abominations.

Leading the children's contingent is the film's protagonist, Joseph Belzer, a teacher in the Jewish school of Zagreb whose headmaster is his father, a rabbi and community leader. When the Jews of Zagreb are rounded up for deportation, Joseph evades Nazi capture and is invested by his father with the task of individual and collective survival. The protagonist reluctantly accepts this responsibility, overcoming a series of personal scruples in order to save his young charges through the use of ingenious expedients: dressing them up as Croatian Eustache youths to get them across the border to Slovenia; inviting an accomplished con artist, Rainer Goldsand, to join the group and aid with illegal transactions; disguising himself as a priest; and bribing a smuggler to lead the way to Switzerland.

It is the youthfulness of these refugees – the fact that they are children and therefore *innocenti* – that both targets them for Nazi persecution and ensures their rescue at the hands of others. The SS commander is especially chagrinned that *children* could elude Nazi entrapment and insists that their capture would have supreme symbolic value in affirming the authority of the Reich. But, of course, it is their very innocence and vulnerability that elicits the custodial impulses of the various adults with whom the children come in contact: the Italian military of Ljubljana and Verona; the partisan groups of Slovenia and Emilia; and, finally, the Swiss border guards. In addition to evoking adult protectiveness, the children personify the *tabula rasa* perspective that invites even the most jaded observers to experience anew the enormity of the Shoah. In this respect, *La fuga degli innocenti* joins the subgenre of Holocaust films (*La linea del fiume, Jona che visse nella balena, La vita è bella, Il cielo cade*) that make children the focalizers of the horror against which we adults, privy to historical knowledge, have built up a series of cognitive and moral defences. Not surprisingly, then, it is the children who serve as spokesmen or sounding boards for the most agonizing possible questions: 'Why does God permit evil?' 'We're always fleeing – is it because we've done something bad?' Most dramatically, five-year-old Rachel stands before a crucifix (covered in canvas) and asks Jesus to go to God and plea for His return to the children of Israel.

Linked to the theological problem of reconciling divine benevolence with the existence of evil is the biblical theme of Jewish accession to the Promised Land. As in *Jona che visse nella balena*, Palestine is the cherished but unattainable destination of every lap in the 'flight of the innocents.' Diego Levi lures the group to Ljubljana with the prospect of immediate embarkation for the Holy Land, and when they are diverted to Italy, the most vocal of the children, Otto, complains, 'We were supposed to go to Palestine. We're screwed.' Instead, the film makes a strong argument for Italian ascent to the rank of Terra Promessa. Though Italy is just a way station on the road to safety in Switzerland, the sojourn in Villa Iris outside Modena is presented as an idyllic oasis amidst the horrors of war, and Italians emerge as the true redeemers of this imperiled group, the natural guardians of the children's fragile and precious *innocenza*. Indeed, it is no mere coincidence that in titling the film *La fuga degli innocenti*, Pompucci strategically invokes two Gospel episodes that confirm the Italians' salvific role in this story. I speak of *La strage degli innocenti* (the massacre of the innocents), and the *Fuga in Egitto* (the flight into Egypt) – references that elevate the Italian efforts on behalf of these children to the level of Salvation History. In so doing, the film gives its unconditional support to the stereotype of *italiani brava gente*.

From the very start of the film, Italy assumes a conspicuous, if somewhat unspecified, role in the rescue operation. 'We have to hope that the Italians hurry up,' remarks Rabbi Belzer, as the SS noose tightens around the Jewish community of Zagreb. Though at this point we do not know who these mysterious Italians are, and what mechanism needs to be speeded up, the link between Italy and Jewish salvation has been firmly established. We soon learn that Italians are the organizers of Delasem and that the children will be better protected in Fascist-occupied Slovenia than in Nazi-affiliated Croatia. The belief in Italian benevolence is reinforced by Helene, a French refugee who meets the *innocenti* on the train to Ljubljana and announces her desire to seek sanctuary in that part of Yugoslavia controlled by forces from Italy. Though Rainer Goldsand harbours profound misgivings – 'I don't like the face of these Italians, they're Nazis, why should they help us?' and though the co-commander of the military unit is a staunch anti-Semite, preferring the term *giudei* to *ebrei* because 'they are descendents of Judah, the one who betrayed our Lord,' it is the *italiani brava gente* label that will underwrite the group's survival in Slovenia. Joseph will invoke that stereotype in his initial plea to Major Ferretti upon arriving at Ljubljana. 'We heard that you Italians behave with honour in war and don't persecute men, women, and children because they're of a different religion.' In Major Ferretti, Joseph has found a receptive audience for such an appeal – ready to activate his own membership in a collective of *italiani brava gente* and, as a platoon leader, able to realize that ideal in microcosm. We eventually learn that Ferretti is a kind of Italian Everyman, a farmer from the north whose experience of the annual pig slaughtering had sensitized him to the horrors of violence and to the atrocity of subjecting 'true Christians' (and here the term refers to human beings in general, in their capacity for spiritual salvation) to such suffering. Like the Italian collectivity for which he stands, Ferretti had been swept up in the mass enthusiasm for the regime – 'Mussolini gave us dignity and pulled us up' – but he now adds ruefully that Il Duce 'got us into this war,' reflecting the growing disenchantment of his *brava gente* with the catastrophic results of the Axis alliance.

The second half of the film may be seen as a sustained effort to discredit Rainer Goldsand's blanket condemnation of *italianità*. Again and again, the film will insist on the distinction between Fascism and Nazism, and Italian benevolence will take the form of a simple geographic observation: 'We're not in Germany, we're in Italian territory. Where do you think you are?' These are the words of the Fascist commander in Verona, where the train bound for Modena is stopped by Nazi officials who want to reroute the children to Germany. There follows a dramatic stand-off between Italian and German troops, rifles pointed at each other, against the background of the single train car containing the child refugees, point of contention between 'allies' who obviously differ on questions of territorial jurisdiction and race. The stand-off comes to a non-violent end when the Fascist commander receives a phonogram from the Ministry of the Interior (thanks to the timely intervention of Diego Levi) that orders the Nazis to desist on the grounds that the refugees may have distant Italian ancestries that need to be determined. In the German commander's rejoinder – 'How could you be our allies? You lack the minimum necessary honourability' – the film offers the most eloquent possible testimony to the *italiani brava gente* reading of Holocaust history.

The final scene dedicated to the distinction between Italian and German racial policy has a striking meta-cinematic component. A car has pulled up to Villa Iris and the military cameraman who has been documenting the 'Nazi' side of events proceeds to film the building and grounds. Enraged by this infringement on a government-protected facility, Professor Mortara, the director of Villa Iris, snarls, 'You can't do anything. Here we're not in Germany!' This statement redounds not only to the limited political authority of these Nazi intruders (the time period of this scene precedes the fall of Mussolini and the subsequent German occupation of Italy), but to the specious truth-claims of a movie camera promising to 'document' its monolithic, authoritative, and soon-to-be-defeated version of history. The rebuke 'You can't do anything. Here we're not in Germany' may well apply both to the alternative history that the *italiani brava gente* are capable of producing in defiance of an unpopular regime and also to the cinema that represents that exceptional historical course.

Epilogue: The Holocaust, the Cinema, and 'the Italian Case' in Ettore Scola's '43–'97[1]

In the summer of 2002, while shopping on Rome's Via dei Giubbonari, named for the jacket-makers who ply their trade there, I noticed that the cashier who rang up my purchase was wearing a necklace with a mezuzah, a pendant encasing a parchment inscribed with verses from the Torah. Never one to pass up a research lead, I asked the gentleman, named Angelo Di Cori, about his background, and explained to him my project on Italian Holocaust memory. Without further prompting, Di Cori poured out the saga of his family's travails during the Nazi occupation of Rome, and offered to give me a copy of the written testimony he had produced at the behest of his grandchildren. Di Cori's account was one of narrow escape, of hiding, of subsistence-level survival tactics, and, finally, of his fifteen-year-old brother's arrest, internment in Regina Coeli prison, and ultimate deportation to Auschwitz.

Among the many moving elements of this wrenching tale, I was struck by its title, '16 ottobre 1943.' Though the events of Di Cori's narration spanned a period of many months, he had singled out the day of the Nazi raid on the ghetto of Rome to conjure up the entirety of his family's Holocaust ordeal. My subsequent research came to confirm the synecdochal value of that date for all Italian Jewry. It signified a kind of primal wound, an unprecedented outrage, the violation of the protective cocoon that the ghetto walls – once prison-like, but ever since the Risorgimento, welcoming and reassuring – had come to offer.

It is with this primal wound that Ettore Scola's short film, significantly entitled '43–'97, begins. By now no expository captions are needed to identify the day and month, nor the location of this nefarious

---

1 Scola's film is included in the DVD accompanying this book.

event. It is enough to show the licence plate of a waiting truck featuring the stylized double S, or the careening motorcycles, or the lines of guards, or the solemn parade of people meekly advancing with their suitcases and satchels, to know what is taking place. Scola's black-and-white camera-work is restrained in its documenting of this relentless round-up, showing tenements emptying out in sad processions under assorted arches, down staircases, and across walkways, alternating group shots with close-ups of beautifully sculpted faces and, in one instance, of a white-bearded, black-scarfed old man who could come right out of an art-historical engraving. There is one particular little boy who recurs throughout the sequence and who we expect to become the focalizer of this event – the set of eyes through which we will experience the narration. With his jaunty cap and his calf-length pants, he recalls the heartbreaking and well-known image of the child with the yellow star immortalized in the Warsaw ghetto photograph that has entered into the archive of collective memory as a prime signifier of Holocaust atrocity.

The film cuts to an interior scene of a woman draping a blanket over a folded-up bed pushed up against a wall. After brutally ushering her out, the SS recede down the steps and Scola's camera closes in on the mattress to reveal a boy peeking his head out, putting on his glasses, and emerging from hiding once the coast is clear. Escaping by a back doorway and leaping to the ground, the boy catches the eye of an SS soldier who takes off after him at breakneck speed. Using parallel montage to great advantage, Scola inter-cuts between the frantic chase through the curved and cobblestone streets of the ghetto and the solemn, slow round-up of passive deportees. Acoustically, this contrast takes the form of a musical counterpoint: the escape is accompanied by an animated and anxious piano score, while the round-up takes place against the backdrop of a mournful violin piece resembling a Hebraic lament. The Italian characters in this sequence remain in utter silence, and the only words we hear are the German orders *Raus, Schnell*. Significantly, the last shot of the Nazi sweep features the little boy with the cap who climbs onto the truck and vanishes from the film. He is the boy who doesn't make it, and his image remains etched in our memory, even as we cheer on the other boy in his successful efforts to evade Nazi capture.

It is the marquee of the neighbourhood 'Cine' that beckons our protagonist towards safety. As he ducks into the theatre, the woman in the ticket booth feigns indifference, and his Nazi pursuer continues down the street. Within the theatre, a newsreel announcer boasts of the 'crushing victories' of German forces and touts the complete agreement of the Axis countries 'in the political and military sphere.' Documentary footage of the Hitler-Mussolini partnership is succeeded by a clip of the Führer's deranged and incendiary speech-making. This then modulates into its parodic re-enactment in the frenzied oratorical gibberish of Charlie Chaplin's *The Great Dictator*, followed by a montage of Italian film clips that traverse the period from 1945 to 1997, including:

1 *Roma, città aperta* (Rome, Open City, Roberto Rossellini, 1945) – Pina (Anna Magnani) runs after the Nazi truck carrying off her fiancé Francesco (Francesco Grandjacquet). She is shot down before the eyes of her son, Marcello (Vito Annichiarico), the priest Don Pietro (Aldo Fabrizi), and the entire community of which she has been so important a part.

2 *Ladri di biciclette* (Bicycle Thief, Vittorio De Sica, 1948) – Antonio (Lamberto Maggiorani) races off on a stolen bike to the shock and horror of his son, Bruno (Enzo Staiola).

3 *I soliti ignoti* (Big Deal on Madonna Street, Mario Monicelli, 1958) – Dante Cruciani (Totò) demonstrates his system of safe-cracking for the benefit of his incompetent cohorts.

4 *Il sorpasso* (The Easy Life, Dino Risi, 1962) – Roberto Mariani (Jean-Louis Trintignant) and Bruno Cortona (Vittorio Gassman) careen around a curve in their sports car and are met by an oncoming truck.

5 *Il gattopardo* (The Leopard, Luchino Visconti, 1963) – Don Fabrizio, Prince of Salina (Burt Lancaster) dances a waltz with Angelica (Claudia Cardinale), signalling the induction of his nephew's wealthy bourgeois bride into the upper reaches of the Sicilian aristocracy.

6 *Amarcord* (Federico Fellini, 1974) – When the ocean liner *Rex*, symbol of Fascist pretensions to world power, appears to an awe-struck populace, a blind member of the gathering insistently asks, 'What's it like?'

7 *Una giornata particolare* (A Special Day, Ettore Scola, 1977) – The Fascist housewife Antonietta (Sophia Loren) confesses her infatuation with the gay, politically subversive Gabriele (Marcello Mastroianni), admitting, 'Ever since this morning I've been watching you' as they fold the laundry on their apartment rooftop.

8 *Ricomincio da tre* (I'm Starting from Three, Massimo Troisi, 1981) – Marta (Fiorenza Marchegiani) announces to her boyfriend Gaetano (Massimo Troisi) that she is pregnant and they discuss what to name the child.

9 *Nuovo cinema paradiso* (Cinema Paradiso, Giuseppe Tornatore, 1988) – Alfredo (Philippe Noiret) explains to the child Totò (Sal-

vatore Cascio) his philosophy for choosing enemies and friends.

10 *Palombella rossa* (Red Wood Pidgeon, Nanni Moretti, 1989). Michele Apicella (Moretti) inveighs against a journalist (Mariella Valentini) for her use of trendy jargon.

11 *Ladro di bambini* (Stolen Children, Gianni Amelio, 1992). In a train compartment, Antonio (Enrico Lo Verso) looks at the two hapless children, Rosetta (Valentina Scalici) and Luciano (Giuseppe Ieracitano), whom he must escort to an orphanage.

12 *La tregua* (The Truce, Francesco Rosi, 1997) – A throng of survivors rushes towards freedom as the gate of Auschwitz is torn down.

Guiding Scola's selection of films to be included in this montage are a variety of factors, including the most obvious one of personal taste. A number of the clips are from ground-breaking films within the history of postwar Italian cinema, as well as some that represent an array of genres – neorealism, *commedia all'italiana*, *cinema politico* – and auteurs – Rossellini, De Sica, Visconti, Fellini, Moretti, Tornatore, Amelio, Rosi, and, needless to say, Scola himself. Many of the clips include child protagonists, and most foreground both their own spectacular nature and internalized responses to their uses of cinematic spectacle.

At the end of the montage, the lights of the theatre go on to reveal that, in place of the boy escapee of 1943, there sits a white-haired gentleman cleaning his glasses. We have transitioned now to colour, but there is an acoustic throwback to the 1940s segment in the sound of footsteps echoing on the cobblestones and the return of the hurried piano music that had accompanied the Nazi chase. At this point, an adolescent of African descent runs panting into the theatre and sits one row behind our aged protagonist. Recognizing his younger self in this desperate fugitive, the Jewish gentleman bestows upon him a knowing smile – one of understanding and consolation. Then, both of them sink down into their seats as the lights go off and the credits for Scola's film scroll down the screen-within-the-screen.[2]

At its most obvious, '43-'97 is about the link between the past and the

---

2 There are, in fact, two versions of the film '43–'97 and they vary slightly with regard to the film clips shown in the montage. Because Schola's closing credits were missing from the digitized version of the film provided to me, I spliced those from the longer VHS copy onto the end of the DVD. For this reason, the list of films cited in the closing credits does not quite correspond to the clips actually included in the DVD. Whereas the credits mention *Blowup*, *Il portiere di notte*, and *Il postino*, the DVD version has substituted for these titles *Il gattopardo* and *Ricomincio da tre*.

present of racial intolerance, about the urgent need to revisit Holocaust history now, lest the logic of persecution visit itself upon the new Italian 'other' of Third World immigration. As Scola will write in the preface to the screenplay of *Concorrenza sleale*, 'to discover being considered "different" due to birth or race – it happened in the past to Jews and blacks, it is happening today to immigrants and *extracomunitari* (those outside the European Union).'[3] On the meta-cinematic level, the film is a complex study of the relationship between off-screen historical context and on-screen cinematic representation – in other words, the film asks us what it means to seek sanctuary in a movie theatre. Cynically understood, such a turning away from the cobblestone streets suggests that cinema is a place of denial, escape, or withdrawal from the arena of necessary historical action. But the relationship that Scola posits between the montage on the screen-within-the-screen and the frame story of the two minority fugitives from persecution is far more complex and nuanced. By embedding a panoramic chronicle of Italian film within a narrative of searing historical allusiveness, Scola is confronting one of the largest and most abstract of theoretical issues: the connection between the film medium and its referent in the life of the country, or, in specifically semiotic terms, he is exploring the link between cinematic signifier and historic signified. In the Italian case, Scola has always been a proponent of the particularly close ties between film and national history. 'The specificity of Italian cinema,' he claimed in a recent interview, 'as opposed to the cinemas of France or Germany, is that of being so intertwined with reality that it scans *la vicenda Italia* (the Italy case). Our cinema has always been social chronicle.'[4]

Scola's montage of clips from 1943 to 1997 forms a kind of para-history – one that at every point asks us to question the way in which what is happening outside the theatre is mirrored, critiqued, transformed, transcended, overlooked, sanitized, etc., on screen. Perhaps more than a para-history, the montage creates a simulacrum of history – each clip has the power to conjure up and signify the moment of its making – *Roma città aperta* is equated with the struggles of the Roman Resistance, *Il sorpasso* is the Italy of 'Il boom,' *Palombella rossa* heralds the waning of the Italian Left, and so forth. In his choice of clips, then, Scola has selected cinematic signifiers that not only represent, but have

---

3 Ettore Scola, *Concorrenza sleale* (Turin: Lindau, 2001), 5.
4 See the interview with Maria Pia Fusco, 'Scola: uno specchio per i giovani,' *La repubblica*, 16 July 2004, 45.

actually come to replace in the public mind, the historical and cultural signifieds that produced them. This blurring of the distinction between the cinematic medium and its external referents is made explicit in the confusion of levels between Scola's 'outer film' – the story of the Jewish escapee from the ghetto round-up – and the montage we see on the screen-within-the-screen. Such a collapsing of levels occurs when the closing credits for Scola's outer film are projected on the screen-within-the screen, so that the boundaries between outside and inside, container and contained, break down. The implications for us in the viewing audience are not far to seek. When the elderly gentleman turns around to acknowledge the young victim of persecution within his own audience, it is as if the film were turning to us and asking us to confront the social injustices in our midst.

Thus, '43–'97 makes a strong case for the defence of the cinema against charges of escapist withdrawal from the cobblestone streets of the historical arena. It is the cinema's commitment to monitor, critique, and engage in the progress of *la vicenda Italia* that can provide the impetus to corrective action. The refuge offered by the movie theatre points to the ultimate power of the medium to intervene in the off-screen world, to bring about a condition of enlightenment and social desire that will render obsolete the very rescue operation that the film performs for the protagonists in the years 1943 and 1997.

It is significant that Scola's plea for the Utopian potential of cinema should pivot on the issue of Holocaust representation. By bracketing his short film with an allusion to the round-up of Roman Jewry on 16 October 1943 and Rosi's cinematic treatment of the Shoah in 1997, Scola is foregrounding the process by which this repressed history has belatedly become the subject of cinematic representation. In his decision to frame the film with a Holocaust narrative, but to embed within it a micro-history of Italian cinema, Scola is constructing a 'representational parable' – an instructive tale about the medium's need to take on this repressed chapter of the Second World War past. Such a strategy vindicates both the specificity and the greater applicability of the Italian Holocaust case. While '43–'97 asserts the uniqueness of this particular 'recovered memory,' it also insists on the cinema's responsibility to challenge all such instances of public unwillingness to face disquieting truths, past or present.

I began this study by arguing that Italian films devoted to the Jewish plight under Fascism and the Nazi Final Solution failed to coalesce into a coherent, continuous cinematic tradition. Filmmakers choosing to broach this subject seemed unaware of a corpus of previous works that they could reference in constructive, polemic, or even parodic ways. In other words, there was no representational memory on which such directors could draw. Scola's film both addresses that absence and resolves it. By locating *La tregua* at the end of his montage, he suggests that Rosi's achievement in his Holocaust epic, and by extension the outpouring of films that followed the end of the Cold War, is not the product of a specific subgenre within Italian film production, but of the entire course of a national medium dedicated to chronicling *la vicenda Italia*. It took nearly five decades for Italian film history to meet this particular representational challenge – one that, it is hoped, will help usher in a new phase of historiographic openness and demographic inclusiveness in the forging of the Italian national self.

Bibliography

Antonutti, Raffaella, and Paolo Finn. 'Quando il cielo cade.' *Cinemasessanta* 41 (September–October 2000).

Bacon, Henry. *Visconti: Explorations of Beauty and Decay.* Cambridge: Cambridge University Press, 1998.

Benigni, Roberto, and Vincenzo Cerami. *La vita è bella.* Turin: Einaudi, 1998.

Bonatesta, Giorgio Vincenzo. *'Perlasca – un eroe italiano.'* Available at http://www.itismaglie.it/html/pdidattici/Perlasca.

Caffaz, Ugo, ed. *Discriminazione e persecuzione degli ebrei nell'Italia fascista.* Florence: La Giuntina, 1988.

Cannistraro, Philip V. 'Mussolini and Fascist Anti-Semitism: Turning Point of a Regime.' In *The Italian Jewish Experience*, ed. Thomas P. DiNapoli. Stony Brook, NY: Forum Italicum Publishing, 2000.

Cozzi, Emilio. 'L'ombra del passato che ritorna.' *Cineforum* 43 (April 2003).

Creed, Barbara. 'Horror and the Monstrous-Feminine: An Imaginary Abjection.' In *Feminist Film Theory: A Reader*, ed. Sue Thornham. New York: New York University Press, 1999.

Deaglio, Enrico. *La banalità del bene: Storia di Giorgio Perlasca.* Milan: Feltrinelli, 2002.

– 'Perlasca, l'uomo che sfidò Hitler.' *L'unità*, 19 January 2002. Also available at http://www.ilportoritrovato.net/html/perlasca.html.

de Gennaro, Adele. *'Perlasca – un eroe italiano.'* Available at http://www.televisione.it/articoli/2002/01/24/251316/phP.

Deleuze, Gilles. *The Time Image.* Trans. Hugh Tomlinson and Robert Galeta. Minneapolis: University of Minnesota Press, 1997.

Della Seta, Daniel. 'Quell'eroe un po' guascone che imbrogliò i nazisti.' Available at http://www.shalom.it/2.02/P.html.

Derrida, Jacques. *The Specters of Marx.* Trans. Peggy Kamuf. New York: Routledge, 1994.

De Santi, Gualtiero. *Carlo Lizzani.* Rome: Gremese, 2001.

Ellero, Roberto. *Ettore Scola.* Florence: La Nuova Italia, 1988.

Finn, Paolo. 'Concorrenza sleale.' *Cinemasessanta* 42 (March–April 2001).

Foa, Anna. *Ebrei in Europa: Dalla Peste Nera all'emancipazione.* Milan: Mondadori, 2001.

Foucault, Michel. *Discipline and Punish: The Birth of the Prison.* Trans. Alan Sheridan. New York: Random House, 1977.

Freud, Sigmund. 'Beyond the Pleasure Principle.' In *The Standard Edition of the Complete Psychological Works,* trans. and ed. James Strachey, vol. 18. London: Hogarth Press, 1953–74.

– 'Mourning and Melancholia.' In *The Standard Edition of the Complete Psychological Works,* vol. 14.

Fusco, Maria Pia. 'Scola: uno specchio per i giovani.' *La repubblica,* 16 July 2004.

Galluccio, Fabio. *I Lager in Italia: la memoria sepolta nei duecento luoghi di deportazione fascisti.* Civezzano: Nonluoghi, 2003.

Ghirelli, Massimo. *Gillo Pontecorvo.* Florence: La Nuova Italia, 1978.

Girelli-Carasi, Fabio. 'Italian-Jewish Memoirs and the Discourse of Identity.' In *The Most Ancient of Minorities,* ed. Stanislao G. Pugliese. Westport, CT: Greenwood Press, 2002.

Gramsci, Antonio. *Il Risorgimento.* Ed. Maria Corti. Turin: Einaudi, 1952.

Guslandi, Valerio. 'Doppio colpo di fulmine: *La finestra di fronte.*' *Ciak,* April 2003.

Incontri con il cinema italiano, ed. Antonio Vitti. Caltanisetta: Salvatore Sciascia, 2003.

Insdorf, Annette. *Indelible Shadows: Film and the Holocaust.* Cambridge: Cambridge University Press, 2002.

Jews in Italy under Fascist and Nazi Rule 1922–1945, ed. Joshua D. Zimmerman. New York: Cambridge University Press, 2005.

Langer, Lawrence. *Holocaust Testimonies: The Ruins of Memory.* New Haven: Yale University Press, 1991.

Levi, Primo. *The Reawakening.* Trans. Stuart Woolf. New York: Touchstone, 1995.

– *Se questo è un uomo, La tregua.* Turin: Einaudi, 1989.

– *I sommersi e i salvati.* Turin: Einaudi, 1991.

– *Survival at Auschwitz.* Trans. Stuart Woolf. New York: Touchstone, 1996.

Liberti, Fabrizio. 'Il cielo cade.' *Cineforum* 40 (August–September 2000).

Loy, Rosetta. *First Words: A Childhood in Fascist Italy.* Trans. Gregory Conti. New York: Henry Holt, 2000.

- *La parola ebreo*. Turin: Einaudi, 1997.
- 'Per Rosetta Loy la memoria è anche assunzione di responsabilità.' At http://www.wuz.it/archivio/cafeletterario.it/intervista/loy.html.

Lukács, Georg. *The Historical Novel*. Trans. Hannah and Stanley Mitchell. London: Merlin, 1962.
- *Realism in Our Time: Literature and the Class Struggle*. Trans. John and Necke Mander. New York and Evanston: Harper & Row, 1964.

Lusardi, Stefano. 'Il dolce è la vita.' *Ciak*, March 2003.

Magretta, Joan, and William Magretta. 'Lina Wertmuller and the Tradition of Italian Carnivalesque Comedy.' *Genre* 12 (Spring 1979).

Marcus, Millicent. *After Fellini: National Cinema in the Postmodern Age*. Baltimore: Johns Hopkins University Press, 2002.
- *Filmmaking by the Book: Italian Cinema and Literary Adaptation*. Baltimore: Johns Hopkins University Press, 1993.

Marrone, Gaetana. *The Gaze and The Labyrinth: The Cinema of Liliana Cavani*. Princeton, NJ: Princeton University Press, 2000.

Martini, Emanuela. '*Canone inverso*.' *Film TV*. 22 February 2000. Reprinted in *Rassegna stampa cinematografica*. Bergamo: S.A.S., 2000.

Maurensig, Paolo. *Canone inverso*. Milano: Oscar Mondadori, 1996.
- *Canone Inverso: A Novel*. Trans. Jenny McPhee. New York: Holt, 1999.

Mazzetti, Lorenza. *Il cielo cade*. Palermo: Sellerio, 2000.

Miccichè, Lino. 'Il cinema non cambia il mondo ma può farci riflettere. Una conversazione con Ettore Scola.' In *Trevico-Cinecittà: L'avventuroso viaggio di Ettore Scola*, ed. Vito Zagarrio. Venice: Marsilio, 2002.
- *Luchino Visconti: Un profilo critico*. Venice: Marsilio, 1996.

Morandini, Morandino. 'Il bello di Benigni.' *Cineforum* 370 (December 1997).

Morante, Elsa. *History, A Novel*. Trans. William Weaver. New York: Random House, 1984.
- *La Storia, Romanzo*. Turin: Einaudi, 1974.

Mulvey, Laura. 'Visual Pleasure and Narrative Cinema.' *Screen* 16:3 (1975).

The New Harvard Dictionary of Music, ed. Don Michael Randel. Cambridge, MA: The Belknap Press of Harvard University Press, 1986.

Pasolini, Pier Paolo. 'Cinema di poesia.' In *Empirismo eretico*. Milan: Garzanti, 1981.

Perlasca, Giorgio. *L'impostore*. Bologna: Il Mulino, 1997.

Piccardi, Adriano. 'La merlettaia e il canarino.' *Cineforum* 41 (August–September 2001).

Picchietti, Virginia. 'Representations of Judaism and the Jewish Experience in Italian Cinema.' Presented at American Association of Italian Studies Conference, 2005.

Picciotto, Liliana. 'The Shoah in Italy: Its History and Characteristics.' In *Jews in Italy under Fascist and Nazi Rule, 1922–1945*, ed. Joshua D. Zimmerman. New York: Cambridge University Press, 2005.

Pitassio, Francesco. 'Finestre superficiali.' *Cineforum* 41 (August–September 2001).

Politi, Marco. 'La Chiesa non dimentica gli orrori dell'Olocausto.' *La repubblica*, 24 March 2000.

Pratolini, Vasco. *Romanzi 1*. Ed. Francesco Paolo Memmo. Milan: Mondadori, 1993.

Ravetto, Chris. *The Unmaking of Fascist Aesthetics*. Minneapolis: University of Minnesota Press, 2001.

The Representation of the Holocaust in Literature and Film. 2 vols. Ed. Marc Lee Raphael. Williamsburg: College of William and Mary, 2003, 2006.

Ribiony, Simona. 'Il fascista Perlasca eroe per 5000 ebrei.' *La stampa*, 24 January 2002. Also available at http://culturitalia.uibk.ac.at/gmerz/ESERCIZ/TEMI/ARTind/Perlasca.htm.

'Ringraziamo il Signore per la ritrovata fratellanza e per la più profonda intesa tra la Chiesa e l'Ebraismo.' *L'osservatore romano*, 14–15 April 1986.

Romoli, Gianni, and Ferzan Ozpetek. *La finestra di fronte*. Milan: Idea Books, 2003.

Rondi, Gian Luigi. '*Canone inverso*.' *Il tempo*, 14 February 2000. Repr. in *Rassegna stampa cinematografica*. Bergamo: S.A.S., 2000.

Salvadori, Roberto G. *Auschwitz perché: La realtà del male*. Arezzo: Limina, 2004.

Samuels, Charles Thomas. *Encountering Directors*. New York: Putnam, 1972.

Santi, Pier Marco, and Rossano Vittori. *I film di Ettore Scola*. Rome: Gremese, 1987.

Santner, Eric. 'History beyond the Pleasure Principle: Some Thoughts on the Representation of Trauma.' In *Probling the Limits of Representation: Nazism and the 'Final Solution*,' ed. Saul Friedlander. Cambridge, MA: Harvard University Press, 1992.

Sassone, Gabriella. 'Luca Zingaretti/attore.' Available at http://www.tamtamcinema.com/persona.asp?ID=348&lang=ita.

Scola, Ettore. *Concorrenza sleale*. Turin: Lindau, 2001.

Southall, James. 'Perlasca.' Available at http://www.movie-wave.net/titles/perlasca.html.

Steinberg, Jonathan. *All or Nothing: The Axis and the Holocaust, 1941–43*. London and New York: Routledge, 2002.

Viano, Maurizio. '*Life Is Beautiful*: Reception, Allegory, and Holocaust Laughter.' *Annali d'Italianistica* 17 (1999).

Waller, Marguerite. 'Signifying the Holocaust: Liliana Cavani's *Portiere di notte*, In *Feminisms in the Cinema*, ed. Laura Pietropaolo and Ada Testaferri. Bloomington: Indiana University Press, 1995.

Wertmüller, Lina. *The Screenplays of Lina Wertmüller*. Trans. Steven Wagner. New York: Warner Books, 1977.

Wieviorka, Annette. *Déportation et génocide: Entre la mémoire et l'oubli*. Paris: Plon, 1992.

Zapponi, Niccolò. 'Fascism in Italian Historiography, 1986–93: A Fading National Identity.' *Journal of Contemporary History* 29 (October 1994).

Zingaretti, Luca. 'Perlasca.' Available at http://www.rai.it/RAInet/cinema.

Zuccotti, Susan. *The Italians and the Holocaust: Persecution, Rescue and Survival*. Lincoln: University of Nebraska Press, 1996.

Film Index

'43–'97 (Scola), 19, 161–7
18,000 Days Ago (Gabrielli). See
  18.000 giorni fa
18.000 giorni fa (Gabrielli), 15, 72–5
8½ (Fellini), 57, 68

Amarcord (Fellini), 120, 163
Andremo in città (N. Risi), 44–5, 46,
  70, 153n
Apocalypse Now (Coppola), 57

Bicycle Thief (De Sica). See Ladri di
  biciclette
Big Deal on Madonna Street (Monicelli). See Soliti ignoti

Caduta degli dei, La (Visconti), 44n
Canone inverso (Tognazzi), 15, 85–98,
  153n, 154–6
Cielo cade, Il (Frazzi brothers), 15, 59,
  99–110, 156, 158
Cinema Paradiso (Tornatore). See
  Nuovo cinema paradiso
Concorrenza sleale (Scola), 15, 111–24,
  164

Cry of the Land, The (Coletti). See
  Grido della terra

Damned, The (Visconti). See Caduta
  degli dei
Diario di un italiano (Capogna),
  48–51
Diary of an Italian (Capogna). See
  Diario di un italiano
Dolce vita, La (Fellini), 113
Donna nella Resistenza, La (Cavani),
  52

Easy Life, The (D. Risi). See Sor-
  passo
Ebreo errante, L' (Alessandrini), 30–2,
  70, 153n
Enfants terribles, Les (Cocteau), 44
Everybody Home (Comencini). See
  Tutti a casa

Facing Windows (Ozpetek). See
  Finestra di fronte
Fascist Jew, The (Molé). See Prima della
  lunga notte – L'ebreo fascista

Finestra di fronte, La (Ozpetek), 15, 70, 140–52

Flight of the Innocents, The (Pompucci). See *Fuga degli innocenti*

Fuga degli innocenti, La (Pompucci), 15, 156–60

Garden of the Finzi-Continis, The (De Sica). See *Giardino dei Finzi-Contini*

Gattopardo, Il (Visconti), 68, 163

Giardino dei Finzi-Contini, Il (De Sica), 29, 46–8, 49, 58, 69, 89, 102, 109, 116–17

Giornata particolare, Una (Scola), 114, 115, 118, 123, 145, 163

Girl with a Suitcase (Zurlini). See *Ragazza con la valigia*

Golden Eyeglasses, The (Montaldo). See *Occhiali d'oro*

Gold of Rome, The (Lizzani). See *Oro di Roma*

Great Dictator, The (Chaplin), 163

Grido della terra, Il (Coletti), 32–3, 71, 153n

History (Comencini). See *Storia, La*

Holocaust (Chomsky), 64

Hungarian Servant, The (Molteni and Piesco). See *Servo ungherese*

I'm Starting from Three (Troisi). See *Ricomincio da tre*

Jona che visse nella balena (Faenza), 15, 19, 59, 70–2, 153, 157

Jonah Who Lived in the Whale (Faenza). See *Jona che visse nella balena*

Kapò (Pontecorvo), 29, 37–9, 41, 46, 58, 70, 139, 153n

Ladri di biciclette (De Sica), 113, 163

Ladro di bambini, Il (Amelio), 164

Leopard, The (Visconti). See *Gattopardo*

Life Is Beautiful (Benigni). See *Vita è bella*

Line of the River, The (Scavarda). See *Linea del fiume*

Linea del fiume, La (Scavarda), 59–62, 64, 153n, 158

Luciano Serra pilota (Alessandrini), 63

Making Love (Tognazzi). See *Canone inverso*

Monastero di Santa Chiara, Il (Segui), 33–5, 139

Monastery of Saint Clare (Segui). See *Monastero di Santa Chiara*

Night of the Shooting Stars (Taviani brothers). See *Notte di San Lorenzo*

Night Porter (Cavani). See *Portiere di notte*

Notte di San Lorenzo, La (Taviani), 108–9

Nuovo cinema paradiso (Tornatore), 164

Occhiali d'oro, Gli (Montaldo), 69–70

Oro di Roma, L' (Lizzani), 39–42, 46, 58, 64

Paisà (Rossellini), 108

Palombella rossa (Moretti), 164, 165

Pasqualino settebellezze (Wertmüller), 29, 55–8, 76, 153n

Perlasca: The Courage of a Just Man (Negrin). See *Perlasca, un eroe italiano*

Perlasca, un eroe italiano (Negrin), 15, 125–39, 153n, 156

Portiere di notte, Il (Cavani), 29, 52–5, 58, 153n

Prima della lunga notte – L'ebreo fascista (Molé), 62–3

Ragazza con la valigia, La (Zurlini), 68

Red Wood Pigeon (Moretti). See *Palombella rossa*

Ricomincio da tre (Troisi), 163

Roma, città aperta (Rossellini), 14, 33, 156, 163, 165

Rome, Open City (Rossellini). See *Roma, città aperta*

Sandra (Visconti). See *Vaghe stelle dell'Orsa*

Schindler's List (Spielberg), 78, 129, 139

Senza confini (Costa), 15, 137–9, 153n

Servo ungherese, Il (Molteni and Piesco), 15, 153–6

Seven Beauties (Wertmüller). See *Pasqualino settebellezze*

Sky Is Falling, The (Frazzi). See *Cielo cade*

Soliti ignoti, I (Monicelli), 163

Sorpasso, Il (D. Risi), 163, 165

Special Day, A (Scola). See *Giornata particolare*

Squadrone bianco (Genina), 63

Stolen Children, The (Amelio). See *Ladro di bambini*

Storia, La (Comencini), 59, 65–9, 72

Storia d'amore e d'amicizia (Rossi), 28, 64–5, 72

Storia del Terzo Reich (Cavani), 52

Story of Love and Friendship (Rossi). See *Storia d'amore e d'amicizia*

Three Brothers (Rosi). See *Tre fratelli*

Tre fratelli (Rosi), 108

Tregua, La (Rosi), 15, 78–81, 153n, 164, 166–7

Truce, The (Rosi). See *Tregua*

Tutti a casa (Comencini), 35–7, 65, 66, 67

Unfair Competition (Scola). See *Concorrenza sleale*

Vaghe stelle dell'Orsa (Visconti), 42–4, 68

Vita è bella, La (Benigni), 15, 45, 59, 75–8, 117, 158

Wandering Jew, The. See *Ebreo errante*

White Squadron, The (Genina). See *Squadrone bianco*

Without Borders (Costa). See *Senza confini*

General Index

'16 ottobre 1943' (Di Cori), 161

Abatantuono, Diego, 118
absurdity, 77, 119–20
Academy Awards, 39
adaptation, 44, 46, 46n, 47, 48–51, 62, 65, 68, 69, 70, 78, 86–94, 98, 99, 101–2, 110, 116–17, 126, 127, 131, 131n, 133, 135–7
adventure film, 60, 134
Alessandrini, Goffredo: *Ebreo errante*, 30–2, 70, 153n; *Luciano Serra pilota*, 63
allegory, 54, 155–6; social, 52–5
alliance, Axis, 5–6, 62, 63, 78, 114–15, 119, 159–60, 163
Allianza Nazionale, 20
Amelio, Gianni: *Ladro di bambini*, 164
Amendola, Claudio, 64
Amsterdam, 70–1
anachronism, 90–1
Andremo in città (Bruck), 44
anti-Fascism, 18; anti-Fascists, 59, 72, 74, 119–20
anti-Semitism, 8, 30, 31, 45, 47–50, 60, 63, 66, 69, 70–1, 89, 96–8, 102, 112,

119; Fascist, 5–6, 9, 13–15, 23, 47–8, 49, 59, 63, 67, 74, 78, 119, 120, 124
Antonioni, Michelangelo, 60
Antonutti, Omero, 138
Antonutti, Raffaella, 28
anxiety, 17, 21, 104
architecture: use of in Holocaust film, 103; students of, 112, 122
Arendt, Hannah: *The Banality of Evil*, 126
Arezzo (Italy), 75
arts, 98, 102–3, 109–10, 154–5, 156; cartoons, 115; genealogy of, 117; painting, 153–6
atonement, 9, 30–1, 117, 124
Auschwitz, 3, 14, 16, 20, 26, 28, 32, 37, 38, 42, 52, 66, 72, 76n, 79–80, 144, 161. *See also* concentration camp
autobiography, 22, 45, 112, 113–15

Badoglio, Pietro, 8
Banalità del bene, La (Deaglio), 126, 129
Bassani, Giorgio: *Giardino dei Finzi-Contini*, 44, 46–8, 69, 89, 102, 109, 116–17; 'Gli Occhiali d'oro,' 69

Benigni, Roberto: *La vita è bella*, 15, 45, 59, 75–8, 117, 158
Berlin, 18, 153–4
Berlusconi, Silvio, 20–1
Bertolucci, Bernardo, 15, 60
Beyond the Pleasure Principle (Freud), 17n
biblical allusions: Calvary, 43; crucifiction of Jesus, 30; Eden, 46, 101–2, 106, 109; Elijah, 48; flight into Egypt, 158; Good Samaritan, 33; Isaiah, Book of, 44; Jesus Christ, 30, 31, 32; Jewish return to the Promised Land, 33, 158; Jonah, 70; massacre of the innocents, 158; Messiah, 48; miracles, 31, 104; Passion, 31; Psalms, 61–2; prophecy, 48; Salome, 54; salvation, 61
Bologna, 62
Bonetti, Massimo, 64
Bova, Raoul, 148
Bruck, Edith: *Andremo in città*, 44–5
Budapest, 125–6, 129, 130, 131, 133–6, 156; myth of, 90n, 133–4

'Caccia, La' (Paganini), 96
Caffaz, Ugo, 3n, 5
Calabria, 72, 75
Camilleri, Andrea, 127
Canone inverso (Maurensig), 86–94, 98
Capogna, Sergio: *Diario di un italiano*, 48–51
Capogreco, Carlo Spartaco, 72
Cardinale, Claudia, 42, 68–9
Castellitto, Sergio, 118
Catholic Church. *See* Roman Catholic Church
Cavani, Liliana: *La donna nella Resistenza*, 52; *Il portiere di notte*, 29, 52–5, 153n; *Storia del Terzo Reich*, 52

Cervantes, Miguel de: *Don Quixote*, 109
Chaplin, Charlie: *The Great Dictator*, 163
Chaplin, Geraldine, 45
children, 36, 45, 75–8, 86, 94, 118, 120, 123, 131–2, 156–7; helplessness of, 36, 104–8, 105, 157; as protagonists, 21–4, 59–61, 70–1, 99–100, 103–8, 112, 115–16, 122, 157–8, 162, 164
Chomsky, Marvin: *Holocaust*, 64
Chopin, Frédéric, 110
Cielo cade, Il (Mazzetti), 99, 101–2, 110
Cinecittà, 114
cinema politico, 29, 80, 164
'Clair de lune' (Debussy), 95
Cocteau, Jean: *Les enfants terribles*, 44
Cold War, 18, 18n. *See also* post–Cold War Italy; post–World War Two Italy
Coletti, Duilio: *Grido della terra*, 32–3, 71, 153n
Colombo, Furio, 7–8, 9n
comedy, 58, 64, 73, 75–8, 96, 103–4, 106, 113, 117– 20, 121, 156. See also *commedia all'italiana*
Comencini, Luigi: *La Storia*, 59, 65–9, 72; *Tutti a casa*, 35–7, 65
commedia all'italiana, 29, 117–19, 124, 164. *See also* comedy
commercial cinema, 45, 62, 117, 139
comparisons: Fascism vs Nazism, 63, 69, 73–4, 78, 158, 160
concentration camp, 3, 30, 32, 37, 52–5, 57–9, 63, 70–1, 73, 74, 76, 77, 80, 86, 153–4; in Italy, 72–5. *See also* Auschwitz
controversy, surrounding Italian Holocaust films, 52, 75
conversion, 31, 34–5, 66, 69, 139, 154

Cooper, Gary, 120
Coppola, Francis Ford: *Apocalypse Now*, 57
Cortese, Valentina, 30
Costa, Fabrizio: *Senza confini*, 15, 137–9, 153n
Cucciola, Riccardo, 60

D'Alatri, Alessandro, 112
D'Annunzio, Gabriele: Fiume campaign, 63; *Forse che sì, forse che no*, 44
Darwinism, 57, 64; social, 59
Deaglio, Enrico: *La banalità del bene*, 126, 129, 135, 137
Debussy, Claude: 'Clair de lune,' 95
deicide, 30, 31
Delasem, 156, 158
Deleuze, Gilles, 104–5, 108
deliverance, 70
Del perduto amore (Placido), 142
denial, 47
Depardieu, Gérard, 120
deportation, 28, 35, 37, 41, 46, 47, 59, 64, 66, 67, 68, 70, 71, 72, 76–8, 86, 105–6, 112, 115, 122, 131, 137–8, 141, 144, 157, 161–2, 165. *See also* Rome: 16 October 1943
De Rossi, Barbara, 64
De Sica, Vittorio, 15, 105, 116, 164; *Giardino dei Finzi-Contini*, 29, 46–8, 69, 89, 102, 109, 116–17; *Ladri di biciclette*, 113, 163
diaspora, 30, 32, 40
Di Cori, Angelo, 161; *16 ottobre 1943*, 161
didacticism, in Italian Holocaust film, 73, 156
Dietrich, Marlene, 34, 54, 156
Difesa della razza, 6, 123

displaced-persons camp, 32
documentary footage, 47–8, 60, 108, 134–5, 157, 160, 162–3
Don Quixote (Cervantes), 109
Dvorak, Anton, 95

Ebreo nel fascismo, Un (Preti), 62
editing, 97–8, 107, 135. *See also* montage
Eichmann, Adolf, 126, 131
Einstein, Albert, 99
Electra (Euripides), 43
Electra (Sophocles), 43
ellipsis, 87–9
Enfants terribles, Les (Cocteau), 44
Ethiopian campaign, 62–3, 126. *See also* imperialism
Euripides: *Electra*, 43
expiation, 30–1, 53, 115, 141, 144, 152

Faenza, Roberto: *Jona che visse nella balena*, 15, 19, 59, 70–2, 153, 158
Farkas, Zoltán, 129–31
Fascism: Jewish participation in, 5, 62–3; rehabilitation of, 20–1, 127; representation in film of, 29, 49, 120–1, 126–7, 138. *See also* comparisons
Fellini, Federico, 164; *Amarcord*, 120, 163; *La dolce vita*, 113; *8½*, 57, 68
feminist analysis, 55n
Ferramonti-Tarsia (camp), 72–5. *See also* concentration camps
Ferrara (Italy), 16, 46, 69–70
Ferrero, Anna Maria, 41
Fini, Gianfranco, 20
Finn, Paolo, 14, 28
Fiume (Istria), 137–8
flashback, 30, 54, 55, 63, 66, 85–6, 94, 108, 132, 142, 143, 145

Florence, 49, 51, 62, 106
Foa, Anna, 5
Forse che sì, forse che no (D'Annunzio), 44
Fossoli (camp), 72
Foucault, Michel, 114
Franck, César: *Prelude, Chorale and Fugue*, 43; in *Remembrance of Things Past*, 43
Franco, Francisco, 125, 126
Frankfurt (Germany), 30, 31
Frazzi brothers (Andrea and Antonio): *Il cielo cade*, 15, 59, 99–110, 156, 158
Freud, Sigmund, 16–17, 21; *Beyond the Pleasure Principle*, 17n; *Mourning and Melancholia*, 16n, 143–4

Gabrielli, Gabriella: *18.000 giorni fa*, 15, 72–5
Gallucio, Fabio: *I Lager in Italia*, 7, 72n
games. *See* play
Gassman, Vittorio, 30
gaze, 52n, 100, 105–6, 108–9, 115, 119, 136–7, 145, 147–9, 152
gender roles, 55, 58, 147. *See also* stereotypes: gender
geneology, 93–4
Genina, Augusto, 63
George VI (King of England), 61–2
ghetto, 4–5, 14, 28, 39–42, 64–7, 112, 115, 122, 136, 141, 143, 146, 161–2, 165
Giannini, Giancarlo, 55
Giardino dei Finzi-Contini, Il (Bassani), 44, 46–8, 49, 69, 89, 102, 109, 116–17
Giordana, Marco Tullio, 113
Girelli-Carasi, Fabio, 15, 18
Girotti, Massimo, 142–4

Gramsci, Antonio: on reading history, 15
guilt, 31, 32, 39, 42, 66, 117, 145, 152. *See also* survival

historiography, 18–19, 80–1, 126, 167
history: characters' perspective on, 146, 150–1; erasure of, 54; as a force, 26, 46, 51, 68, 69, 96–7, 105, 109, 119–20; gamble with, 76; ghettoization of, 28; impression of immunity to, 26, 102, 106, 118; knowledge of, 22, 43, 49–50, 78, 110, 142–3, 158; as mode of analysis, 16; prominence of, 35, 87, 93; questioning of, 114; representation of, 43, 50, 60–1, 100–1, 113, 142, 162–5; selective reading of, 18; suppression of, 43, 80–1, 166
Hitchcock, Alfred, 146
Hitler, Adolf, 5, 63, 114, 163
Hollywood, Golden Age Cinema of, 134, 156
Holocaust: history of, 18–19, 126; indifference to, 36, 81; memorialization, 15–16, 37; non-representation of, 87–9; representation of, 17, 36–7, 42, 45, 46, 47, 55, 57, 59, 67–8, 75–8, 81, 100–1, 104–5, 117, 156–7, 166–7; statistics of Italian victims, 3, 8–9
homosexuality, 54, 69–70, 114, 118, 141, 145, 151. *See also* sexuality
Hungary, 93. *See also* Budapest

identity: in the camps, 73; change of, 37–8; German, 58; homosexual, 145; Italian, 8, 17–19, 21, 24, 35, 49, 75, 79, 108, 114, 123–4, 126–30, 156, 158–60, 167; —, in the post–Cold

War era, 129; Jewish, 5, 7, 26, 30, 34, 35, 37, 40, 43, 44, 50, 61, 66–7, 69, 71, 86, 90, 121, 124, 132, 133; loss of, 59; recovery of, 71, 126
ideology: end of, 18, 80–1, 126–7, 137; polarization of, 18
immigrants, in Italy, 19, 164–5
imperialism, Italian, 62, 75, 123, 138–9. *See also* Ethiopian campaign
Impostore, L', 126, 135
internationalization, of Italian Holocaust film, 30, 37, 70, 79, 153
intertextuality, 128
irony, 25, 36, 57–9, 73–4, 76, 94, 108–9, 115, 119–20, 148
Israel, 32–3, 71–2, 137, 158
Italian Comunist Party. *See* Partito comunista italiano
Italy: immigration into, *see* immigrants; Jewish history, 3–5; national history of, 18. *See also* post–World War Two Italy

Jerusalem, 30, 48
Jews: under Fascism, 6–9, 14, 19, 20, 22–3, 64, 158–9; folk culture of, 32; under German occupation in Italy, 8–9, 14, 39–42, 64, 161; history of, 3–9, 13–14, 31, 32; identity, *see* identity: Jewish; of Rome, 3–4, 13, 39–42
John Paul II, Pope, 19–20
John XXIII, Pope, 20
Jona che visse nella balena (Oberski), 70

Koch, Ilse, 58
Kokoschka, Oskar, 153–4

Levi, Diego, 156, 158

Levi, Primo, 14, 38, 72, 116; *Se questo è un uomo*, 80; *La tregua*, 78–80
liberation, 8, 16, 32–5, 56, 66, 73, 76–7, 79, 100–1, 108–9, 126
Lithuania, 121
Lizzani, Carlo: *L'oro di Roma*, 39–42, 46, 64
Ljubljana (Slovenia), 156–9
London, 59, 60, 85, 91
Loren, Sophia, 116
Loy, Rosetta, 20–7; *La parola ebreo*, 20–7
Lukács, Georg, 40, 113

Manfredi, Nino, 34
'Manifesto della razza,' 6. *See also* Racial Laws
Marc'Aurelio, 115
Marrone, Gaetana, 52n, 53
Marxism, 47, 80, 137n
Massari, Lea, 60
Mastroianni, Marcello, 116
Maurensig, Paolo: *Canone inverso*, 86–94, 98
Mazzetti, Lorenza: *Il cielo cade*, 99, 101–2, 110
media culture, Italian, 142–3
melodrama, 33; in Holocaust films, 29, 33, 43, 51, 94, 96, 97, 140–1, 143, 156. *See also* romance
memorials, 25, 44, 49. *See also* Holocaust: memorialization
memory, 16–17, 25–7, 28–9, 36, 42, 53–4, 67, 90–1, 93–4, 101, 108, 116, 122, 126, 141–3, 152, 166. *See also* repression
Mezzogiorno, Giovanna, 148
Milan, 79, 111
mini-series. *See* television
mise-en-scène, 41–2, 65, 67, 74, 118, 135, 156

Mitteleuropa, as film setting, 45, 79, 85, 90, 93, 125, 133–4, 153. *See also* Budapest; Hungary; Prague

Modena (Italy), 62, 72, 156, 159

Molé, Francesco: *Prima della lunga notte – L'ebreo fascista*, 62–3

Molteni, Giorgio: *Il servo ungherese*, 15, 153–6

Monicelli, Mario: *I soliti ignoti*, 163

montage, 31, 35, 41–2, 56, 57–8, 90, 98, 115, 135, 155, 156, 162–6. *See also* editing

Montaldo, Giuliano: *Gli occhiali d'oro*, 69–70

Morandini, Morandino, 77

Morante, Elsa, 13–14, 26–7; *La Storia*, 13–14, 26–7, 65, 68

Moravia, Alberto, 34

Moretti, Nanni: *Palombella rossa*, 164, 165

Morricone, Enrico: *Canone inverso*, 95, 97–8

mourning, 15n, 16–17, 42, 49, 71–2, 90, 109, 132, 143–4, 146. See also *Trauerarbeit*

Mourning Becomes Electra (O'Neill), 43–4

Mourning and Melancholia (Freud), 15n, 143–4

Muccino, Gabriele, 112, 142

Mulvey, Laura, 147

music: diegetic, 33–5, 72, 86, 88–8, 99–100, 108, 110, 112, 121, 122, 133, 153–6; as metaphor, 70, 91–2; non-diegetic, 43, 51, 56–8, 60, 62, 95, 101, 139, 162, 164

Mussolini, Benito, 5–6, 8–9, 62, 105, 114, 116, 125, 126

Naples, 3n, 33–4, 35, 55–6, 58, 76

narrative: desire, 79–80, 100–1; fetishism of, 17; forms, 50–2, 94; structure, 22, 25–6, 91–2, 95; theory, 95; tradition, 96. *See also* travel narrative

Negrin, Alberto: *Perlasca, un eroe italiano*, 15, 125–9, 153n, 156

neorealism, 14–15, 33, 47, 80, 104, 108, 113, 116–17, 149, 164

Noiret, Philippe, 69

nostalgia, 80, 90, 110, 118, 153

Nostra Aetate, 20

Oberski, Jonah: *Jona che visse nella balena*, 19, 70

'Occhiali d'oro, Gli' (Bassani), 69

occupation, German: of Czechoslovakia, 85–6, 90n, 93; of Italy, 8, 60, 99, 145, 161

O'Neill, Eugene: *Mourning Becomes Electra*, 43–4

Ozpetek, Ferzan: *La finestra di fronte*, 15, 70, 140–52

Paganini, Niccolò: 'La Caccia,' 96

Palatucci, Giovanni, 137–9

panopticon, 114

parable, 30, 49, 76–7, 166

Paris, 30, 37, 42, 63

parody, 58, 73–4, 155–6, 163

Parola ebreo, La (Loy), 20–7

partisans. *See* resistance: partisans

Partito comunista italiano (PCI), 18

Pasolini, Pier Paolo, 15, 155

Paul VI, Pope: *Nostra Aetate*, 20

Perlasca, Giorgio, 125–9, 135, 138, 139; *L'impostore*, 126, 135

perspective, 18–19, 22–5, 33, 47, 107, 109, 119, 130, 141, 152, 156–7. *See also* children: as protagonists; gaze

Petraglia, Sandro, 131n
Picciotto, Liana, 3n, 9, 29n, 72n
Piesco, Massimo: *Il servo ungherese*,
    15, 153–6
Pitassio, Francesco, 146–7
Pius XII, Pope, 8
Placido, Michele: *Del perduto amore*,
    142
play: games, 17n, 76–7, 96, 101–2,
    115–16, 118, 120, 122–3
Pompucci, Leone: *La fuga degli inno-
    centi*, 15, 156–60
Pontecorvo, Gillo: *Kapò*, 29, 37–9, 41,
    46, 70, 139, 153n
Ponti, Carlo, 116
post–Cold War Italy: lack of histori-
    cal memory in, 142–3; lack of
    socially conscious films in, 112–13;
    proliferation of Holocaust films, 9,
    15, 16–17, 70–81, 87, 126–7, 146, 167
post–World War Two Italy: film his-
    tory of, 30–5, 80, 98, 108, 113, 117,
    142–3, 164, 166; reticence regard-
    ing Holocaust, 13–18, 28–9, 55, 67,
    81, 143, 166; social problems of, 15,
    101, 108. *See also* neorealism
Prague, 90n; Prague Spring (1968),
    85, 89, 93
Pratolini, Vasco: 'Wanda,' 48–51
prayer. *See* religion: prayer
Preti, Luigi: *Un ebreo nel Fascismo*,
    62
Proust, Marcel: *Remembrance of
    Things Past*, 43
psychoanalytic analysis, 16–17, 21–3,
    43, 47, 52–3, 71, 147
Psychomachia, 156

Racial Laws (1938–9), 6–7, 9, 14, 18,
    22, 26, 40, 46, 49, 59, 62–3, 69, 75,

112, 114, 123, 138. *See also* 'Mani-
    festo della razza'
RAI (Radiotelevisione italiana), 19,
    126
realist-historical fiction, 14–15, 20, 33,
    36, 39–41, 40n, 43, 46, 47, 50–1, 62
redemption, 37, 48, 52, 59, 108
Reggiani, Serge, 36
religion: prayer, 105, 106; —, Chris-
    tian, 34–5; —, Jewish, 38, 40, 44; rit-
    ual, 24, 40, 44, 48, 64, 103–4, 109
Remembrance of Things Past (Proust),
    43
repression (psychological), 9, 17, 21,
    28, 55, 57, 68–9, 143, 145, 146. *See
    also* trauma
rescue, 8, 36, 45, 59–60, 73–4, 103–4,
    106, 125–6, 129, 131, 132, 135, 137–
    9, 156, 158
resistance, 38, 40, 45, 63, 64, 76, 155,
    160; Italian, 8, 18, 35, 62–3, 65, 80–
    1, 100–1, 146, 165; partisans, 35, 45,
    59, 61, 64, 68, 80, 157
resolution, 96, 119; lack of, 116
retro-reading, 142, 144–5
'Ride of the Valkyries' (Wagner), 57–
    8
righteous gentiles, 59, 137, 138
Risi, Dino, 45; *Il sorpasso*, 163, 165
Risi, Nelo: *Andremo in città*, 44–5, 70,
    153n
Risiera di San Saba (camp), 72
Risorgimento, 5
Roman Catholic Church: Jewish rela-
    tions with, 8, 19–20; Vatican II, 20
romance, in Holocaust films, 29, 39,
    40–1, 46–8, 50–1, 54, 56, 58, 64, 69,
    76, 77, 86, 88, 94–5, 114, 122, 123,
    131, 134, 140–1, 145, 150–2, 156. *See
    also* melodrama

Rome, 3, 13–14, 20, 22, 26–7, 75, 79, 106, 161; Empire, 4–5; as film setting, 28, 33, 39–42, 61, 64–65, 108, 111, 114, 140–3, 146, 162; Jewish history of, 3–4, 28, 39, 42n; 16 October 1943, 3, 39, 59, 64, 66, 105, 141, 146, 161, 165–6; via dei Giubbonari, 161

Romoli, Gianni, 143

Rosi, Francesco: *Tre fratelli*, 108; *La tregua*, 15, 78–81, 153n, 164, 166–7

Rossellini, Roberto, 15, 108, 134, 164; *Paisà*, 108; *Roma, città aperta*, 14, 33, 156, 163, 165

Rossi, Franco: *Storia d'amore e d'amicizia*, 28, 64–5, 72

Rubini, Sergio: *L'amore ritorna*, 142

Rulli, Sandro, 131n

Russian front, 72

sacrifice, 39, 46, 48, 52, 58, 141, 145. *See also* self-sacrifice

Salvadori, Roberto G., 3

Santner, Eric, 16–17, 21, 71

Sarfatti, Michele, 17

satire, 58, 117, 120–1

Scavarda, Aldo, 60; *Linea del fiume*, 59–62, 64, 153n, 158

Scimeca, Pasquale, 113

Scola, Ettore, 14, 15, 19; *Concorrenza sleale*, 15, 111–24, 164; *Una giornata particolare*, 114, 115, 118, 123, 145, 163; *'43–'97*, 19, 161–6

Segui, Mario: *Il monastero di Santa Chiara*, 33–5, 139

Sekulovic, Aleksander: *Kapò*, 39

self-sacrifice, 30–2, 36, 38–9, 45, 76, 133. *See also* sacrifice; suicide

Se questo è un uomo (Levi), 80

sexuality: eroticization, 131n; in

Holocaust films, 29, 38, 42, 44, 46, 52, 54–5, 68, 95, 131, 139, 144, 145, 147–8; sado-masochism, 52. *See also* homosexuality

Sicily, 79

sickness, 30, 31, 37, 47, 65, 68, 71, 86

Simonides of Ceos, 154

social consciousness, in Italian film, 112–13, 117–18, 124, 165–7

Socialism, 49, 52, 63

Solinas, Franco: *Kapò*, 39

Somma, Sebastiano, 138

Sophocles: *Electra*, 43

Sordi, Alberto, 35

Soviet Union, 18, 37, 38, 79–80, 85, 93

Spain, 31: Spanish Civil War, 126, 127

Spielberg, Steven: *Schindler's List*, 78, 129, 134, 139

spy films, 134, 139, 156

star discourse, 68, 118, 127, 128, 142–3, 148

stereotypes: Fascist, 78, 120–1; gender, 145; Hungarian, 90, 127, 130; Italian, 127–30, 158–60; Jewish, 5, 30, 70, 121–2, 130–1, 155–6; Nazi, 127, 134, 139, 155–6

Stern, Isaac, 129

Storia, La (Morante), 13–14, 26–7, 65, 68

Strasberg, Susan, 37

suicide, 9, 34, 40, 44n, 48, 51, 62, 63, 69, 91, 100, 107, 120. *See also* self-sacrifice

survivors, 13–14, 26–7, 32, 45, 52–5, 56–7, 59, 67, 70, 80, 94, 136, 141, 157; guilt of, 53; salvation fantasy, 103–4

Switzerland, 125, 156–7

Sydow, Max von, 156

synagogues, 4, 20, 40–2, 49, 65

Taviani brothers (Paolo and Vittorio), 15; *La notte di San Lorenzo*, 108–9
television, 126; mini-series, 28, 62–70, 72, 126, 128, 137–8; soap operas, 149–50, 152
Terzieff, Laurent, 37
testimony, 36, 43, 94, 98, 101, 113–14, 161; *see also* witness
time, 53–5, 106, 142–5, 164–5
Toaff, Elio, 20
Tognazzi, Ricky: *Canone inverso*, 15, 85–98, 153n, 156
Tornatore, Giuseppe: *Nuovo cinema paradiso*, 164
trains, 36, 45, 61, 62, 63, 66–7, 72, 79, 106, 131, 134, 159
Trauerarbeit, 16–17, 49, 53, 71–2. *See also* mourning
trauma (psychological), 16–17, 21, 27, 52–5, 57, 68, 71–2, 101, 108, 131–2, 141, 143, 145, 146, 152. *See also* repression
travel narrative, 59–60, 79
Tregua, La (Levi), 78–80
Trieste, 72, 79
Troisi, Massimo: *Ricominciamo da tre*, 163
trolley, 118, 119
Turin, 79
Tuscany, 99–102. *See also* Arezzo; Florence; Volterra

utopia, 33, 37, 61, 68, 74, 80, 101, 109, 113, 116, 122, 166

Valli, Alida, 49
Vanoni, Ornella, 60
Venice, 4, 46, 79

Verona, 157, 159
Victor Emmanuel III (King of Italy), 8
Vienna, 53, 89, 90n, 96
Visconti, Luchino, 15, 164; *La caduta degli dei*, 44n; *Il gattopardo*, 68, 163; *Vaghe stelle dell'Orsa*, 42–4, 43n, 68
Volterra (Italy), 42, 44
voyeurism, 23–4, 54–5, 141, 145–9. *See also* windows

Wagner, Richard: 'The Ride of the Valkyries,' 57–8
Waller, Marguerite, 55n
'Wanda' (Pratolini), 48–51
war, 8, 22, 26, 40, 45, 47–8, 116
Warsaw (Poland), 162
Wertmüller, Lina: *Pasqualino settebellezze*, 29, 55–9, 76, 153n
Wiesenthal, Simon, 73, 74
Wieviorka, Annette, 18n
windows, 22–4, 26, 36, 42, 66, 103, 112, 119, 141, 145–50, 152. *See also* voyeurism
witness, 36, 53, 55, 77, 79, 80, 86, 92–4, 101, 110, 115, 116, 117, 119–20, 131, 141, 152. *See also* testimony
writing, 36, 80, 92, 105, 115, 150, 152

Yugoslavia, 45

Zagreb (Croatia), 156–8
Zapponi, Niccolò, 14, 18–19
Zingaretti, Luca, 127–8
Zionism, 32–3, 37, 71–2
Zuccotti, Susan: *The Italians and the Holocaust*, 4n
Zurlini, Valerio: *La Ragazza con la valigia*, 68